CHILDREN'S ISSUES, LAWS AND PROGRAMS

CHILD NUTRITION AND THE WIC PROGRAM

CHILDREN'S ISSUES, LAWS AND PROGRAMS

Additional books in this series can be found on Nova's website under the Series tab.

Additional E-books in this series can be found on Nova's website under the E-books tab.

NUTRITION AND DIET RESEARCH PROGRESS

Additional books in this series can be found on Nova's website under the Series tab.

Additional E-books in this series can be found on Nova's website under the E-books tab.

CHILDREN'S ISSUES, LAWS AND PROGRAMS

CHILD NUTRITION AND THE WIC PROGRAM

DOMINIC J. LOMBARDI
EDITOR

Nova Science Publishers, Inc.
New York

For permission to use material from this book please contact us:
Telephone 631-231-7269; Fax 631-231-8175
Web Site: http://www.novapublishers.com

LIBRARY OF CONGRESS CATALOGING-IN-PUBLICATION DATA

Child nutrition and the WIC program / [edited by] Dominic J. Lombardi.
p. cm.
Includes index.
ISBN 978-1-61209-142-6 (hardcover)
1. Special Supplemental Nutrition Program for Women, Infants, and Children (U.S.) 2. Food relief--United States. 3. Children--Nutrition--United States. I. Lombardi, Dominic J.
HV696.F6C485 2011
363.8'830830973--dc22
2010047618

Published by Nova Science Publishers, Inc. ✝ New York

CONTENTS

PREFACE

Federally supported child nutrition programs and initiatives, along with the Special Supplemental Nutrition Program for Women, Infants, and Children (the WIC program) reach more than 40 million children and some 2 million lower-income pregnant/post-partum women. The basic goals of federal child nutrition programs are to improve children's nutrition, increase lower-income children's access to nutritious meals and snacks, and help support the agricultural economy. This new book explores the background, history and topical issues of child nutrition and the WIC Program.

Chapter 1- Federally supported child nutrition programs and initiatives, along with the Special Supplemental Nutrition Program for Women, Infants, and Children (the WIC program) reach more than 40 million children and some 2 million lower-income pregnant/post-partum women. In FY2007, federal spending on these programs totaled over $19 billion.

The basic goals of federal child nutrition programs are to improve children's nutrition, increase lower-income children's access to nutritious meals and snacks, and help support the agricultural economy. Child nutrition programs are "entitlements." Federal cash funding and commodity support is "guaranteed" to schools and other providers based on the number of meals/snacks served, who is served (e.g., free meals for poor children get higher subsidies), and legislatively established (and inflation-indexed) per-meal subsidy rates. On the other hand, the WIC program is a "discretionary" grant program where specific annual appropriations to pay for benefits and nutrition services and administration are distributed by formula.

Chapter 2- The Special Supplemental Nutrition Program for Women, Infants, and Children (WIC) was created to safeguard the health of low-income women, infants, and children ages 1-4 who are at nutritional risk. WIC provides supplemental food, nutrition education, and referrals to health care and other social services. Almost half of all infants and about a quarter of all children ages 1-4 in the United States participate in the program. WIC is the U.S. Department of Agriculture's third-largest food and nutrition assistance program, with Federal expenditures of $6.2 billion in fiscal year (FY) 2008.

Chapter 3- A comprehensive congressional review ("reauthorization") of the primary laws governing child nutrition and WIC programs (the Richard B. Russell National School Lunch Act and the Child Nutrition Act) was scheduled for 2009 (the last reauthorization was in 2004). Congress did not meet the September 30, 2009, deadline for comprehensive reauthorization. Instead, a one-year extension (through September 30, 2010) was included in the FY2010 Agriculture Department appropriations measure to give Congress time to consider a full reauthorization bill. The delay in child nutrition/WIC reauthorization was primarily due to a lack of agreement on how to fund any new child nutrition initiatives subject to congressional "pay-go" rules. The Administration had proposed spending $10 billion over the next 10 years on expanding child nutrition efforts to "end childhood hunger by 2015," but did not offer specific policy changes or spending/revenue offsets. In 2010, Congress has moved to begin the process of enacting the most sweeping changes in child nutrition and WIC programs since the 1970s.

Chapter 4- USDA's Special Supplemental Nutrition Program for Women, Infants, and Children (WIC) provides participating infants with free infant formula. Federal law requires that WIC State agencies enter into cost-containment contracts with infant formula manufacturers, with agencies typically receiving substantial discounts (rebates) from manufacturers for each can of formula purchased through the program. Each WIC State agency or group of agencies awards a contract to the manufacturer offering the lowest net wholesale price, defined as the difference between the manufacturer's wholesale price and the rebate. In exchange for the rebate, a manufacturer is given an exclusive right to provide its infant formula to WIC participants in the State. In fiscal 2008, infant formula rebates totaled $2.0 billion, compared with total WIC expenditures (after rebates) of $6.2 billion.

Chapter 5- One of the most worrisome aspects of the growing tide of obesity in the United States is the high rate of overweight among children. Over one in five young children, ages 2 to 5, are at risk of being overweight—meaning their Body-Mass-Index-for-age is at or above the 85th percentile. These children face both current and long-term health problems, and their numbers have grown in the past two decades (Must and Strauss, 1999). Th e number of young children whose families participate in the Special Supplemental Nutrition Program for Women, Infants, and Children (WIC) also grew in that time period, more than doubling from 1.7 million in 1988 to 4.0 million in 2007 (USDAERS, 2008).

Chapter 6- The Special Supplemental Nutrition Program for Women, Infants, and Children (WIC) is one of the central components of the Nation's food and nutrition assistance programs. With Federal expenditures of $5.5 billion in fiscal 2007—or almost 10 percent of total Federal Government expenditures for food and nutrition assistance—WIC is the third largest food assistance program, trailing only the Supplemental Nutrition Assistance Program (SNAP, formerly the Food Stamp Program) and the National School Lunch Program (USDA, 2008). WIC serves over 8 million participants per month, including almost half of all infants and a quarter of all children ages 1-4 in the United States.

In: Child Nutrition and the WIC Program
Editor: Dominic J. Lombardi
ISBN: 978-1-61209-142-6

Chapter 1

CHILD NUTRITION AND WIC PROGRAMS: A BRIEF OVERVIEW

Joe Richardson

SUMMARY

Federally supported child nutrition programs and initiatives, along with the Special Supplemental Nutrition Program for Women, Infants, and Children (the WIC program) reach more than 40 million children and some 2 million lower-income pregnant/post-partum women. In FY2007, federal spending on these programs totaled over $19 billion.

The basic goals of federal child nutrition programs are to improve children's nutrition, increase lower-income children's access to nutritious meals and snacks, and help support the agricultural economy. Child nutrition programs are "entitlements." Federal cash funding and commodity support is "guaranteed" to schools and other providers based on the number of meals/snacks served, who is served (e.g., free meals for poor children get higher subsidies), and legislatively established (and inflation-indexed) per-meal subsidy rates. On the other hand, the WIC program is a "discretionary" grant program where specific annual appropriations to pay for benefits and nutrition services and administration are distributed by formula.

In addition to the WIC program (and its ancillary farmers' market program), the child nutrition programs covered in this report include the School Lunch and Breakfast programs (providing federal subsidies for meals served in schools), day-care, summer and other outside-of-school programs assisting sponsors in providing meals/snacks, and payments to states covering administrative oversight costs, expenses for a Fresh Fruit and Vegetable program, the Special Milk program, and various support activities (e.g., various administrative oversight and nutrition education activities).

The underlying laws covering child nutrition and WIC programs were last reauthorized in 2004 in the Child Nutrition and WIC Reauthorization Act (P.L. 108-265). The next reauthorization is scheduled for 2009. The Administration's FY2010 budget calls for increased funding of approximately $1 billion a year for child nutrition programs (for "program reforms aimed at improving program access, enhancing the nutritional quality of school meals, expanding nutrition research and evaluation, and improving program oversight").

This report will be updated as warranted by significant changes in the programs covered and major legislative initiatives.

BACKGROUND

Child nutrition programs and the WIC program provide cash, commodity, and other assistance (including funds for nutrition services and food packages in the WIC program and technical assistance and administrative cost aid in child nutrition programs) under three major federal laws: the Richard B. Russell National School Lunch Act (originally enacted as the National School Lunch Act in 1946), the Child Nutrition Act (originally enacted in 1966), and Section 32 of the Act of August 24, 1935 (7 U.S.C. 612c). The Agriculture Department's Food and Nutrition Service (FNS) administers the programs at the federal level; most funding is included in the annual Agriculture Department appropriations laws; and congressional jurisdiction over the underlying three laws is exercised by the Senate Agriculture, Nutrition, and Forestry Committee; the House Education and Labor Committee; and, to a limited extent (relating to commodity assistance and Section 32 issues), the House Agriculture Committee. Congress periodically reviews and reauthorizes expiring authorities under these laws. The most recent reauthorization was in 2004 (P.L. 108-265); the next reauthorization is scheduled for 2009.

Child nutrition and WIC programs are operated by a wide variety of local public and private providers, and the degree of direct state involvement varies by program and state - e.g., in the WIC program, state health agencies exercise substantial control; in the school meal programs, local educational agencies (LEAs) and local "school food authorities" most often have the major role; in a very few instances, the federal government (FNS) takes the place of state agencies (for example, where a state has chosen not to operate a specific program or where there is a state prohibition on aiding private schools). At the state level, education, health, social services, and agriculture departments all have roles; at a minimum, they are responsible for approving and overseeing local providers such as schools, summer program sponsors, and child care centers and day care homes, as well as making sure they receive the federal support they are due. At the local level, program benefits are provided to more than 40 million children and infants, and some 2 million lower-income pregnant and post-partum women, through some 100,000 public and private schools and residential child care institutions, about 200,000 child care centers and family day care homes, approximately 30,000 summer program sites, and (in the case of the WIC program) about 10,000 local health care clinics/sites operated by nearly 2,000 health agencies.

All programs are available in the 50 states and the District of Columbia. Virtually all operate in Puerto Rico, Guam, and the Virgin Islands (and, in differing versions, in the Northern Marianas and American Samoa), and there are no restrictions on eligibility related to citizenship or legal residence status. In addition, WIC-like benefits are available to overseas military personnel, and Defense Department overseas dependents' schools participate in the school meal programs.

In the meal service programs like the School Lunch and Breakfast programs, summer programs, and assistance for child care centers and day care homes, federal aid is in the form of legislatively set subsidies ("reimbursements") paid for each meal/snack served that meets federal nutrition guidelines. Most subsidies are cash payments to schools or other providers, but about 10% of the total value of all aid is in the form of federally donated food commodities. Although all meals/snacks served by participating providers are subsidized, those served free or at a reduced price to lower-income children are supported at higher rates. All federal meal/snack subsidy rates are indexed annually (each July) for inflation, as are the income standards of eligibility for free and reduced-price meals/snacks. However federal subsidies do not necessarily cover the full cost of the meals and snacks offered by providers, and states and localities contribute to cover program costs—as do children's families (by paying charges for nonfree or reduced-price meals/snacks). Required nonfederal cost sharing is relatively minimal - states must expend at least an amount totaling some $200 million a year nationally in order to receive federal school lunch funds. Federal per-meal/snack child nutrition subsidies may cover local providers' administrative/operating costs, but separate direct federal payments for administrative/operating costs are limited to expense grants to state oversight agencies, a small set-aside of funds for state audits of child care sponsors, and special administrative payments to sponsors of summer programs and family day care homes. Under the WIC program, federal appropriations pay the cost of specifically tailored food packages and include legislatively set amounts for costs of administrative and nutrition services.

Other relevant CRS reports include CRS Report RL33829, *Domestic Food Assistance: The Farm Bill and Other Legislation in the 110th Congress* and CRS Report RL33299, *Child Nutrition and WIC Legislation in the 108th and 109th Congresses.* In addition, CRS Report RL33 307, *Child Nutrition and WIC Programs: Background and Recent Funding* provides historical background. Extensive information about child nutrition and WIC programs also may be found at the Agriculture Department's Food and Nutrition Service website, http://fns.usda.gov.

School Lunch and School Breakfast Programs

The School Lunch and School Breakfast programs provide federal cash and commodity support for meals meeting minimum federally set nutrition standards. The meals are served by public and private nonprofit elementary and secondary schools and residential child care institutions (RCCIs) that opt to enroll and guarantee to offer free or reduced price meals to eligible low income children. Both programs are "entitlement" programs, and both subsidize participating schools and RCCIs for **all** meals served that meet federal nutrition standards at specific, inflation- indexed rates for each meal; food items not served as part of a meal meeting nutrition standards (e.g., a la carte offerings) are not eligible for subsidies.

Each program has a three-tiered system for cash per meal federal reimbursements to schools and RCCIs.

1. It allows children to receive free meals if they have family income below 130% of the federal poverty guidelines ($27,580 for a four-person family in the 2008- 2009 school year); these meals receive the highest subsidy rate.
2. Children may receive reduced price meals (no more than 40 cents for a lunch or 30 cents for a breakfast) if their family income is between 130% and 185% of the poverty guidelines (between $27,580 and $39,220 for a four-person family in the 2008-2009 school year); these meals receive a subsidy rate either 40 cents (for lunches) or 30 cents (for breakfasts) below the free meal rate.
3. A small per meal subsidy is provided for "full-price" or "paid" meals (the price is set by the school or RCCI) served to children whose families do not apply, or whose family income does not qualify them, for free or reduced price meals.

Children in Temporary Assistance for Needy Families (TANF) programs and the Supplemental Nutrition Assistance Program (the SNAP, formerly the Food Stamp program) may automatically qualify for free school meals. Information across these programs can be shared to facilitate this through "direct certification" and other means.

Table 1. School Lunch Program Participation and Federal Costs, Selected Fiscal Years 1980-2007 (in millions)

	Average Daily Participation[a]				Federal costs	
	Free meals	Reduced-price meals	Full-price meals[b]	Total[c]	Current Dollars[d]	Constant 2007 Dollars[e]
1980	10.0	1.9	14.7	26.6	$3,044.9	$7,813.2
1985	9.9	1.6	12.1	23.6	3,034.4	5,841.2
1990	9.8	1.7	12.6	24.1	3,677.1	5,865.0
1992	11.2	1.7	11.7	24.6	4,439.2	6,543.4
1994	12.2	1.8	11.3	25.3	4,919.9	6,858.3
1996	12.6	2.0	11.3	25.9	5,308.7	7,002.2
1998	13.0	2.2	11.4	26.6	5,744.1	7,260.5
2000	13.0	2.5	11.9	27.3	6,099.5	7,331.6
2001	12.9	2.6	12.0	27.5	6,414.5	7,466.5
2002	13.3	2.6	12.0	28.0	6,770.2	7,772.2
2003	13.7	2.7	11.9	28.4	7,037.5	7,889.0
2004	14.1	2.8	12.0	29.0	7,425.5	8,138.3
2005	14.6	2.9	12.2	29.6	7,879.3	8,359.9
2006	14.8	2.9	12.4	30.1	8,162.1	8,349.8
2007	14.9	3.0	12.6	30.5	8,726.5	8,726.5

Source: Compiled by the Congressional Research Service (CRS) based on data from the U.S. Department of Agriculture, Food and Nutrition Service.

a. In order to reflect participation for the actual school year (September through May), these estimates are based on 9 month averages of October through May, plus September, rather than averages of the 12 months of the fiscal year (October through September).

b. The federal government provides a small subsidy for these meals.

c. Details may not sum to total because of rounding.

d. Includes cash payments and the value of "entitlement" commodities; does not include the value of "bonus" commodities provided at the Agriculture Department's discretion.

e. Constant dollars were calculated using the fiscal year CPI-U.

The School Lunch Program subsidizes lunches (5.1 billion in FY2007) to children in about 6,000 RCCIs and almost all schools (95,000). During FY2007, average daily participation was 30.5 million students (61% of the 50 million children enrolled in participating schools and RCCIs); of these, 49% received free lunches, and 10% ate reduced-price lunches (**Table 1**). The remainder were served full-price (but still subsidized) meals. More than 90% of federal funding is used to subsidize free and reduced-price lunches served to low income children. For the 2008-2009 school year, inflation-indexed per lunch federal subsidies (cash payments, plus a required, and inflation-indexed, 21 cents a meal in "entitlement" commodity support) range from 45 cents for full price lunches to $2.78 and $2.38 for free and reduced price lunches, respectively. FY2007 federal school lunch costs (including commodity assistance) totaled some $8.7 billion (**Table 1**).

The School Breakfast program serves fewer students than does the School Lunch program; about 1.7 billion breakfasts in 80,000 schools (and 6,000 RCCIs) were subsidized in FY2007. Average daily participation was 10.1 million children (23% of the 43 million students enrolled in participating schools and RCCIs). Unlike the School Lunch program, the great majority received free or reduced price meals: 70% received free meals, and 10% purchased reduced price meals. In the 2008-2009 school year, inflation-indexed per breakfast federal subsidies (cash only) range from 25 cents for full price meals to $1.40 and $1.10 for free and reduced price breakfasts, respectively. FY2007 federal school breakfast funding totaled about $2.2 billion (**Table 2**).

In addition to federal cash subsidies, participating schools receive donations of federally acquired **food commodities**. Schools are "entitled" to a specific, inflation-indexed value of federally provided commodities for each lunch they serve (20.75 cents a meal for the 2008-2009 school year); they also may receive "bonus" commodities acquired by the Agriculture Department in support of the farm economy. In recent years, the value of federal commodity aid to schools has totaled well over $1 billion a year, and, by law, commodity assistance must represent at least 12% of the total value (cash + commodities) of aid given under the School Lunch program. Cash and commodity support to participating schools is based on the number and type of meals served (e.g., lunch or breakfast, free or full price). However, once the aid is received by the school, it is used to support the overall school meal service budget, as determined appropriate by the school.

SPECIAL SUPPLEMENTAL NUTRITION PROGRAM FOR WOMEN, INFANTS, AND CHILDREN (THE WIC PROGRAM)

The WIC Program provides food assistance, nutrition risk screening, and related services (e.g., nutrition education and breastfeeding support, medical care referral) to low-income pregnant and postpartum women and their infants, as well as to children up to age 5 from low-income families. Participants in the program generally must have family income at or below 185% of poverty, and must be judged to be nutritionally at risk. Nutrition risk is defined as detectable abnormal nutritional conditions; documented nutritionally related medical conditions; health impairing dietary deficiencies; or conditions that predispose people to inadequate nutrition or nutritionally related medical problems. Most income-eligible applicants meet the WIC program's nutrition risk criteria.

Table 2. School Breakfast Program Participation and Federal Costs, Selected Fiscal Years 1980-2007 (in millions)

	Average Daily Participation[a]				Federal Costs	
	Free meals	Reducedprice meals	Full-price meals[b]	Total[c]	Current dollars[d]	Constant 2007 Dollars[e]
1980	2.8	0.2	0.6	3.6	$287.8	$738.5
1985	2.9	0.2	0.4	3.4	379.3	730.2
1990	3.3	0.2	0.5	4.0	596.2	950.9
1992	4.0	0.2	0.6	4.9	786.5	1,159.3
1994	4.8	0.3	0.7	5.8	959.0	1,336.8
1996	5.3	0.4	0.9	6.6	1,118.7	1,475.6
1998	5.6	0.5	1.0	7.1	1,272.2	1,608.1
2000	5.7	0.6	1.2	7.5	1,393.3	1,674.7
2001	5.8	0.7	1.3	7.8	1,450.1	1,689.4
2002	6.0	0.7	1.4	8.1	1,566.7	1,798.6
2003	6.2	0.7	1.5	8.4	1,651.8	1,851.7
2004	6.5	0.8	1.6	8.9	1,775.7	1,946.2
2005	6.8	0.9	1.7	9.4	1,927.2	2,044.8
2006	7.0	0.9	1.9	9.8	2,042.9	2,089.9
2007	7.1	1.0	2.0	10.1	2,163.8	2,163.8

Source: Compiled by the Congressional Research Service (CRS) based on data from the U.S. Department of Agriculture, Food and Nutrition Service.

a. In order to reflect participation for the actual school year (September through May), these estimates are based on 9 month averages of October through May, plus September, rather than averages of the 12 months of the fiscal year (October through September).

b. The federal government provides a small subsidy for these meals.

c. Details may not sum to total because of rounding.

d. Does not include the value of any federally donated commodities.

e. Note – Constant dollars were calculated using the fiscal year CPI-U.

Beneficiaries of the WIC Program receive monthly vouchers for the purchase of a "package" of specifically prescribed food items in participating retail stores (or, in some cases, actual monthly food packages of supplemental foods directly provided by state agencies). The range of permissible food items is set by federal regulation, although administering state agencies have some latitude in how federal standards are carried out (e.g., specifying "store" brands, decisions as to what types of infant formula are covered, what food may be provided for those with special dietary needs). Among the items that may be included are milk, cheese, eggs, infant formula, cereals, fruit or vegetable juices, and fresh fruits and vegetables. The program requires that vouchers (or food packages) be tailored (by food type and amount) by category of recipient—e.g., infants, children; pregnant, postpartum and nursing mothers. In addition to food benefits, recipients also must receive nutrition education and breast-feeding support (where called for) and may receive other services like referral to medical care providers.

The federal cost of providing WIC benefits varies widely depending on the recipient and the foods prescribed in recipients' vouchers, as well as differences in retail prices (vouchers are denominated in food amounts, not dollars) and administrative and nutrition services expenses (like those for nutrition risk screening, breastfeeding support, and nutrition education). Moreover, the program's food costs are significantly influenced by the degree to which states gain rebates from infant formula (and, in some cases, juice or other) manufacturers under a requirement to pursue "cost containment" strategies; these rebates recently have totaled to over $1.8 billion a year nationwide and pay for the cost of serving a significant portion of the WIC population. In FY2007, the national average federal cost of a WIC food package (after rebates) was $39 a month for each participant. The program also provides states with funding for administrative costs and nutrition services (like nutrition education). In FY2007, the average monthly "nutrition services and administrative" ("NSA") cost, including regular administrative expenses and nutrition risk assessments and nutrition education, was about $16 per case.

The WIC Program has categorical, income, and nutrition risk requirements for eligibility. Only pregnant and postpartum women, infants, and children under age 5 may participate. As noted above, WIC applicants must show evidence of health or nutrition risk, medically verified by a health professional, in order to qualify. They also must have family income below 185% of the most recent annually indexed federal poverty guidelines ($32,560 a year for a three person family for the period July 2008-June 2009; state WIC agencies may (but virtually never) set lower income eligibility cutoff points. Receipt of TANF, SNAP benefits (formerly, food stamps), or Medicaid assistance also can satisfy the WIC Program's income test, and states may consider pregnant women meeting the income test "presumptively" eligible until a nutritional risk evaluation is made. In 2006, 60% of WIC enrollees had family income below the federal poverty guidelines, 9% of WIC enrollees were cash welfare (TANF) recipients, 22% received food stamps, and 63% were covered by Medicaid.

WIC participants receive benefits for a specified period of time, and in some cases must be recertified during this period to show continuing need—e.g., pregnant women may continue to receive benefits throughout their pregnancy and for up to 6-12 months after childbirth. Although it is federally funded, the WIC program actually is administered by some 2,000 state and local health agencies (and more than 30 Indian tribal organizations participating as separate grantees and treated like states). Over 10,000 local clinics/sites carry out the program. State administrative responsibilities extend to certifying eligibility, distributing benefits, issuing benefits, redeeming vouchers, and approving retail stores for participation.

Unlike most other federal nutrition assistance programs, the WIC program is not an "entitlement" program; it is "discretionary" and participation and benefits are limited by the amount of federal funding appropriated, whatever state supplementary funding is provided, and the extent of manufacturers' rebates. However, Congress has historically provided funding at levels that meet participation and food cost requirements—so-called "full funding." In FY2007, federal spending was $5.4 billion, and the program served a monthly average of 8.3 million women, infants, and children: 25% women, 27% infants, and 51% children. In addition to the regular WIC program (which includes special vouchers for fruits and vegetables), annual Agriculture Department appropriations (in a budget account separate from WIC appropriations) fund a small ($20 million a year) **WIC farmers' market nutrition program** under which WIC applicants and recipients receive additional vouchers for the purchase of fresh produce at farmers' markets. **Table 3** summarizes WIC participation and federal spending. Spending is made up of food costs, just over 70% of the total in recent years, and nutrition services and administrative (NSA) expenses (of which approximately two-thirds are typically for service activities like nutrition education and nutrition risk evaluations and one-third is for traditional administrative activities like eligibility determinations and issuing and redeeming vouchers).

Day Care, Summer, and After-School Programs

In addition to the school-day-based lunch and breakfast programs, child nutrition laws include provisions for federal subsidies and commodity support for schools and other institutions/ organizations offering meals and snacks to children in outside-of-school program settings. This assistance is provided to (1) schools and other governmental institutions, (2) private for-profit and nonprofit day care centers, (3) family/group day care homes, and (4) nongovernmental institutions/organizations that offer outside-of-school programs for children. In addition, day care centers for chronically impaired adults and elderly persons are eligible for assistance under the same general terms as centers caring for children.

Table 3. Special Supplemental Nutrition Program for Women, Infants, and Children (WIC) Participation and Federal Spending for Selected Fiscal Years, 1980-2007 In Millions

	Average monthly participation				Federal spending	
	Women	Infants	Children	Total[a]	Current dollars[b]	Constant 2007 dollars[c]
1980	0.4	0.5	1.0	1.9	$727.7	$1,867.3
1985	0.6	0.9	1.6	3.1	1,489.3	2,866.9
1990	1.0	1.4	2.1	4.5	2,122.4	3,385.2
1995	1.6	1.8	3.5	6.9	3,436.2	4,659.5
1996	1.6	1.8	3.7	7.2	2,301.1	3,035.1
1997	1.7	1.9	3.8	7.4	3,843.8	4,939.3
1998	1.7	1.9	3.7	7.3	3,890.4	4,917.5
1999	1.7	1.9	3.7	7.3	3,938.1	4,883.2
2000	1.8	1.9	3.5	7.2	3,982.1	4,786.6
2001	1.8	1.9	3.6	7.3	4,153.3	4,838.6
2002	1.8	1.9	3.8	7.5	4,339.8	4,982.1
2003	1.9	1.9	3.8	7.6	4,524.4	5,071.9
2004	1.9	2.0	4.0	7.9	4,887.3	5,356.5
2005	2.0	2.0	4.0	8.0	4,993.1	5,297.7
2006	2.0	2.1	4.0	8.1	5,075.7	5,192.4
2007	2.1	2.2	4.0	8.3	5,417.9	5,417.9

Source: Compiled by the Congressional Research Service (CRS) based on data from the U.S. Department of Agriculture, Food and Nutrition Service.

a. Details may not sum to totals due to rounding.

b. Includes funding for food costs, administration, nutrition services, studies, surveys, pilots, and farmers' market programs. Does not include support from manufacturer rebates for infant formula and juices.

c. Constant dollars were calculated using the fiscal year CPI-U.

Federal support for day care, summer, and outside-of-school meal/snack programs totaled some $2.5 billion in "entitlement" funding (including a small amount of commodities) for FY2007. More than 5 million children (and 100,000 adults) participated.

Child and Adult Care Food Program (CACFP)

The large majority of assistance for meals and snacks served in outside-of-school settings is provided under the CACFP. This program pays subsidies for meals and snacks served in participating nonresidential child care centers (average attendance 40-5 0 children) and family day care homes (typically caring for 5-10 children). It also supports assistance for meals and snacks in adult day care centers (averaging 40-45 chronically ill or elderly adults), as well as those offered in participating after-school programs (which are discussed later).

The CACFP provides federal payments for breakfasts, lunches, suppers, and snacks served in participating centers or homes. In many cases, sponsors giving administrative support to providers also are paid limited amounts for their costs. Subsidized meals and snacks must meet minimum federal nutrition standards, and providers must fulfill any state or local licensing/approval requirements or minimum alternative federal requirements (or otherwise demonstrate that they comply with government established standards for other child care programs). Federal assistance is made up overwhelmingly of cash subsidies based on the number of meals/snacks served and federally set indexed per-meal/snack subsidy rates; about 3% is in the form of federally donated food commodities. CACFP subsidies are available for meals and snacks served to children age 12 or under, migrant children age 15 or under, handicapped children of any age, and (in the case of adult care centers) chronically impaired and elderly adults; but preschool children form the overwhelming majority of those served by the program. Federal CACFP payments flow to individual providers either directly from the administering state agency (this is the case with many child/adult care centers able to handle their own administrative responsibilities) or through “sponsors” who oversee and provide support for a number of local providers (this is the case with some child/adult care centers and all day care homes).

Child care centers in the CACFP can be: (1) public or private nonprofit centers, (2) Head Start centers, (3) for-profit proprietary centers (if they meet minimum requirements as to the proportion of low-income children they enroll), and (4) shelters for homeless families. Adult day care centers include public or private nonprofit centers and for-profit proprietary centers (if they meet minimum requirements related to serving low-income disabled and elderly adults). In FY2007, some 48,000 child care centers, with average daily attendance of 2.2 million children, participated in the CACFP. Adult care centers totaled 2,500, with an average daily attendance of 105,000 persons.

Participating day care centers may receive daily subsidies for up to two meals and one snack or one meal and two snacks for each child, so long as they meet federal nutrition standards. All meals and snacks served in centers are federally subsidized to at least some degree; different subsidies are provided for breakfasts, lunches/suppers, and snacks, and subsidy rates are set in law and indexed for inflation annually. However, cash subsidies vary according to the family income of each child’s family, and the income demographics of the centers’ recipients is periodically evaluated. Subsidies are annually indexed, and the largest subsidies are paid for meals and snacks served to children with family income below 130% of the federal poverty income guidelines (the income limit for free school meals): for July 2008-June 2009, these subsidies are 71 cents for each snack, $1.40 for each breakfast, and $2.57 for each lunch/supper. Smaller subsidies are available for meals and snacks served at a reduced price (no more than 15 cents for snacks, 30 cents for breakfasts, and 40 cents for lunches/suppers) to children with family income between 130% and 185% of the poverty guidelines (the income range for reduced-price school meals) and for meals and snacks served to children who do not qualify for free or reduced- price meals/snacks. "Independent" centers (those without sponsors handling administrative responsibilities) must pay for administrative costs associated with the CACFP out of non-federal funds or a portion of their meal subsidy payments. In other cases, center sponsors may retain a proportion of the meal subsidy payments they receive on behalf of their centers to cover their costs. Finally, federal commodity assistance is available to centers, valued at some 21 cents a meal for July 2008-June 2009 (the same commodity value provided for school meals).

CACFP subsidized day care homes serve an average of 5-10 children; just under 30% of children in the CACFP (860,000 in FY2007) are served through day care homes, and about one-third of the money spent under the CACFP supports meals and snacks served in homes. In FY2007, 143,000 home sites (with some 900 sponsors) received subsidies.

As with centers, payments to day care homes are provided for no more than two meals and one snack (or one meal and two snacks) a day for each child. Unlike centers, day care homes must participate under the auspices of a public or (most often) private nonprofit sponsor that typically has 100 or more homes under its supervision; CACFP day care home sponsors receive monthly administrative payments (separate from meal subsidies) based on the number of homes for which they are responsible. Also unlike centers, day care homes receive cash subsidies (but not commodities) that generally do not differ by individual children's family income. Instead, there are two distinct, annually indexed subsidy rates. "Tier I" homes (those located in low-income areas or operated by low income providers) receive higher subsidies for each meal/snack they serve: for July 2008-June 2009, all lunches and suppers are subsidized at $2.18 each, all breakfasts at $1.17, and all snacks at 65 cents. "Tier II" homes (those not located in low-income areas or without low income providers) receive smaller subsidies: for July 2008-June 2009, these are $1.31 for lunches/suppers, 43 cents for breakfasts, and 18 cents for snacks. However, Tier II providers may seek the higher Tier I subsidy rates for individual low income children for whom financial information is collected and verified.

Although federal subsidies for day care centers differ by family income, there is no requirement that meals/snacks specifically identified as "free" or "reduced-price" be served. Centers may adjust their regular fees (tuition) to account for federal payments, but the CACFP itself does not regulate these fees; in addition, centers can charge separately for meals/snacks, so long as there are no charges for children meeting free-meal/snack income tests and limited charges for those meeting reduced-price income tests. Federal subsidies for family day care homes differ by the type of home and homes may adjust their tuition to account for federal payments; as with centers, there is no requirement that meals/snacks specifically identified as "free" or "reduced-price" be offered. However, unlike centers, federal rules prohibit any separate meal charges.

In FY2007, the CACFP provided \$2.1 billion in cash subsidies for meal costs and \$77 million worth of commodities. In addition, it paid \$137 million for sponsors' administrative costs and expenses related to auditing local operators.

Summer Food Service Program

The Summer Food Service program provides assistance to local public and private nonprofit “service institutions” running summer youth/recreation programs, summer feeding projects, and camps. Assistance is primarily in the form of cash subsidies for each meal or snack served; however, federally donated commodities also are offered. Participating service institutions (also called sponsors) often, but not of necessity, are entities that provide ongoing year-round service to the community and include schools, local governments, camps, colleges and universities in the National Youth Sports program, and private nonprofit organizations like churches.

Sponsors of three types of summer programs can be approved: (1) “open” sites operating in lower-income areas where 50% or more of the children have family income that would make them eligible for free or reduced-price school meals, (2) “enrolled” sites where at least half of the children enrolled in the sponsor’s program are eligible for free or reduced-price school meals, and (3) summer camps. Summer meals/snacks are provided free to all children at open or enrolled sites and to lower-income children in camps.

Summer sponsors get operating (food, storage, labor) cost subsidies for all meals/snacks they serve—one meal and one snack, or two meals (three meals for children in programs for migrant children) per child per day. In addition, sponsors receive payments for administrative costs, and states are provided with subsidies for administrative costs and health and meal-quality inspections. For the summer of 2008, the combined (operating and administrative cost) subsidies under the summer program were approximately \$3 for each lunch/supper, \$1.70 for each breakfast, and 70 cents for each snack. Actual payments vary slightly (e.g., by about 5 cents for lunches) depending on the location of the site (e.g., rural vs. urban) and whether meals are prepared on-site or by a vendor.

In FY2007, some 3,600 sponsors (with 30,000 food service sites) participated in the summer program and served an average of 1.9 million children daily. Program costs totaled to about \$300 million, including cash, commodities, administrative cost assistance, and health inspection costs.

After-School Programs

Federal assistance for snacks (and, in some cases, meals) served through after-school programs is provided through two basic alternatives. The CACFP offers subsidies to sponsors (schools or community-based nonprofit sponsoring entities) for snacks served during the school year to "at- risk" children in after-school programs located in lower-income areas where at least half the children are eligible for free or reduced-price school meals. In a few states (eight in FY2009), these CACFP payments also are available for meals (typically suppers) through after-school programs. All snacks/meals generally are served free. A second, less-used, avenue is open only to schools as an extension of the School Lunch program. They may operate after-school snack-only programs during the school year that provide free snacks in lower-income areas (like the CACFP component) or offer free, reduced-price, or fully paid-for snacks (differentiated by family income like the School Lunch program) in non-needy areas.

Although non-school sponsors may receive after-school nutrition assistance, the overwhelming majority of sites (more than 80%) are operated by schools. Federal cash subsidies for snacks (and, where available, meals) generally are the same as those paid for snacks and lunches/suppers in the regular CACFP. In FY2007, average daily participation in after-school snack/supper programs was approximately 1.2 million children. Spending on this type of assistance is not separately tracked at the federal level, but is included in the figures for the School Lunch program and the CACFP, noted above.

Other Child Nutrition Programs, Initiatives, and Support Activities

Child nutrition laws also support a range of smaller programs, initiatives, and activities.

States are entitled to federal grants to help cover **administrative and oversight/monitoring costs** associated with child nutrition programs. The national amount each year is equal to about 1.5% of child nutrition cash support. The majority of this money is allocated to states based on their share of spending on the covered programs; about 15% is allocated under a discretionary formula granting each state additional amounts for the CACFP, commodity distribution, and "coordinated review" efforts. In addition, states receive payments for their role in overseeing summer programs (about 2.5% of their summer program aid). States are free to apportion their federaladministrative expense payments among child nutrition initiatives (including commodity distribution activities) as they see fit. State administrative expense funding in FY2007 totaled to more than $160 million.

States receive grants for a **Fresh Fruit and Vegetable program**, under which selected schools in each state get money to purchase and distribute fresh fruits and vegetables to all children in attendance (regardless of family income). Money is distributed by a formula under which about half the funding is distributed equally to each state and the remainder is allocated by state population; states select participating schools (with an emphasis on those with a higher proportion of low-income children) and set annual per student grant amounts (between $50 and $75). Funding is set by law at $40 million for the 2008-2009 school year, $65 million for the 2009- 2010 school year, $101 million for the 2010-2011 school year, $150 million for the 2011-2012 school year, and inflation-indexed for later years.

Schools and institutions like summer camps and child care facilities not otherwise participating in federally subsidized meal service programs, along with schools with split (part-day) sessions for kindergartners or pre-kindergartners where children do not have access to regular school meal programs, can participate in the **Special Milk program**. Under this program, they provide milk to all children at a reduced-price or free. Each half-pint served is federally subsidized at a slightly different rate, depending on whether it is served free or not, but the provision of free milk to needy children is not required. In FY2007, about 90 million half-pints were subsidized at about 15 cents each (7% were served free) to roughly 500,000 children. Federal costs for this program typically run about $15 million a year.

Under a **coordinated review effort (CRE)**, the FNS, in cooperation with state agencies, conducts periodic school compliance and accountability evaluations to improve management and identify administrative, subsidy claim, and meal quality problems. This $5 million-a-year effort is the major ongoing initiative related to maintaining the integrity of child nutrition programs. The Agriculture Department's Economic Research Service (ERS) and the FNS conduct **nutrition research, studies, surveys, and program evaluations** (typically totaling about $10 million a year). A national **Food Service Management Institute (FSMI)** provides technical assistance, instruction, and materials related to nutrition and food service management; it is funded at $4 million a year. An **information clearinghouse** provides information to support communitysponsored food assistance initiatives, using funding of about $250,000 a year. **Special FNS projects** – "Team Nutrition" nutrition education initiatives, a food safety project, technical assistance to program operators, food service training grants, aid with electronic food resource systems, "program integrity" efforts – are aimed at helping schools and other providers with nutrition education materials, assisting them to improve their meal service operations and the quality of meals, and ensuring that federal support is spent correctly; they are typically funded at $15-$20 million a year.

In: Child Nutrition and the WIC Program
Editor: Dominic J. Lombardi

ISBN: 978-1-61209-142-6

Chapter 2

THE WIC PROGRAM: BACKGROUND, TRENDS, AND ECONOMIC ISSUES, 2009 EDITION

United States Department of Agriculture

ABSTRACT

The mission of the Special Supplemental Nutrition Program for Women, Infants, and Children (WIC) is to safeguard the health of low-income women, infants, and children through age 4 who are at nutritional risk. WIC provides nutritious foods to supplement diets, nutrition education, and referrals to health care and other social services. Administered by USDA's Food and Nutrition Service (FNS), almost half of all infants and about a quarter of all children ages 1-4 in the United States participate in the program. WIC is USDA's third-largest food and nutrition assistance program, accounting for 10 percent of total Federal spending on food and nutrition assistance. This report describes the WIC program—how it works, its history, program trends, and the characteristics of the population it serves. It also examines current issues facing WIC, focusing mainly on those with important economic implications.

Keywords: Food and Nutrition Assistance Programs, Special Supplemental Nutrition Program for Women, Infants, and Children, WIC, administrative-based issues, outcome-based issues

ACKNOLEDGMENTS

The authors thank Alice Lenihan of the North Carolina Division of Public Health–Nutrition Services and David Smallwood, John Kirlin, Shelly Ver Ploeg, and Laura Tiehen of the Economic Research Service for their comments on earlier drafts, and Angela Anderson for editorial and design support.

Use of commercial and trade names does not imply approval or constitute endorsement by USDA.

Summary

The Special Supplemental Nutrition Program for Women, Infants, and Children (WIC) was created to safeguard the health of low-income women, infants, and children ages 1-4 who are at nutritional risk. WIC provides supplemental food, nutrition education, and referrals to health care and other social services. Almost half of all infants and about a quarter of all children ages 1-4 in the United States participate in the program. WIC is the U.S. Department of Agriculture's third-largest food and nutrition assistance program, with Federal expenditures of $6.2 billion in fiscal year (FY) 2008.

What Is the Issue?

The Child Nutrition and WIC Reauthorization Act of 2004 (P.L. 108-265), which authorized funds for the WIC program, expires on September 30, 2009. Reauthorization provides an opportunity for policymakers to examine issues associated with the operation and effectiveness of the program. The goal of this report is to provide a better understanding of how WIC works, provide its history and program trends, and inform public debate on major economic issues facing the program.

What Did the Study Find?

Numerous issues are associated with administering a program of WIC's size and complexity. This report identifies and frames some of these issues, focusing mainly on those with important economic implications.

Expansion of the WIC Program. As a discretionary grant program, the number of participants served by WIC depends on the annual appropriation and the cost of operating the program. Participation has grown dramatically over time, due largely to increased congressional appropriations and to savings generated by cost-containment practices. Although funding has been sufficient to serve all eligible people *seeking to enroll* in the program in recent years, many eligible people still do not participate in WIC. Some groups contend that WIC should continue to increase participation among those eligible, but others claim that WIC eligibility requirements are too lenient and that WIC has expanded too much. They also question whether WIC would be more effective providing more intensive services to fewer participants.

Federal Funding and State Incentives. Unlike the other major USDA food assistance programs, such as the Supplemental Nutrition Assistance Program (formerly the Food Stamp Program), WIC is 100 percent federally funded—that is, State matching funds are not required. With little or no State funds at stake, State officials have few incentives to restrict WIC enrollment and may have little interest in WIC operations—factors cited in the increasing number of participants and the proliferation of WIC-only stores (stores that sell only or predominantly WIC foods and serve only or predominantly WIC participants) in the early 2000s.

Funding for Nutrition Services and Administration (NSA). WIC State agencies receive NSA grants to cover the costs of administering the program and the costs associated with providing key services, such as nutrition education and breastfeeding promotion and support. NSA funds are based on a set amount per participant, adjusted annually for infl ation, and currently account for 28 percent of total program costs. NSA funding levels have been a source of considerable confl ict. The debate centers on whether NSA funds are too high and should be capped to allow for a greater proportion of appropriated funds to be used for food benefits or whether the funds merely refl ect the success of the WIC program in keeping food costs low while serving more participants from infant formula rebates.

Food Package Revisions. In December 2007, USDA revised the WIC food packages to encourage positive changes in participants' behaviors and outcomes while minimizing vendor burden and maintaining cost neutrality. These revisions—which must be implemented by October 1, 2009—represent the most significant changes to the WIC program since its inception. The potential impacts of the revised food packages on participants, vendors, and food manufacturers, as well as on non-WIC consumers, are unknown.

Rising Food Prices. Prices for food at home rose 6 percent in 2008—the largest single-year increase since 1990. Because food accounts for almost three-quarters of total WIC costs, changes in food prices have important implications for program funding and the number of participants the program can serve.

Increasing Infant Formula Costs. Federal law requires that WIC State agencies enter into cost-containment contracts to purchase infant formula. Typically, WIC State agencies obtain substantial discounts through negotiated rebates from infant formula manufacturers for each can of formula. In exchange, the manufacturer is given the exclusive right to provide its product to WIC participants in that State. Rebates, totaling about $1.8 billion in FY 2007, support about a quarter of all WIC participants. Recent ERS research indicates, however, that the per can cost of formula to WIC has increased. Because of the large volume of infant formula purchased through WIC—the program purchases over half of all infant formula sold in the United States—even small increases in the per can cost could have far-reaching negative implications for the program.

WIC's Effect on the Health of Participants. Much of the research on WIC's impact on the health of participants has focused on its effect on birth outcomes (e.g., birthweight, preterm delivery, and infant mortality). Less research is available on other health outcomes, such as the growth and development of children, or on other participant groups. Changes in how the program operates and in participant characteristics also contribute to the need for new research. Methodological issues and the complexity of health outcomes complicate researchers' ability to assess the program's impact.

The Effectiveness of WIC's Nutrition Education Program. Evaluating the effectiveness of WIC's nutrition education is complicated by variation among and within States in its content, how it is implemented, and the characteristics of the participants. Efforts to improve nutrition education are constrained by limited staff time with clients and limited financial resources.

WIC and Childhood Obesity. Increasing childhood obesity has raised questions as to whether food and nutrition assistance programs, such as WIC, contribute to the problem by providing too much food and encouraging overeating. The prevalence of overweight, however, is growing among both WIC and non-WIC children, and there is little evidence that participation in WIC is associated with increased prevalence of overweight. WIC food packages have recently been revised, partly to reduce the amount of saturated fat, cholesterol, and total fat provided in the supplemental food package and improve eating patterns that promote healthy weight.

WIC and Breastfeeding Rates. Low breastfeeding rates among WIC participants have raised questions about WIC's effects on breastfeeding. The 2007 WIC food package revisions provide stronger incentives for breastfeeding by increasing the market value of the food packages for infant/ mother pairs who are fully breastfeeding. How effective these increases will be in getting more women to breastfeed and what effects higher breastfeeding rates may have on program costs, given infant formula rebates, remains to be seen.

How Was the Study Conducted?

Researchers from USDA's Economic Research Service (ERS) examined WIC's laws and regulations, program trends in terms of program expenditures, number of participants, and infant formula rebates, and a large number of WIC-related research publications.

INTRODUCTION

The mission of the Special Supplemental Nutrition Program for Women, Infants, and Children (WIC) is to safeguard the health of low-income women, infants, and children ages 1-4 who are at nutritional risk by providing supplemental food, nutrition education, and referrals to health care and other social services. WIC is based on the premise that early intervention programs during critical times of growth and development can help prevent future medical and developmental problems. Administered at the Federal level by USDA's Food and Nutrition Service (FNS), the program provides grants for supplemental foods, nutrition services, and administration to 90 WIC State agencies, including all 50 States, the District of Columbia, 34 Indian Tribal Organizations, and 5 territories (Guam, the U.S. Virgin Islands, American Samoa, the Commonwealth of Puerto Rico, and the Commonwealth of the Northern Mariana Islands).

Since its establishment in 1972, WIC has become one of the central components of the Nation's food and nutrition assistance system. With Federal expenditures of $6.2 billion in FY 2008—or 10 percent of total USDA expenditures for domestic food and nutrition assistance—WIC is the country's third-largest food and nutrition assistance program, trailing only the Food Stamp Program ($37.5 billion) and the National School Lunch Program ($9.3 billion) (USDA, 2008b) (Figure 1).[1] WIC was the fastest growing food assistance program in FY 2008 in terms of Federal expenditures, growing 15 percent over the previous year. WIC served an average of 8.7 million participants per month during FY 2008.

The Child Nutrition and WIC Reauthorization Act of 2004 (P.L. 108-265), which authorized funds for WIC and child nutrition programs, is set to expire on September 30, 2009. Reauthorization provides an opportunity for policymakers to examine the operation and effectiveness of the program. This report updates a previous report released in 2002 (Oliveira et al., 2002).[2] Specifically, this report provides information on how the program works, WIC's legislative and regulatory history, program trends with regard to costs and participation levels, and the characteristics of the population WIC serves. It also examines current issues facing WIC, focusing mainly on those with important economic implications.

OVERVIEW OF THE WIC PROGRAM

WIC has a number of features that make it unique among food and nutrition assistance programs. For example, WIC has a narrowly defined target population. It requires that applicants be at nutritional risk and it uses a priority system to determine who gets served when funds are short. WIC also provides participants with a package of benefits, including supplemental foods, nutrition education, and health care referrals. Food benefits are directed to specific nutritional needs. To increase budgetary efficiency, WIC negotiates substantial rebates from infant formula manufacturers.

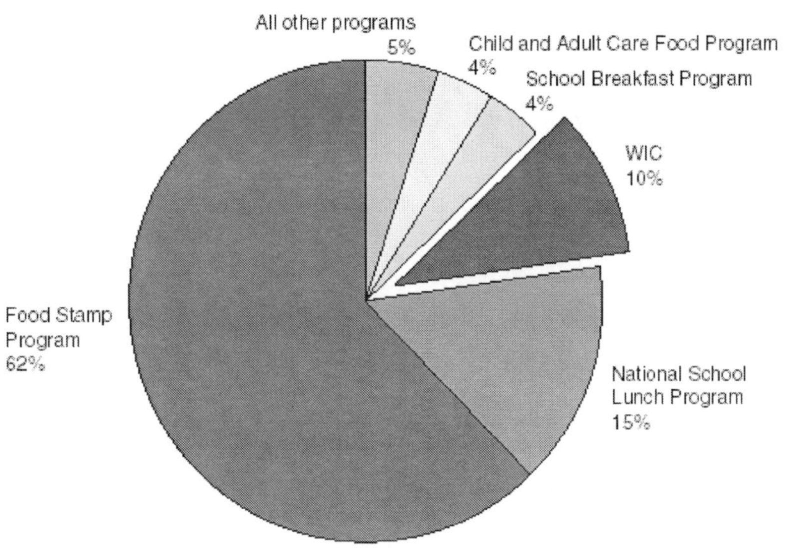

Note: USDA expenditures for food and nutrition assistance totaled $60.7 billion in FY 2008. Source: USDA, 2008b.

Figure 1. USDA expenditures for food and nutrition assistance program, FY 2008

Table 1.WIC income eligibility guidelines for the 48 contiguous States and DC (effective from July 1, 2008 to June 30, 2009)

Family size	Annual income
Number of people	*Dollars*
1	19,240
2	25,900
3	32,560
4	39,220
5	45,880
6	52,540
7	59,200
8	65,860
For each additional member, add	6,660

Note: Alaska and Hawaii have higher guidelines. Source: 73 *Federal Register* 19048.

Participant Eligibility

To qualify for WIC, applicants must meet categorical, residential, income, and nutritional risk eligibility requirements.

Categorical Eligibility

To participate in the WIC program, a person must be either:

- A pregnant woman;
- A nonbreastfeeding woman up to 6 months postpartum;
- A breastfeeding woman up to 1 year postpartum;[3]
- An infant up to his/her first birthday; or
- A child up to his/her fifth birthday.

Residential Eligibility

WIC applicants must reside within the State where they establish eligibility.

Income Eligibility

The family income of WIC applicants must meet specified guidelines.[4] All WIC State agencies currently set the income cutoff at the maximum 185 percent of the Federal poverty guidelines (annual income of $39,220 for a family of four living in the 48 contiguous States as of July 1, 2008) (table 1). Either the income of the family during the past 12 months or the family's current rate of income may be used to determine an applicant's income eligibility, whichever most accurately refl ects the family's status.[5]

Applicants who participate in the Food Stamp, Medicaid, or Temporary Assistance for Needy Families (TANF) programs are adjunctively income eligible; that is, they are deemed to meet the income eligibility criteria automatically and do not have to provide documentation of income when they apply.[6] In addition, WIC State agencies have the option to deem individuals automatically income eligible if they participate in other State-administered programs that use income guidelines at or below 185 percent of the Federal poverty guidelines and routinely require income documentation.

Nutritional Risk

Applicants must be at nutritional risk, as determined by a health professional, such as a physician, nutritionist, dietician, or nurse. During the determination process, the height (or length) and weight of each applicant is measured and a blood test for anemia is administered to everyone except infants under 9 months (Bartlett et al., 2007).[7] The medical history and dietary patterns of participants are also considered. Federal regulations recognize five major types of nutritional risk for WIC eligibility:

- Detrimental or abnormal nutritional conditions detectable by biochemical or anthropometric measurements (such as anemia, underweight, or overweight).
- Other documented nutritionally related medical conditions (such as nutrient deficiency diseases, metabolic disorders, or lead poisoning).
- Dietary deficiencies that impair or endanger health (such as inadequate dietary patterns).
- Conditions that directly affect the nutritional health of a person (including alcoholism or drug abuse).
- Conditions that predispose a person to inadequate nutritional patterns or nutritionally related medical conditions (including, but not limited to, homelessness and migrancy) (7 Code of Federal Regulations (CFR) 246.2).

WIC participants are typically eligible to receive benefits for a 6-month period. They then must be recertified to continue receiving benefits. Pregnant women, however, are certified for the duration of their pregnancy and up to 6 weeks postpartum. Breastfeeding women and their infants can be certified up to the infant's first birthday at the WIC State agency's option (table 2).[8]

Participant Benefits

The WIC program offers three types of benefits to participants: a supplemental food package, nutrition education, and referrals to health care and other services. All benefits are provided to participants free of charge.

Supplemental Food Package

WIC provides participants with a package of supplemental foods designed to address the nutritional needs of the specific population of low-income pregnant, breastfeeding and nonbreastfeeding postpartum women, infants, and children at nutritional risk. Federal regulations define specific WIC foods and the maximum quantities included in the packages (7 CFR 246.10). The food package is supplemental; it is not intended to be a primary source of food or general food assistance. The foods included in the packages are high in nutrients determined to be beneficial for pregnant, breastfeeding, and postpartum women, infants, and children, as prescribed by the Secretary (7 CFR 246.2). A lack of such nutrients may result in adverse health consequences.

Packages are designed to meet the specific needs of each participant category. For example, breastfeeding women whose infants do not receive infant formula from WIC can receive an enhanced food package that includes canned tuna and carrots in addition to other WIC foods, while nonbreastfeeding postpartum women do not. Unlike the Food Stamp Program, the amount of food provided to recipients does not vary with household income. The authorized maximum monthly allowances for all WIC foods must be made available to participants if medically and nutritionally warranted (7 CFR 246.10). WIC State agencies, however, may tailor an individual's food package based upon their nutritional or health status, their nutritional risk factors, food restrictions, intolerances, and preferences.[9] WIC State agencies also have the authority to make adjustments to WIC foods for administrative convenience and to control costs (e.g., restricting container sizes, brands, types, and physical forms).

Prior to revisions in the food packages in 2007, there were seven food packages that included different types and quantities of food depending on participant category and the nutritional needs of the participant:

- Infants through 3 months.
- Infants 4-11 months.
- Children or women with special dietary needs.
- Children ages 1-4.
- Pregnant and breastfeeding women (basic).
- Nonbreastfeeding postpartum women.
- Breastfeeding women (enhanced).

Table 2. Certification Periods, by WIC Participant Categories

Pregnant woman	For the duration of the pregnancy and up to the last day of the month in which the infant becomes 6 weeks old or the pregnancy ends.
Postpartum woman	Up to the last day of the sixth month after the baby is born or the pregnancy ends.
Breastfeeding woman	Approximately every 6 months. The State agency may permit its local agencies to certify a breastfeeding woman up to the last day of the month in which her infant turns 1 year old or until the woman ceases breastfeeding, whichever occurs first.
Infant	Approximately every 6 months. The State agency may permit its local agencies to certify an infant younger than 6 months up to the last day of the month in which the infant turns 1 year old, provided the quality and accessibility of health care services are not diminished.
Child	Approximately every 6 months and ending with the last day of the month in which a child reaches his/her fifth birthday.

Source: 7 CFR 246.7.

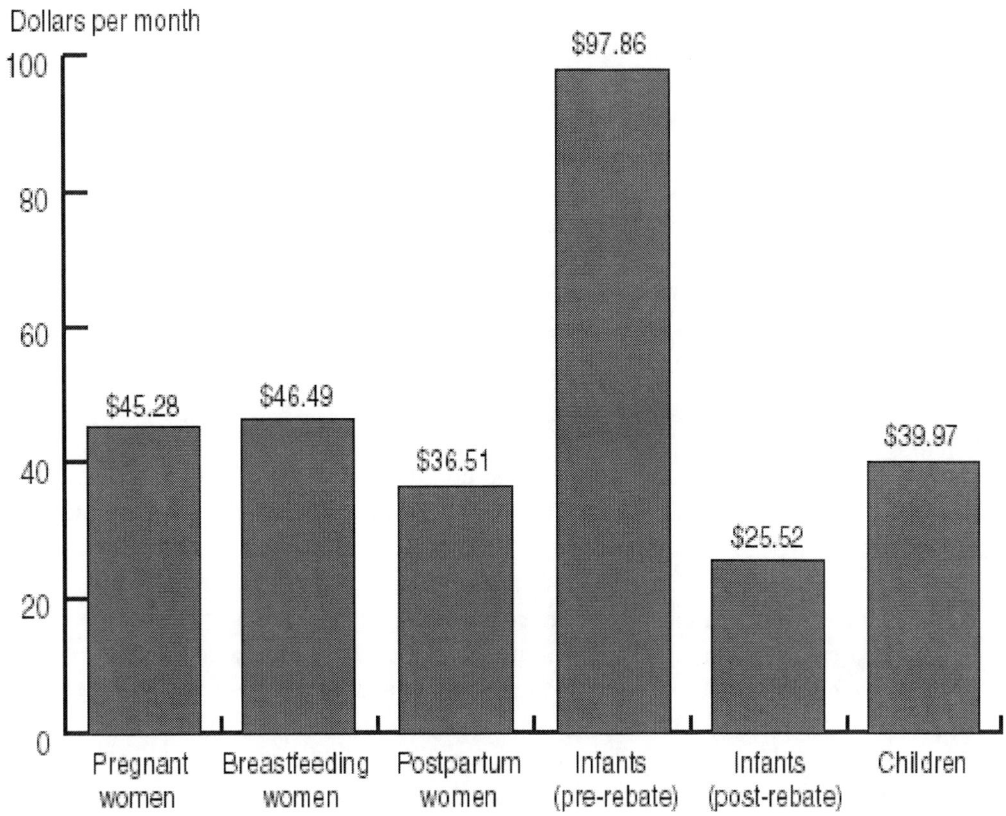

Note: The average cost of the WIC food packages in FY 2005 was $55.18 before rebates.
Source: USDA, 2007b.

Figure 2. Monthly WIC food package costs, by participant category, FY 2005

These packages included combinations of the following foods: iron-fortified infant formula; iron-fortified infant and adult cereal; vitamin C-rich fruit juice and/or vegetable juice; eggs; milk; cheese; peanut butter and/or dried beans or peas; tuna; and carrots. Special infant formulas and certain medical foods could also be provided by the WIC food package when prescribed by a physician or health professional for a specific medical condition. Participants received quantity-based vouchers that entitled them to specific amounts of WIC-approved foods. The monthly cost of the packages varied greatly by participant category, ranging from $36.51 for postpartum women to $97.86 for infants (before rebates) in FY 2005 (Figure 2).[10]

In December 2007, program regulations governing the WIC food packages were revised to better reflect advances in nutrition science and dietary recommendations and to address current supplemental nutritional needs of WIC participants (72 *Federal Register* 68965-69032). WIC State agencies are required to implement the new provisions between February 4, 2008, and October 1, 2009. There are still seven food packages. Food package I now covers infants up to 5 months, food package II covers infants 6-11 months, and food package III covers all individuals with medical needs, including infants.

Other changes to the food packages include reducing the maximum monthly allowances for some foods (e.g., milk, juice, and eggs), allowing additional foods (e.g., soy-based beverages and tofu as alternatives to milk in the women's packages and in children's packages with medical documentation), adding new foods (e.g., fruits, vegetables, and some whole-grain products) to most food packages, and removing juice from the older infant food package (table 3). Under the new food packages, participants will receive vouchers with a fixed monthly cash value for fruits and vegetables ($6 for children, $10 for fully breastfeeding women, and $8 for all other women).[11] For all other WIC foods, WIC participants are still given quantity-based WIC food vouchers. (For additional details about the revised food packages, see the section on "Potential Impacts of the Revised WIC Food Packages," pg. 44.)

Nutrition Education

WIC makes nutrition education available to all participants (or to the parents or caretakers of infant/child participants). The nutrition education is designed to achieve two broad goals:

1. Emphasize the relationship between nutrition, physical activity, and health, with special emphasis on the nutritional needs of pregnant, postpartum, and breastfeeding women, infants, and children younger than 5 and awareness about the dangers of using drugs and other harmful substances during pregnancy and while breastfeeding.
2. Assist individuals at nutritional risk improve their health status and achieve a positive change in dietary and physical activity habits, resulting in improved nutritional status and in the prevention of nutrition-related problems through optimal use of the supplemental foods and other nutritious foods (7 CFR 246.11).

All pregnant participants are encouraged to breastfeed, unless contraindicated for health reasons. Local WIC agencies are required to offer participants or caretakers at least two nutrition education sessions during each 6-month period. Individuals who do not attend the nutrition education activities, however, are not denied the WIC food package.

Referrals to Health Care and Social Services

WIC was designed to serve as an adjunct to good health care during critical times of growth and development. Local WIC agencies assist WIC participants in obtaining health care and social services (such as immunizations, food stamps, and Medicaid) either through onsite health services or referrals to other agencies.

Table 3. WIC food packages, before and after the 2007 revisions

	Food package and participant group						
	I	II	III	IV	V	VI	VII
	Prior to 2007 revisions						
Food	**Infants 0-3 months**	**Infants 4-11 months**	**Children/ women with special dietary needs**	**Children 1-4 years**	**Pregnant and breastfeeding women (basic)**	**Nonbreast-feeding postpartum women**	**Breastfeeding women (enhanced)**
Infant formula	X	X	X				
Juice		X	X	X	X	X	X
Infant cereal		X					
Cereal			X	X	X	X	X
Milk				X	X	X	X
Eggs				X	X	X	X
Cheese							X
Dried beans/peas and/or peanut butter				X	X		X
Tuna (canned)							X
Carrots							X
	After 2007 revisions						
	Infants 0-5 months[1]	**Infants 6-11 months[1]**	**Infants/ children/ women with special dietary needs[2]**	**Children 1-4 years**	**Pregnant/ partially breastfeeding women**	**Postpartum women**	**Fully breastfeeding women**
Infant formula	X	X	X				
Infant cereal		X					
Baby food (fruits/vegetables)		X	X				
Baby food (meat)[3]		X					
Juice			X	X	X	X	X
Cereal			X	X	X	X	X
Milk			X	X	X	X	X
Eggs			X	X	X	X	X
Cheese			X				X
Fruits/vegetables			X	X	X	X	X
Whole-wheat bread and other whole grains			X	X	X	X	X
Legumes and/or peanut butter			X	X	X	X	X
Fish (canned)			X				X

[1] The amount of formula, and the types and quantities of other foods in food package II, varies according to infant feeding option (fully formula feeding, partially breastfeeding, or fully breastfeeding).

[2] Participants receiving food package II ireceive the same types and amounts of food they would be entitled to in their respective categories with the addition of WIC formula, which also includes exempt infant formula and WIC-eligible medical foods.

[3] Allowable only to fully breastfeeding infants who do not receive any WIC formula.

Source: 72 *Federal Register* 68965-69032.

Food Delivery Systems

To provide program participants with supplemental food packages, WIC State agencies may use three types of food delivery systems (or any combination of the three):

- Retail—participants obtain supplemental food by exchanging a food instrument (e.g., check or voucher) at authorized retail outlets.[12]
- Home delivery—supplemental food is delivered to the participant's home.
- Direct distribution—participants pick up supplemental food from storage facilities operated by the State or local agency.

In both home delivery and direct distribution food delivery systems, WIC State agencies may purchase the supplemental food in bulk lots to take advantage of discounts. Most State agencies, however, have found that these systems were not feasible due to the costs associated with administering the program or because of its impact on participants (USDA, 1991). As a result, most participants receive their supplemental foods via retail food delivery systems.[13] Under retail food delivery systems, WIC State agencies provide food instruments to participants who then exchange them for supplemental foods at authorized retail outlets. The food instrument specifies the types and quantities of supplemental foods that can be purchased. Food instruments may be issued to participants every 1, 2, or 3 months (7 CFR 246.12).[14] Most participants pick up their food instruments in person at the local agency or clinic. WIC State agencies, however, may issue the food instrument through alternative means, such as mailing or electronic benefit transfer (EBT).[15]

WIC Vendors

Only vendors authorized by the WIC State agency may accept WIC food instruments. Although WIC State agencies are not required to authorize all qualified stores, they must authorize an appropriate number of stores in a geographic distribution that ensures the lowest practicable food prices consistent with adequate participant access and effective WIC State agency management and oversight (7 CFR 246.12). WIC State agencies are also required to establish minimum requirements for the variety and quantity of WIC foods that vendors must stock. Vendors are authorized for a maximum of 3 years, at which time they must apply for reauthorization. To ensure that vendors charge competitive prices for WIC foods, WIC State agencies are required to establish a vendor peer group system with distinct competitive price criteria and allowable reimbursement levels for each peer group.[16] By regulation, WIC food purchases are not subject to State or local sales taxes (7 CFR 246.12).

At the end of FY 2005 (the latest data available), there were 44,458 authorized WIC vendors nationwide (USDA, 2008c).[17] Ninety percent of authorized vendors were regular retail vendors, 6 percent were pharmacies, 3 percent were "WIC-only" or "above-50-percent" vendors, 1 percent participated in the home delivery or direct distribution systems, and less than 1 percent were military commissaries.[18]

The WIC Farmers' Market Nutrition Program

The WIC Farmers' Market Nutrition Program (FMNP) was established in 1992 to provide fresh, unprepared, locally grown fruits and vegetables to WIC participants and to expand the awareness of, use of, and sales at farmers' markets (7 CFR 248.1). In FY 2007, the FMNP operated in parts of 38 States, the District of Columbia, Guam, Puerto Rico, and 5 Indian Tribal Organizations (ITOs). Federal funds support 100 percent of the program's food costs and 70 percent of its administrative costs. States operating the FMNP must therefore contribute at least 30 percent of the program's total administrative cost. Women, children, and infants over 4 months who have either been certified to receive WIC program benefits or who are on a waiting list for WIC certification are eligible to participate in the program. Eligible WIC participants are issued FMNP coupons in addition to their regular WIC food instruments. These coupons can be used to buy fresh, unprepared fruits, vegetables, and herbs from farmers, farmers' markets, or roadside stands approved by the FMNP State agency to accept FMNP coupons. Until the December 2007 revisions to the WIC food packages, FMNP provided the only source of fruits and vegetables not in juice form to WIC participants other than the provision of carrots to breastfeeding women. The Federal food benefit level for FMNP recipients may not be less than $10 or more than $30 per year per recipient. During FY 2007, 2.3 million WIC participants received benefits from farmers' markets. That same year, 15,062 farmers, 3,217 farmers' markets, and 2,371 roadside stands were authorized to accept FMNP coupons.[19] Coupons redeemed through the FMNP resulted in over $20 million in revenue to farmers for FY 2007.

Administration of WIC

WIC operates through a Federal/State/local partnership.

- At the Federal level, WIC is administered by USDA's Food and Nutrition Service (FNS), which provides separate cash grants for food benefits and for Nutrition Services and Administration (NSA) to the 90 WIC State agencies. In addition, FNS issues regulations, monitors compliance with these regulations, provides technical assistance to the WIC State agencies, and conducts studies of program operations and compliance.
- WIC State agencies are responsible for program operations within their jurisdictions.[20] They allocate funds to local WIC sponsoring agencies, negotiate rebate contracts with infant formula manufacturers, and provide assistance to local agencies with respect to program operations. WIC State agencies have considerable latitude in operating their programs within broad regulatory guidelines (Macro International, 1995).[21] For example, WIC State agencies decide the specific brands, forms, and package sizes to include in their list of approved WIC foods.
- About 2,000 local WIC agencies, mostly State and county health departments, but also some public and private nonprofit health or human service agencies, provide services to WIC participants either directly or through about 10,000 local service sites or clinics, including county health departments, hospitals, mobile vans,

community centers, schools, and migrant health centers and camps. Local WIC clinics certify applicants, provide nutrition education, make referrals to health care and other social services, and distribute food instruments.

Unlike other food and nutrition assistance programs, WIC is 100 percent federally funded (i.e., State matching funds are not required).[22] Federal grants to WIC State agencies are divided into food grants and NSA grants. Total spending for the WIC program in FY 2008 was $6.2 billion, of which $4.5 billion (73 percent) was spent on food and $1.7 billion (27 percent) was spent on NSA (USDA, 2008b).[23] Food grants cover the cost of supplemental foods, while NSA grants cover nonfood costs, such as certifying participants, determining nutritional risks, conducting blood tests for anemia, providing outreach and nutrition education services, breastfeeding promotion and support, referrals to health and social services, printing food instruments, administering the food delivery system, and staff salaries. At least a sixth of a State agency's NSA expenditures must be used for nutrition education, and an additional portion of NSA funds must be used for breastfeeding promotion and support (7 CFR 246.14). (For more information on NSA, see the section on "Funding for Nutrition Services and Administration (NSA)," p. 39.)

Priority System

WIC is a discretionary grant program funded annually by appropriations law. The number of participants that can be served each year depends on the annual appropriation and WIC's operating costs.[24] Because WIC may not be able to serve all eligible people, WIC uses a seven-point priority system to ensure that people with the greatest nutritional risk and most likely to benefit from WIC intervention receive program benefits (table 4).

Once a local agency has reached its maximum participation level (i.e., is serving the maximum number of participants under its current budget), the priority system is applied to people on the local agency's waiting list. In general, priority is given to people demonstrating medically based nutritional risks over dietary based nutritional risks, to infants and pregnant and breastfeeding women over children, and to children over postpartum women. Increases in funding and savings from infant formula rebates during the 1990s allowed a greater number of lower priority applicants, such as children, to participate. As a result, the role of the seven-point priority system in allocating available program slots among applicants decreased in importance relative to previous years when program funds were more limited. As of spring 2008, anecdotal evidence indicates that funding in recent years has been sufficient to provide benefits to all eligible people seeking to enroll in the program, including those at the lowest priority levels.

Table 4. WIC Nutritional Risk Priorities

Priority (from highest to lowest)	Description
I	Pregnant women, breastfeeding women, and infants at nutritional risk as demonstrated by hematological or anthropometric measurements or other documented nutritionally related medical conditions that demonstrate the need for supplemental foods.
II	Except those infants who qualify for Priority I, infants up to 6 months of age of program participants who participated during pregnancy, and infants up to 6 months of age born of women who were not program participants during pregnancy but whose medical records document that they were at nutritional risk during pregnancy due to nutritional conditions detectable by biochemical or anthropometric measurements or other documented nutritionally related medical conditions that demonstrated the person's need for supplemental foods.
III	Children at nutritional risk as demonstrated by hematological or anthropometric measurements or other documented medical conditions that demonstrate the child's need for supplemental foods.
IV	Pregnant women, breastfeeding women, and infants at nutritional risk because of an inadequate dietary pattern.
V	Children at nutritional risk because of an inadequate dietary pattern.
VI	Postpartum women at nutritional risk.
VII	Individuals certified for WIC solely due to homelessness or migrancy and, at State agency option, previously certified participants who might regress in nutritional status without continued provision of supplemental foods.

Notes: Priorities I through VI must be used in all States. State agencies may, at their discretion, expand the priority system to include Priority VII.

Source: 7 CFR 246.7.

Cost-Containment Measures

Because WIC can serve only as many participants as funding allows, WIC State agencies have tried to reduce food costs through a variety of cost-containment measures. The most effective cost-containment measure is the use of infant formula rebates. WIC accounts for over half of all infant formula sales in the United States (Oliveira et al., 2004). Since 1989, Federal law has required that WIC State agencies enter into cost-containment contracts for the purchase of the infant formula used in WIC. Typically, WIC State agencies obtain significant discounts in the form of rebates from infant formula manufacturers for each can of formula purchased. In exchange for the rebates, a manufacturer is given the exclusive right to provide its product to WIC participants in that State. As a result, WIC pays the lowest price for infant formula. (See the section on "Infant Formula Costs," p. 51, for more information on the WIC infant formula rebate system.)

In FY 2005, pre-rebate food package costs (i.e., estimated retail cost of WIC foods at the time of purchase) averaged $55.18 per participant compared with $37.42 per participant post-rebate (i.e., after taking into account savings from infant formula rebates) (USDA, 2007b). Estimated infant formula rebates for FY 2007 totaled $1.8 billion, an amount that supported about a quarter of WIC participants (USDA, 2008d).

Some WIC State agencies have instituted rebate systems for other foods, such as infant cereal and infant fruit juice, but their savings are much smaller than for infant formula.[25] Additional cost-containment practices used by some WIC State agencies include limiting authorized food vendors (such as supermarkets and grocery stores) to outlets with lower food prices and limiting food-item selection according to brand, package size, form, or price (for instance, requiring purchase of least-cost items) (Kirlin et al., 2003).

Legislative and Regulatory History of the WIC Program

During WIC's history, a number of legislative acts and Federal regulations have shaped the program (table 5). This chapter describes WIC's evolution by examining its legislative and regulatory history.

Table 5. WIC Timeline

1972	Legislation created the Special Supplemental Food Program as a 2-year pilot project (Public Law (P.L.) 92-433).
1973	The program was renamed the Special Supplemental Food Program for Women, Infants, and Children (WIC), and two food packages were created—one for infants and one for children and pregnant and breastfeeding women. WIC supplemental foods included infant formula, milk, cheese, eggs, infant and adult cereals, and fruit juice.
1974	The first WIC site officially opened in Pineville, KY.
1975	Legislation established WIC as a permanent national health and nutrition program (P.L. 94-105).
1977	USDA issued regulations that established a priority system based on nutritional need to determine who shall receive program benefits first. The regulations also allowed State agencies to operate up to three types of food distribution systems (home delivery, retail purchase, and direct distribution) and added a third WIC food package (for children with special dietary needs).
1978	The Child Nutrition Amendments of 1978 (P.L. 95-627) established a national income standard for program eligibil-ity based on the income standards prescribed for reduced-price school lunches. The standards in 1978 stated that a household's income had to be 195 percent of the Federal poverty guidelines or lower. The act also strengthened WIC's nutrition education component by requiring that nutrition education be provided to all program participants.
1980	The number of food packages increased from three to six. Dry beans and peas or peanut butter were added to the food packages for children and pregnant and breastfeeding women, and a maximum level of 6 grams of sugar per dry ounce for adult cereals was set. Wyoming became the last State to implement WIC (the District of Columbia imple- mented its program in 1981).
1981	The maximum income level for reduced-price lunches was lowered to 185 percent of the Federal poverty guidelines. Since the WIC income eligibility standard was tied to the National School Lunch Program's eligibility standard, the maximum income level for WIC was also lowered to 185 percent of poverty.
1987	Tennessee became the first State to implement an infant formula rebate program.
1988	The Hunger Prevention Act of 1988 (P.L. 100-435) provided grants in up to 10 States to conduct Farmers' Market Demonstration Projects.
1989	The Child Nutrition and WIC Reauthorization Act of 1989 (P.L. 101-147) required WIC agencies with retail food distribution systems to use competitive bidding to procure infant formula unless another cost-containment approach yielded equal or greater savings. The act established adjunct income eligibility for Food Stamp, Medicaid, and Aid to Families with Dependent Children (AFDC) recipients. The act also required that USDA promote breastfeeding.
1992	To encourage breastfeeding among WIC mothers, an enhanced WIC food package (food package VII) was created that added two new food items—carrots and canned tuna—along with increased amounts of juice, cheese, and beans/peas and peanut butter for women who exclusively breastfeed their infants. The WIC Farmers' Market Nutrition Act of 1992 (P.L. 102-314) established the WIC Farmers' Market Nutrition Program.
1994	The Healthy Meals for Healthy Americans Act of 1994 (P.L. 103-448) changed the name of the program to the Special Supplemental Nutrition Program for Women, Infants, and Children to emphasize its role as a nutrition program.
1997	USDA kicked off the National Breastfeeding Promotion Campaign to encourage WIC participants to begin and con- tinue breastfeeding.
1998	The William F. Goodling Child Nutrition Reauthorization Act of 1998 (P.L. 105-336) required at certification that, except in limited circumstances, all applicants for WIC must be physically present, document their income, and present proof of residency.
1999	WIC State agencies are required to use definitions of nutritional risk from a national list established for the WIC pro- gram. States are not required to use all of the nutritional risk criteria on the list.
2004	The Child Nutrition and WIC Reauthorization Act of 2004 implemented provisions to maintain competitive pricing among WIC vendors, including peer group pricing.
2007	Interim final rule revises regulations governing the WIC food packages by adding fruits, vegetables, and whole grains; reducing the amounts of certain foods in the existing packages (e.g., juice and milk); and allowing more food substitution that accommodates different cultural eating patterns.

The 1960s and 1970s: Establishment of the WIC Program

The origins of WIC date back to the 1960s when the Nation began to recognize that many low-income Americans were suffering from malnutrition. Various studies identified hunger as a major problem in this country. Events such as the Poor Peoples' March on Washington, DC, and the CBS documentary "Hunger in America" helped publicize the problem (USDA, 1999). In 1968, a group of physicians met with officials from the U.S. Department of Health, Education, and Welfare (HEW) and USDA in Washington, DC (Leonard, 1994). The physicians described young women, often pregnant, in their clinics with various ailments caused by lack of food. Out of this meeting came a plan to build food commissaries attached to neighborhood clinics. Doctors or clinic staff would prescribe needed foods and the prescription served as a voucher that the women would take to the commissary to obtain a food package. Later that year, the first USDA commissary program was established in Atlanta, GA.[26] Independently, another voucher program to distribute foods in a Baltimore, MD, neighborhood was developed by Dr. David Paige of Johns Hopkins University (Leonard, 1994).

In response to the growing public concern about malnutrition among low-income mothers and children, USDA established the Commodity Supplemental Food Program (originally named the Supplemental Food Program) in 1969 (Institute of Medicine, 1996). The program provided commodities to feed low-income pregnant women, infants, and children up to age 6. It was eventually recognized, however, that the available food assistance programs, including the Food Stamp Program and the Commodity Supplemental Food Program, were not meeting the special needs of pregnant women and infants (USDA, 1999).

In December 1969, the White House Conference on Food, Nutrition and Health focused national attention and resources on the problem of malnutrition and hunger due to poverty. Among the recommendations stated in the conference report was the need for special attention to be given to the nutritional needs of low-income pregnant women and preschool children (White House Conference on Food, Nutrition and Health, 1970).

On September 26, 1972, WIC was formally authorized by an amendment to the Child Nutrition Act of 1966. The legislation (P.L. 92-433), sponsored by Senator Hubert H. Humphrey, established the Special Supplemental Food Program as a 2-year pilot program.[27] The legislation's writers used the earlier Johns Hopkins voucher program as a model and designed the program to be a 2-year demonstration, with the expectation that the program's benefits would be so overwhelming that it would continue as a full program (Leonard, 1994).

The legislation assigned USDA the responsibility of administering a program to provide supplemental foods to participants. Specific foods were not identified; however, supplemental foods were defined as foods containing nutrients currently lacking in the diets of populations at nutritional risk, particularly foods containing high-quality protein, iron, calcium, vitamin A, and vitamin C.[28] Also, no mention was made of providing nutrition education or health care referrals. The legislation, however, which grew out of concern that low-income families were not receiving good health care or proper nutrition, created a close association between the supplemental food aspect of the program and health care services by requiring that WIC eligibility depend on participants being at nutritional risk as determined by health professionals (U.S. General Accounting Office, 1979).[29]

Because USDA took little action, the Food Research and Action Center (FRAC) filed suit against USDA, and a Federal court judge ordered USDA to issue regulations to implement the program (Leonard, 1994; 38 *Federal Register* 18447-18451). The regulations, issued in July 1973, created two food packages—one for infants and one for children and pregnant and breastfeeding women—and specified the maximum monthly quantities of each food to be made available to participants. Authorized WIC foods were infant formula, milk, cheese, eggs, infant and adult cereals, and fruit juice. Later that year, legislation (P.L. 93-150) was enacted that authorized federally recognized Indian tribes to act as their own WIC State agencies.

The first WIC site officially opened in Pineville, KY, on January 15, 1974 (USDA, 1999). By the end of the year, WIC was operating in parts of 45 States.[30] At this time, WIC provided supplemental foods only to pregnant and breastfeeding women, infants, and children ages 1–3.[31] Nonbreastfeeding postpartum women and children age 4 and older were excluded.

On October 7, 1975, P.L. 94-105 established WIC as a permanent program. The legislation stated, "Congress finds that substantial numbers of pregnant women, infants, and young children are at special risk in respect to their physical and mental health by reason of poor or inadequate nutrition or health care, or both. It is, therefore, the purpose of the program authorized by this section to provide supplemental nutritious food as an adjunct to good health during such critical times of growth and development in order to prevent the occurrence of health problems." Categorical eligibility was extended to nonbreastfeeding women (up to 6 months postpartum) and children up to their fifth birthday.[32] Eligibility was limited to people determined by the program to be at nutritional risk because of inadequate nutrition and inadequate income. What constituted inadequate nutrition and inadequate income, however, was not defined. The program was designed to supplement food stamps and, as a result, participation in the Food Stamp Program did not preclude a person from participating in WIC.[33] The legislation required that the program begin in areas most in need of special supplemental food and allowed costs for nutrition education as administrative expenses.

In 1977, regulations were issued that established a priority system based on nutritional need to ensure that people most in need received program benefits first (42 *Federal Register* 43206-43220). The system specified priorities for serving categories of participants within the target population. Because of the difficulties associated with determining inadequate dietary patterns as indicators of nutritional need, it was deemed that people with clinical indicators of nutritional need (e.g., people suffering from anemia, abnormal growth patterns, or medical conditions) deserved higher priority levels than people with no clinical indicators. The regulations also allowed State agencies to operate up to three types of food distribution systems (home delivery, retail purchase, and direct distribution) and added a third WIC food package (for children with special dietary needs).[34]

In 1978, P.L. 95-627 defined nutritional risk and established income eligibility standards linked to the income standards prescribed for free and reduced-price school meals.[35] The legislation required that nutrition education be provided to all program participants (or their parents/caretakers) and that not less than a sixth of administrative funds be used for nutrition education activities. The act removed any reference to specific nutrients by defining supplemental foods as "those foods containing nutrients determined by nutrition research to be lacking in the diets" of the target population, as prescribed by the Secretary of Agriculture. The Secretary ("to the degree possible") was also to ensure that the fat, sugar, and salt content of the foods prescribed by WIC were appropriate. The act strengthened the link between WIC and the third component of its benefit package—referrals to health and other services—by requiring that WIC State agencies describe their plans to coordinate WIC operations with special counseling services, such as family planning, immunization, child abuse counseling, and alcohol and drug abuse prevention counseling.

The 1980s and 1990s: WIC Expands

The WIC program saw a number of changes in the 1980s and 1990s, during which time program caseloads nearly quadrupled. Prior to 1980, WIC provided three food packages: one for infants, one for women and children, and one for children with special dietary needs. These food packages were designed so that local WIC agencies could tailor the packages to suit the nutritional needs of the individual. In 1980, new regulations increased the number of food packages from three to six: infants 0-3 months, infants 4-11 months, children/women with special dietary needs, children 1-4 years, pregnant and breastfeeding women, and nonbreastfeeding postpartum women (45 *Federal Register* 74854-74877). The additional food packages took into account the different nutritional needs of participants and the belief that little tailoring was taking place.[36] Dry beans and peas or peanut butter were added to the food packages for children and pregnant and breastfeeding women to increase food variety and enhance nutrient value. The regulations also set a maximum level of 6 grams of sugar per dry ounce for adult cereals due to concerns over sugar's contribution to tooth decay.

In 1989, P.L. 100-435 established a Farmers' Market Coupon Demonstration Project in which 3-year grants were awarded in 10 States to create demonstration projects designed to provide WIC participants with coupons that could be exchanged for fresh, unprepared foods at farmers' markets. Largely as a result of the success of these demonstration projects, P.L. 102-314 in 1992 permanently established the WIC Farmers' Market Nutrition Program (FMNP). Because of limited funding, the FMNP is only available in some geographical areas. Participants in the FMNP receive $10-$30 worth of coupons per year to be spent at approved farmers' markets (a set of vouchers can be provided to a household or to an individual.)[37]

One of the most important legislative acts required WIC State agencies to implement cost-containment practices. In the mid-1980s, infant formula accounted for nearly 40 percent of total WIC food costs and infant formula retail prices were rising more quickly than prices for other foods. These factors led several WIC State agencies to look into cost-containment practices to reduce infant formula costs. In 1987, Tennessee became the first State with a retail food delivery system to implement a rebate system to control costs associated with infant formula. It used competitive bidding to award a contract to an infant formula manufacturer for the exclusive right to provide its product to WIC participants in the State in exchange for a rebate on the formula. The practice proved to be so successful in containing costs that P.L. 101-147 was enacted in 1989, requiring that all WIC State agencies enter into cost-containment contracts for the purchase of infant formula. Because funding for WIC is fixed by congressional appropriations, cost-containment practices allow the program to serve more participants or absorb higher food costs. Since establishment of the infant formula rebate system, rebates have increased dramatically. (For more information on the infant formula rebate program, see the section on "Infant Formula Costs," p. 51.)

While the savings from infant formula rebates allowed WIC State agencies to serve more participants, the escalation in participation increased States' administrative burden (Macro

International, 1995). When infant formula rebates were first implemented, the NSA portion of the States' Federal appropriations was fixed at 20 percent of the total appropriation.[38] As a result, the increase in participation reduced the amount of NSA dollars per participant. To address this funding constraint, P.L. 101-147 (enacted in 1989) changed how the total Federal WIC appropriation to WIC State agencies is allocated for NSA. The new law changed the funding for NSA to a per participant basis based upon the 1987 national average NSA grant per participant (i.e., before the large-scale implementation of infant formula rebates) adjusted annually for inflation.

P.L. 101-147 also established adjunct income eligibility for Food Stamp, Medicaid, and Aid to Families with Dependent Children (AFDC) participants.[39] This was intended to simplify the WIC application process since, at that time, the income eligibility criteria for these other programs were lower than those for WIC.[40] This eligibility provision also had the effect of increasing the coordination between WIC and these other programs (Bartlett et al., 2000). Through the provision of onsite health services or referrals to other health care and social service providers, WIC became an important source for an array of health and social services as it "evolved from being an adjunct to maternal and child health services to becoming an important gateway program through which many low-income households entered the public health system" (Macro International, 1995).

The late 1980s also saw an increased emphasis on breastfeeding promotion and support in WIC.[41] Concern about low breastfeeding rates among WIC mothers prompted Congress in 1989 to mandate $8 million to support breastfeeding promotion activities in WIC and allow the use of administrative funds to purchase breastfeeding aids by WIC agencies as part of P.L 101-147 (U.S. General Accounting Office, 1993). A Breastfeeding Promotion Consortium was established in 1990 to exchange ideas on how the Federal Government and private health organizations can collaboratively promote breastfeeding as the optimal form of infant feeding to WIC participants and the general public. The 1991 Act (P.L. 102-342) required that the Secretary of Agriculture establish a promotion program to promote breastfeeding as the best method of infant nutrition and to foster wider public acceptance of breastfeeding in this country. In 1992, USDA established an enhanced WIC food package for breastfeeding mothers whose infants do not receive WIC infant formula. The enhanced package added two new food items—carrots and canned tuna—along with increased amounts of juice, cheese, and beans/ peas and peanut butter, to the items provided in the food package for pregnant and breastfeeding women. In 1994, P.L. 103-448 required WIC to spend at least $21 (to be adjusted annually for infl ation) for breastfeeding promotion on every pregnant and breastfeeding woman participating in the program.

As WIC expanded rapidly in the 1990s, the potential for misuse of program funds and violation of program regulations increased. Legislative and regulatory actions were enacted to strengthen the integrity of the program. For example, the 1998 William F. Goodling Child Nutrition Reauthorization Act (P.L. 105-336) required that, except in limited circumstances, applicants must be physically present at certification to document their income if they were not adjunctively income eligible based on enrollment in other programs and provide proof of residency (to prevent dual participation).[42] P.L. 105-336 also required WIC State agencies to permanently disqualify WIC vendors convicted of trafficking food instruments (i.e., accepting food instruments for cash).

In 1999, the WIC program standardized nutritional risk criteria for determining program eligibility and assigning individual priority levels. As noted earlier, the priority system was designed to ensure that, in the event that program funds were not sufficient to serve all eligible people, WIC benefits would be provided to those most in need. Prior to April 1, 1999, each WIC State agency developed its own nutritional risk criteria subject to broad Federal parameters. As of April 1, 1999, however, WIC State agencies are required to use consistently defined nutritional risk criteria selected from a list of nearly 100 risk factors established specifically for use in the WIC program and issued by FNS (USDA, 1998).[43] WIC State agencies may choose to use some or all of the nutritional risk criteria on the national list.

2000 to the Present: Recent Developments

The beginning of the decade saw a rapid increase in the number of "WIC-only" stores (i.e., stores that sell only or predominantly WIC foods and serve only or predominantly WIC participants). Under the retail food delivery system used by most WIC State agencies, WIC participants exchange food vouchers (or instruments) for supplemental foods at authorized retail outlets. Although WIC participants receive their WIC foods for free, market forces discourage regular WIC vendors from taking advantage of the price insensitivity of WIC participants and charging higher prices for WIC foods. That is because regular WIC vendors serve both WIC and non-WIC customers and if a WIC vendor charges too high a price for the WIC foods, the non-WIC customers—who pay out of pocket for their food—may shop at another store, resulting in a loss of revenue for the vendor. Since WIC-only stores do not serve non-WIC customers, there is less economic incentive for them to keep prices low. As a result, the prices at WIC-only stores are generally higher than those of other WIC vendors.[44] Neuberger and Greenstein (2004) estimated that WIC-only stores in California increase WIC food costs by about $33 million per year. Because WIC participants are not required to obtain all the foods listed on their food instrument, it is not clear to what extent WIC-only stores have higher costs because of higher prices or because WIC vouchers are more likely to be redeemed in full there.

To address concerns about the increasing number of WIC-only stores with higher food costs, the Child Nutrition and WIC Reauthorization Act of 2004 (P.L. 108-265) included several vendor cost-containment provisions. The new law required that WIC State agencies establish a vendor peer group system, distinct peer competitive price criteria, and allowable reimbursement levels for each peer group. WIC State agencies must use the competitive price criteria to evaluate the prices a vendor applicant charges for supplemental foods compared with the prices charged by other vendor applicants and authorized vendors. State agencies must establish peer groups to determine the competitive-price criteria and maximum reimbursement levels applicable to vendors; vendors are assigned to peer groups based on characteristics such as geographic location, number of cash registers, WIC sales volume, type of ownership (sole proprietorship, corporate, or partnership) and other criteria indicating that all of the vendors in a peer group would be expected to have similar prices. The law also mandated special cost-containment requirements for "above-50-percent vendors," (i.e., vendors that derive more than 50 percent of their annual food sales revenue from WIC food instruments). P.L. 108-265 requires that WIC State agencies ensure that the prices of above-50-percent vendors do not result in higher total food costs.[45]

This decade also saw major changes to WIC food packages. Prior to 2007, WIC food packages had remained largely unchanged since the 1970s, even as the WIC population became more diverse, food patterns and participants' nutritional risks changed, and nutritional science advanced. For many years, WIC program administrators, medical and scientific communities, advocacy groups, and Congress had expressed an interest in updating the food packages. In December 2007, USDA published an interim final rule that overhauled the WIC food packages (72 *Federal Register* 68965-69032).[46]

The interim final rule's revisions largely refl ect recommendations made by the Institute of Medicine (IOM) of the National Academies in its report, "WIC Food Packages: Time for a Change," with certain cost-containment and administrative modifications that ensure cost neutrality (Institute of Medicine, 2005).[47] The interim final rule revised regulations to align WIC food packages with the *Dietary Guidelines for Americans* (U.S. Department of Health and Human Services and U.S. Department of Agriculture, 2005) and with the current infant feeding guidelines set by the American Academy of Pediatrics. This alignment was aimed at promoting and supporting the establishment of successful long-term breastfeeding, providing WIC participants with a wider variety of food and WIC State agencies with greater fl exibility in prescribing food packages for participants with cultural food preferences. In order to serve the greatest number of eligible applicants, the revised food packages were designed to be cost-neutral (i.e., to cost no more than the packages they replaced). Although WIC State agencies could begin to phase in the revised food packages by February 2008, none did so.[48] All WIC State agencies are required to implement the new provisions no later than October 1, 2009. (For additional details about the WIC food packages revisions, see the section on "Potential Impact of the Revised WIC Food Packages," p. 44.)

PROGRAM TRENDS

This section examines trends in program expenditures, participation, infant formula rebates, and food costs per person. Some of the trends appear to have changed in FY 2008. (For more information on converting nominal dollars to real dollars, see box, "Adjusting for Infl ation," p. 23.)

WIC Expenditures

Since WIC's initiation in 1974, nominal (i.e., not adjusted for infl ation) Federal expenditures for the program have increased each year, reaching $6.2 billion in FY 2008 (Figure 3).[49] In real terms (i.e., adjusted for infl ation), the increases in WIC expenditures have not been nearly so dramatic. Real expenditures for WIC increased each year—except for 1989—up to FY 1997. This increase was due to Congressional appropriations that were stimulated largely by favorable program evaluations that showed WIC to be a successful and cost-effective program.[50] As the program reached full participation (whereby every eligible person who applies for WIC is accepted into the program), annual Congressional appropriations fl attened out and the increase in real expenditures slowed. In fact, between 1998 and 2007, real expenditures decreased in 4 of the 10 years.[51] In a break from recent years, however, expenditures in real terms increased by almost 9 percent in 2008. This increase, the largest in 15 years, refl ected both an increase in participation and an increase in per person food costs.

Participation

Since WIC's formal inception, the number of program participants has expanded dramatically. From an average of 88,000 participants per month in 1974, the number of participants increased each year reaching 7.4 million per month in 1997 (Figure 4). (See box, "Number of Births in the United States Is Increasing," p. 25, for more information about participation trends.) Congressional funding for WIC increased steadily during this period. The rapid growth in participants from 1989 to 1997, when participation increased by an average 8 percent per year, coincided with the startup of the infant formula rebate program. The only decrease in participation in WIC's history occurred from 1998 to 2000, when the number of participants fell 1-2 percent each year. During this period, Federal expenditures for WIC in real terms (i.e., after adjusting for infl ation) decreased by 2 percent. From 2000 to 2007, participation once again increased, but at a slower rate (about 2 percent per year). In FY 2008, however, participation increased 5 percent, the largest single-year increase since 1995.

ADJUSTING FOR INFLATION

To account for the effects of infl ation or general price changes over time, the estimates for WIC expenditures, infant formula rebates, and per person food costs in this section were converted into real (i.e., infl ation-free) dollars. This raised the question—which index should be used to adjust these WIC-related variables for infl ation? Various price indices, based on different market baskets of goods, are used to measure different aspects of infl ation. The most widely used measure of infl a-tion is the Consumer Price Index (CPI) for all items, which is a broad, comprehensive price index that measures the average change over time in prices paid by urban consumers for a fixed market basket of consumer goods and services. Because WIC foods (which are usually consumed at home) account for about three-quarters of total WIC expenditures, this report uses the CPI for food at home (i.e., foods purchased at retail food stores) to defl ate costs associated with WIC expenditures and food costs per person. For consistency, the CPI for Food at Home was also used to defl ate the dollar amount of infant formula rebates received by WIC. Although not presented in this report, WIC expenditures, per person food costs, and infant formula rebates were also defl ated using the CPI for all items. The same general trends were observed regardless of which CPI was used.

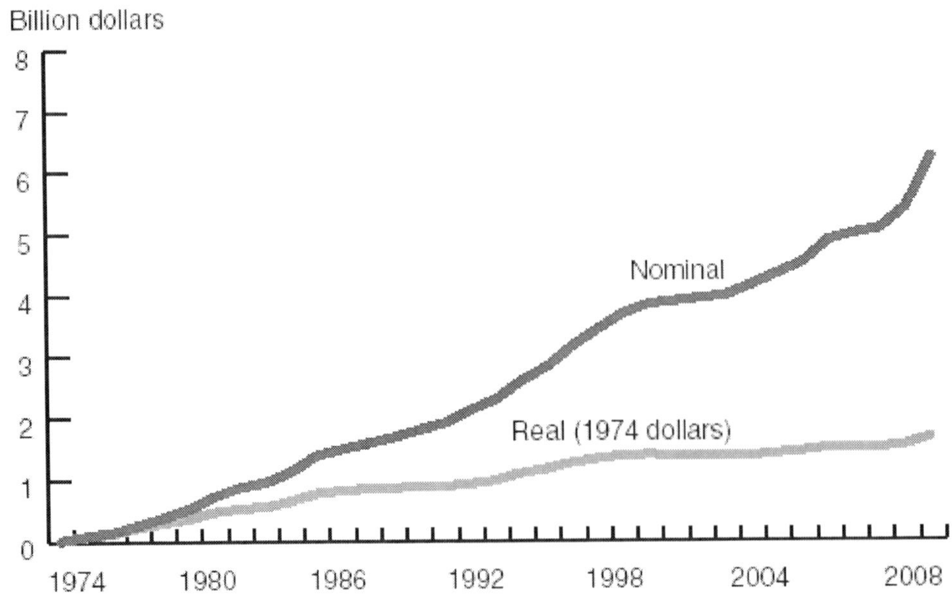

Source: ERS calculations of real expenditures based on USDA Food and Nutrition Service estimates of nominal expenditures adjusted by the Bureau of Labor Statistics' Consumer Price Index for food at home.

Figure 3. Federal expenditures for WIC, FY 1974-2008

Participation patterns have varied among the three main participant categories. For example, since the program began in 1974, the number of women and infants participating in the program has increased each year except for 2000 when the number of infants decreased by less than 1 percent. The number of children in WIC has experienced greater fl uctuation, increasing sharply from 1988 to 1997 (by 128 percent) before decreasing by 7 percent from 1997 to 2000. The number of children also decreased slightly in 2006. In FY 2008, the number of children experienced a large increase—7 percent compared with only 3 percent for women and infants. In general, infants and pregnant and breastfeeding women have a higher priority in WIC than do children, so they may be more "protected" when program funds are limited. Because children have a lower priority, they will be less likely to be able to participate when funding is tight. Conversely, as funding increases, there may be greater outreach efforts aimed at bringing children into the program since eligible infants and pregnant and breastfeeding women are more likely to already be in the program.

Per Person Food Costs

In the first 15 years of the WIC program, the nominal per person cost of the WIC food package increased by 112 percent (from $16 in FY 1974 to $33 in FY 1988) (Figure 5). From 1988 to 2007, however, nominal costs increased by a total of only 17 percent, increasing by almost 12 percent in FY 2008 alone.

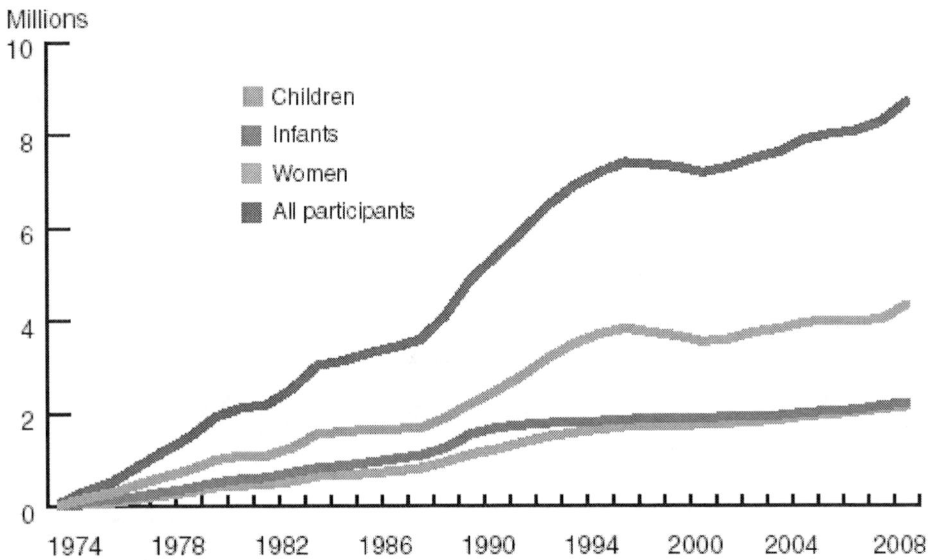

Source: USDA, Food and Nutrition Service.

Figure 4. Average number of WIC participants per month, FY 1974-2008

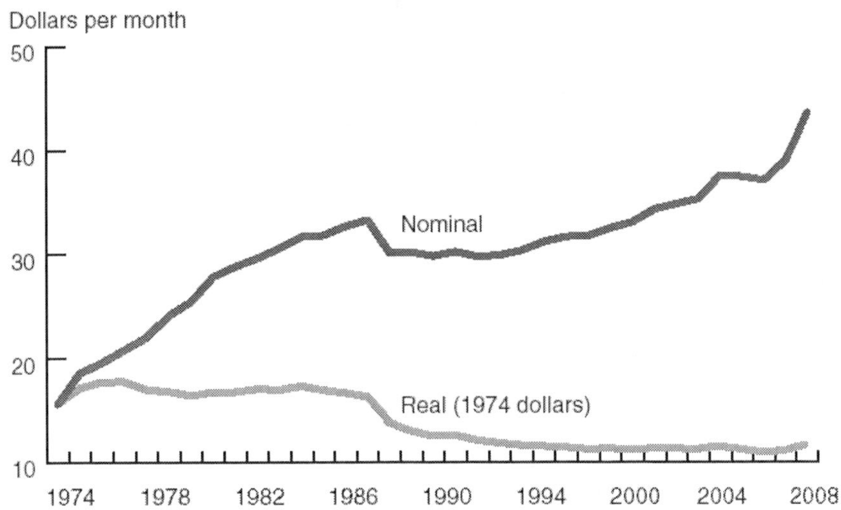

Source: ERS calculations of real average WIC food cost per person based on USDA, Food and Nutrition Service estimates of WIC per person food costs adjusted by the Bureau of Labor Statistics' Consumer Price Index for food at home.

Figure 5. Average WIC food costs per person, FY 1974-2008

In real terms (1974 dollars, after adjusting for infl ation), the average monthly cost per person of the WIC food package actually decreased by 28 percent from 1974 to 1998. Much of this decrease occurred in the late 1980s and early 1990s as a result of the infant formula rebate program that WIC State agencies began to implement during that time. Real average WIC food costs per person were fl at for most of the last decade—decreasing by 1 percent between 1998 and 2007—before increasing by 5 percent in FY 2008. This increase, largely the result of rising food prices, represented the largest single-year increase in percentage terms since 1975 when WIC was only in its second year of operation.

NUMBER OF BIRTHS IN THE UNITED STATES IS INCREASING

The number of persons eligible for WIC is largely a function of economic conditions and the number of people in the target subpopu-lations. Provisional data from the Centers for Disease Control and Prevention indicate that, in 2007 (the latest year in which data are available), the number of live births in the United States reached over 4.3 million, the largest number of births recorded since the WIC program began in 1974. After a downward trend from 1990 to 1997, the number of live births has increased in 8 of the last 10 years.

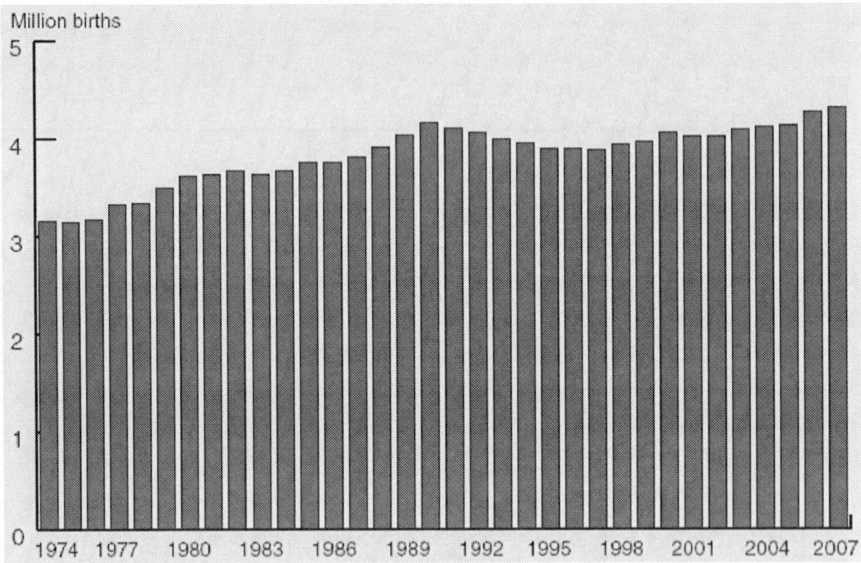

Note: Data for 2006 and 2007 are provisional.

Source: Tejada-Vera and Sutton, 2008 and Martin et al., 2007.

Live births in the United States, 1974-2007

Infant Formula Rebates

Rebates from infant formula manufacturers have become an integral component of the WIC program. Since the use of rebates began in the late 1980s, the amount of the rebates in nominal terms has increased each year, reaching an estimated $1.8 billion in FY 2007 (Figure 6). In real terms, rebates have largely leveled off. Since 1999, real rebates have increased by only 4 percent.

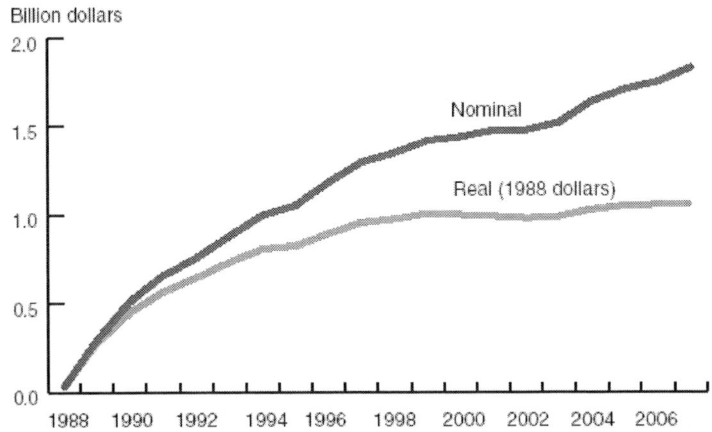

Source: ERS calculations of real infant formula rebates based on USDA, Food and Nutrition Service estimates of infant formula rebates adjusted by the Bureau of Labor Statistics' Consumer Price Index for food at home.

Figure 6. Infant formula rebates, FY 1988-2007

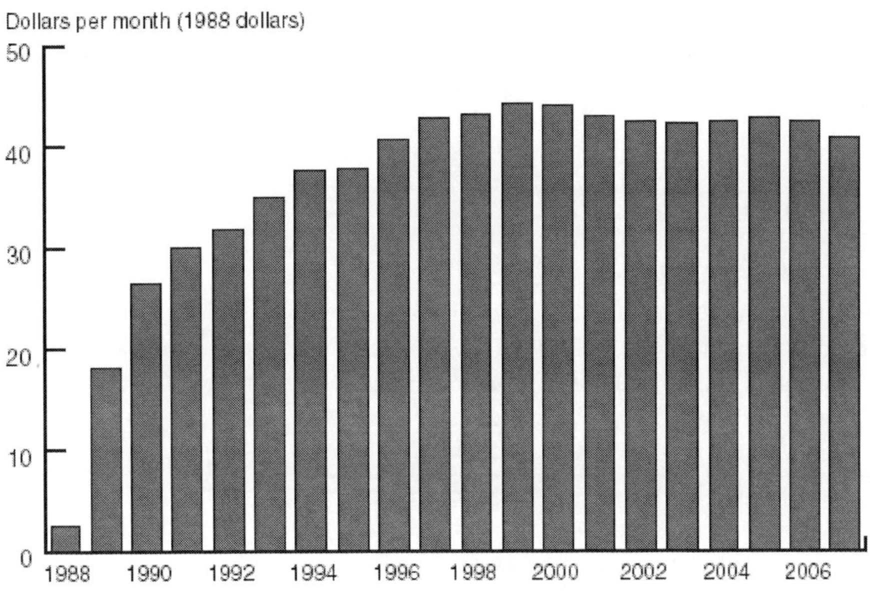

Source: ERS calculations of real infant formula rebates based on USDA, Food and Nutrition Service estimates of infant formula rebates adjusted by the Bureau of Labor Statistics' Consumer Price Index for food at home divided by the number of infants participating in WIC.

Figure 7. Average real rebate per infant, FY 1988-2007

The amount of total rebates received by WIC tells only part of the story. While the total amount of rebates received by WIC has leveled off, the number of infants participating in the program has continued to increase.[52] As a result, the average rebate per WIC infant (in real terms) has decreased in recent years (Figure 7).[53] Since peaking at almost $44.18 (in 1988 dollars) per month in FY 1999, the average real rebate per infant has decreased in 6 of the last 8 years, falling to about $40.77 in FY 2007.

Characteristics of WIC Participants

Descriptive information on the characteristics of WIC participants is available from USDA's Food and Nutrition Service (see box below, "FNS Data on WIC Participant Characteristics"). This chapter describes participants' characteristics in terms of participant categories, race and ethnicity, nutritional risks, participation in other programs, and income and poverty status.

Participant Category

Children accounted for 49 percent of all WIC participants in April 2006 (Figure 8). The number of children in WIC decreased as their ages increased: 17 percent of all WIC participants were 1 year of age, 13 percent were 2 years of age, 11 percent were 3 years of age, and 8 percent were 4 years of age. Infants made up another 26 percent of all WIC participants. Women accounted for 25 percent of all WIC participants, with pregnant women making up 11 percent of all participants and nonbreastfeeding postpartum women and breastfeeding women each accounting for 7 percent of all participants. Among pregnant women, over half (51 percent) enrolled in the program during their first trimester and 38 percent in the second. Only 10 percent of pregnant women enrolled in their third trimester.

Race and Ethnicity

One of the more dramatic trends that has emerged since the early 1990s is the change in the racial/ethnic composition of WIC participants. Accounting for only 23 percent of all participants in 1992, Hispanics accounted for 41 percent in 2006—more than any other racial/ethnic group (Figure 9). During the same period, the percentage of Whites and Blacks combined decreased from 72 percent to 52 percent.

FNS Data on WIC Participant Characteristics

Every 2 years, USDA's Food and Nutrition Service (FNS) sponsors a study on the characteristics of WIC participants and the agencies administering the program, publishing the results in the *WIC Participant and Program Characteristics* (PC) series of reports. The most recent report (PC2006) is based on a near-census of people enrolled in WIC in April 2006 (Bartlett et al., 2007). In that month, 8.8 million women, infants, and children were enrolled in the program. Only about 91 percent of enrollees, however, actually picked up their WIC food instruments. For simplicity and comparability with the PC reports' terminology, enrollees (including the 9 percent who did not pick up their WIC food instrument) are referred to as participants in the discussion of participant characteristics.

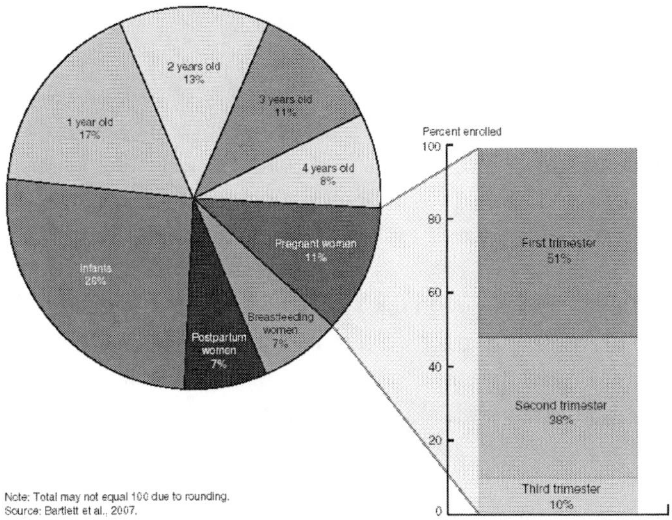

Figure 8. Distribution of WIC participants, by participation category, 2006

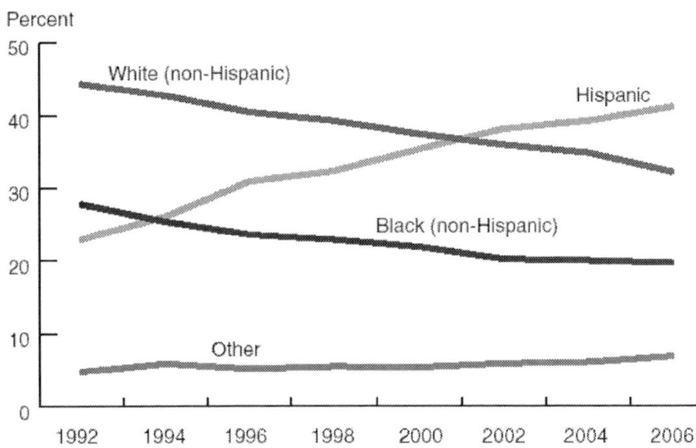

Source: Bartlett et al., 2007.

Figure 9. WIC participants, by race/ethnicity, 1992-2006

Nutritional Risks

For the PC2006, States could report each applicant's 10 highest priority nutritional risks present at certification.[54] For women, high weight-for-height (46 percent), "other dietary" risks (40 percent), and inappropriate weight gain (30 percent) were the risks most often reported. Eighty-one percent of infants were recorded at risk due, at least in part, to the WIC-eligibility of their mothers or because their mothers were at risk during pregnancy. "Other dietary" risks (61 percent), inadequate or inappropriate nutrient intake (27 percent), and high weight-for-height (23 percent) were the most frequently recorded risks for children.

Participation in Other Programs

Participants from Medicaid, Food Stamp, or TANF programs are automatically income eligible for WIC. In 2006, 66 percent of WIC participants received benefits from at least one of these other public assistance programs at the time of their WIC certification, 16 percent received benefits from two of these programs, and 6 percent received benefits from all three.[55] Medicaid was received by 63 percent of WIC participants, food stamps by 22 percent, and TANF by 9 percent.

From 1992 to 2006, participation in the TANF or AFDC programs by WIC participants at time of certification decreased from 27 percent to 9 percent, refl ecting the overall decline in participation in these programs since passage of the Personal Responsibility and Work Opportunity Reconciliation Act (PRWORA) of 1996 (a.k.a., the Welfare Reform Act of 1996) that replaced AFDC with TANF (Figure 10). Similarly, participation among WIC participants in the Food Stamp Program fell from 40 percent to 22 percent due, at least in part, to fewer WIC participants meeting income eligibility requirements of the Food Stamp Program.[56] On the other hand, participation in the Medicaid program by WIC participants at time of certification increased from 48 percent in 1992 to 63 percent in 2006. Implementation of two legislative changes, the State Children's Health Insurance Program (SCHIP) and Title XXI of the Balanced Budget Act of 1997—which expanded Medicaid eligibility for children—contributed to the increase in Medicaid participation among WIC participants (Bartlett et al., 2007). (For additional information on the effect of Medicaid participation on WIC, see the section on the "Expansion of the WIC Program," p. 31.)

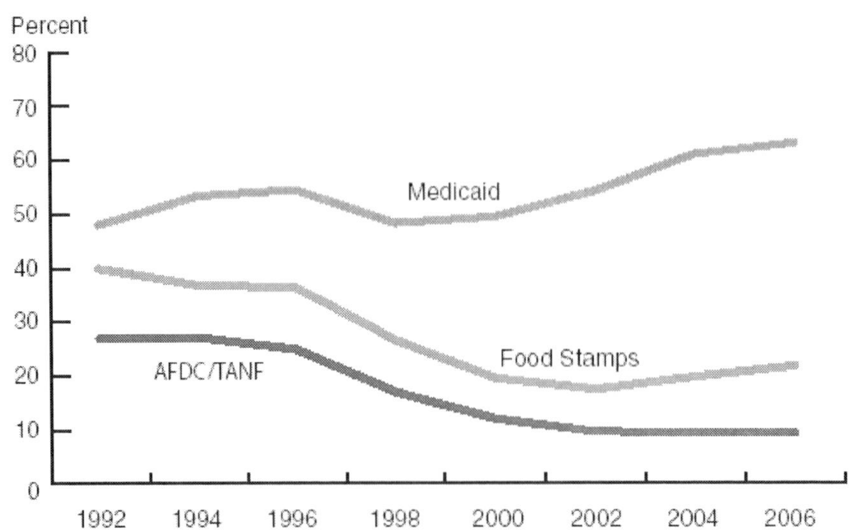

Source: USDA, Food and Nutrition Service, PC data, various years.

Figure 10. Share of WIC participants participating in other public assistance programs,1992-2006

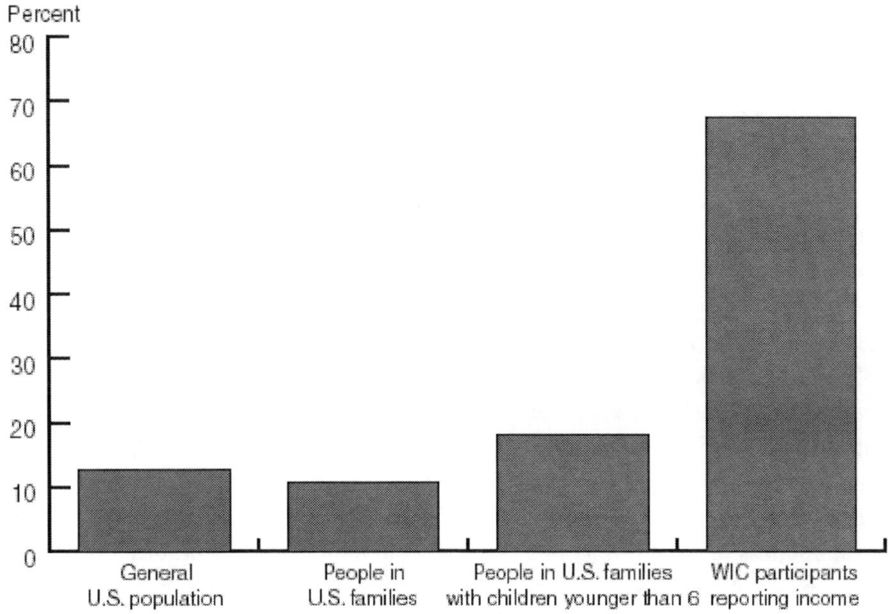

Source: Bartlett et al., 2007.

Figure 11. People in poverty, 2006

Income and Poverty Status

In the PC2006, almost 10 percent of participants had missing values for income (86 percent of those with missing income were adjunctively income eligible due to their participation in the Medicaid, Food Stamp, or TANF Programs). Among WIC participants with reported income in 2006, the average annualized income of their family/economic units was $15,577. Most WIC participants were poor; two-thirds (67 percent) of those reporting income were at or below the poverty level compared with 13 percent of the general population (Figure 11). In contrast, 2 percent of participants reporting income had incomes above the 185 percent of poverty guidelines that cap WIC participation (some participants with incomes above the cap can legally participate in WIC because Medicaid participation makes them income eligible and Medicaid participation in several States is capped at income levels greater than 185 percent of the poverty guidelines).

Administrative-Based Issues in WIC

Numerous issues are associated with administering a program of WIC's size and complexity, including administrative-based issues and their economic implications. These administrative issues include expanding WIC enrollment, Federal funding and State incentives, funding for NSA, potential impacts of revisions to the WIC food packages, food prices, and infant formula costs. Many of these issues are interrelated. For example, food prices may affect the expansion of the WIC program, which, in turn, could impact the costs of infant formula to WIC. Administrative-based issues may also impact program outcomes, which are discussed in the next chapter.

Expansion of the WIC Program

The number of WIC participants has increased dramatically over time (see Figure 4). By 2006, almost half of all infants and a quarter of all children ages 1-4, pregnant women, and postpartum women (up to 1 year after giving birth) in the United States were estimated to have participated in the program (Figure 12). Although funding has been sufficient to serve all eligible people seeking to enroll in recent years, many eligible people still do not participate in WIC. The latest estimates of 2003 WIC program coverage show that only 57 percent of the 13.5 million people eligible for WIC actually participated (USDA, 2006). The proportion of the eligible population that participated varied by participant category, ranging from 45 percent of children to 83 percent of infants (Figure 13). Some groups contend that WIC should continue efforts to increase participation among those eligible. For example, the Food Research and Action Center (FRAC) claims that having unserved eligibles in WIC "is especially disturbing in light of the obesity epidemic and the continuing hunger, poverty, poor nutrition, and ill health among the Nation's low-income families" (Food Research and Action Center, 2005). On the other hand, Besharov and Germanis (2001) contend that the WIC program has expanded beyond the truly disadvantaged and that cutbacks should be made at the upper levels of income eligibility.

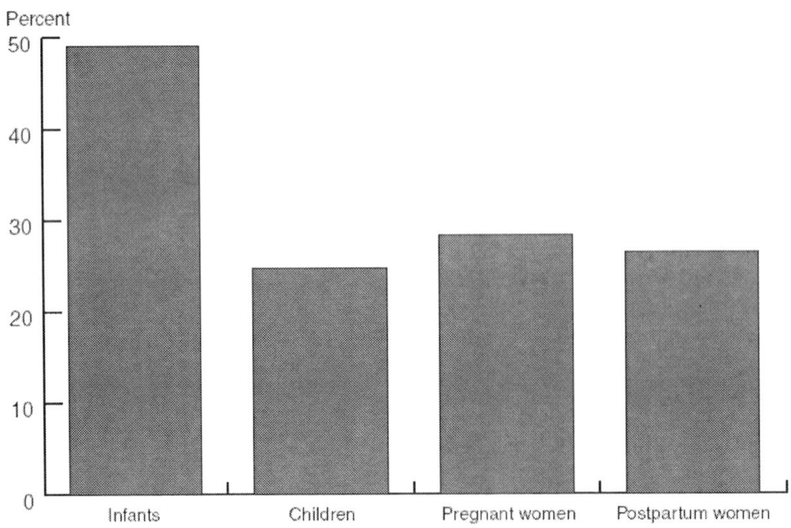

Note: Postpartum women include both breastfeeding and nonbreastfeeding women. Source: Economic Research Service estimates (see appendix on p. 82 for information on how the percentages were estimated).

Figure 12. WIC recipients as a share of U.S. population subgroups, 2006

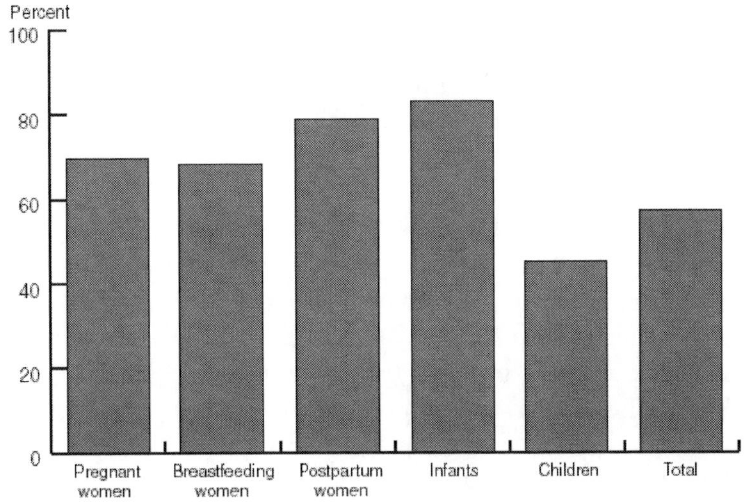

Note: Coverage rate equals the number of WIC participants as a share of persons estimated to be eligible for WIC.
Source: USDA, 2006.

Figure 13. WIC program coverage rates, by participant category, 2003

WIC's Eligibility Requirements Are Less Restrictive than Those of Food Stamps

Among the arguments for tightening WIC's eligibility requirements is that many of WIC's eligibility requirements are too lenient, especially when compared with those of the Food Stamp Program (the country's principal food and nutrition assistance program). For example:

- Undocumented immigrants are eligible to receive WIC benefits, but are not eligible for food stamp benefits.
- A family's assets play no role in determining its income eligibility for WIC, unlike the rules governing the Food Stamp Program.[57]
- The income eligibility limit for WIC is 185 percent of poverty, which is higher than the 130 percent of poverty limit required for participation in the Food Stamp Program.
- WIC regulations allow for considerable flexibility in how WIC agencies interpret the period used in determining an applicant's income eligibility. WIC State agencies may "consider the income of the family during the past 12 months and the family's current rate of income to determine which indicator more accurately refl ects the family's status" (7 CFR 246.7).[58] (Note that WIC regulations leave the period for determining a family's "current rate" of income undefined.) As a result, people whose *annual* income is above 185 percent of poverty, but who are experiencing a temporary decline in monthly earnings (e.g., from deciding not to work right before and/or right after childbirth), may still meet the income eligibility criteria for WIC. FNS estimates that 29 percent of the 13.5 million people eligible for WIC (but not necessarily participating in WIC) in 2003 had annual incomes above 185 percent of poverty (USDA, 2006). These people were presumably eligible because they had periods of low income during the year or because they were adjunctively eligible due to enrollment in Medicaid (see next section).

- WIC regulations do not require WIC participants to report changes in income that would make them ineligible if they were applying for bene-fits (that is, their income increases to above 185 percent of poverty). On the other hand, food stamp recipients are required to report changes in income that would make them ineligible for benefits.

Expansion of Adjunctive Eligibility Through Medicaid

A number of States now allow some people with incomes greater than 185 percent of the poverty guidelines to participate in Medicaid programs, and participation in Medicaid makes them automatically income eligible for WIC.[59] As of January 2008, 24 States and the District of Columbia had Medicaid programs for *infants* with income eligibility guidelines greater than 185 percent of the Federal poverty guidelines, including four States (Hawaii, Maryland, New Hampshire, and Vermont) and the District of Columbia that had income eligibility guidelines at 300 percent of the Federal poverty guidelines.[60] Twelve States and the District of Columbia had Medicaid programs for *children* with income eligibility guidelines greater than 185 percent of the Federal poverty guidelines, including three States (Hawaii, Maryland, and Vermont) and the District of Columbia that had income eligibility guidelines at 300 percent of the Federal poverty guidelines. Nineteen States and the District of Columbia had Medicaid programs for *pregnant women* with income eligibility guidelines greater than 185 percent of the Federal poverty guidelines, with the District of Columbia having income eligibility guidelines at 300 percent of the Federal poverty guidelines.

As shown earlier in figure 10, almost two-thirds (63 percent) of all WIC participants at the time of certification in 2006 participated in Medicaid, up from 48 percent in 1992. This increase in the proportion of WIC participants who also participate in Medicaid (and who may therefore have income greater than 185 percent of the Federal poverty guidelines) has led some to suggest that WIC may be increasingly serving those who are less economically needy. Questions have also been raised as to whether WIC can continue to absorb increases in participation associated with the expansions in Medicaid eligibility (Thiel, 2008). Examination of WIC participants' family income as a percentage of the Federal poverty guidelines shows that it has shifted modestly over time—a smaller proportion of participants report incomes at or below 50 percent of poverty, while a larger proportion report incomes between 101 and 185 percent of poverty (table 6). The number of WIC participants reporting income above 185 percent of poverty, however, remains relatively small—only 2 percent in 2006 (Bartlett et al., 2007). Thus, even with the more relaxed income eligibility guidelines in some States, program data do not indicate that WIC has been fl ooded in recent years by participants with incomes above the 185-percent level.[61] Furthermore, analysis conducted by the Center on Budget and Policy Priorities indicates that WIC caseloads in States with Medicaid eligibility limits greater than 185 percent of poverty have not grown more rapidly than caseloads in States with Medicaid limits at or below 185 percent of poverty (Greenstein, 2008).[62]

Differing Medicaid eligibility standards across States raise issues of equity in WIC. For example, Fox et al. (2003) asks, "should individuals in states with Medicaid eligibility higher than 185 percent of poverty qualify for WIC while those in other states do not?" Others have argued for eliminating adjunctive eligibility for people with incomes above some specified level. For example, the President's FY 2009 budget for USDA proposed limiting automatic

WIC income eligibility to Medicaid participants with household incomes that fall below 250 percent of the Federal poverty guidelines (USDA, 2008e). One of the arguments against capping adjunctive eligibility above some level of household income is that adjunctively eligible applicants do not have to provide information about family income, thereby speeding up the application process for applicants and staff and lowering administrative costs. The National WIC Association claims that the proposal to cap adjunctive eligibility would eliminate eligibility for only a small number of individuals and would increase costs due to additional administrative burden in affected States by requiring duplicative income documentation for all Medicaid recipients applying for WIC and discouraging otherwise eligible applicants from applying to WIC if they think they are not eligible (National WIC Association, 2008).

Table 6. Distribution of WIC Participants by Percentage of Federal Poverty Level among Those Reporting Income, 1992-2006

Percent of Federal Poverty level	1992	1994	1996	1998	2000	2002	2004	2006
			Percent					
0-50	40.7	43.4	39.1	34.0	30.9	31.7	33.4	33.0
51-100	34.4	33.4	34.2	34.7	34.0	32.8	33.5	34.3
101-130	12.1	12.0	12.9	15.1	15.9	16.1	15.3	15.1
131-185	12.0	10.6	13.0	15.4	18.0	17.8	16.2	15.6
Over 185	0.7	0.7	0.7	0.7	1.1	1.6	1.7	2.0

Source: USDA, Food and Nutrition Service, program characteristics (PC) data, 1992-2006.

Nutritional Risk Eligibility Requirements Are Nonbinding

WIC applicants seemingly face one eligibility requirement that applicants of other food and nutrition assistance programs do not. In order to participate in WIC, applicants must meet one of several nutritional risk criteria.[63] These criteria include detrimental or abnormal nutritional conditions detectable by biochemical or anthropometric measurements; other documented nutritionally related medical conditions; dietary deficiencies that impair or endanger health; conditions that directly affect the nutritional health of a person, including alcoholism or drug abuse; and conditions that predispose people to inadequate nutritional patterns or nutritionally related medical conditions, including, but not limited to, homelessness and migrancy (7 CFR 246.12). However, an FNS-sponsored study by the Institute of Medicine (2002) to evaluate the dietary assessment methods used by WIC to establish nutritional risk estimated that more than 96 percent of all people in the United States (and an even greater percentage of the low income) do not usually consume the number of servings recommended by the Food Guide Pyramid and would therefore be at dietary risk based on the criteria *failure to meet Dietary Guidelines*. IOM concluded that because "nearly all U.S. women and children" are at dietary risk and therefore meet the nutritional risk criteria established by WIC, in practice the WIC nutritional risk criteria have little effect on restricting program participation.

Instead of Expanding Enrollment, Should WIC Target Those Most in Need?

WIC has also been criticized because all WIC recipients in the same participant category (i.e., children, postpartum women, etc.) basically receive the same package of benefits despite differences in need among the individuals within each participant group (Besharov and Germanis, 2001). That is, although family income is used to determine eligibility for WIC, once a person is deemed eligible for WIC, income is not used to determine the amount of benefits they receive. For example, a child in a family with income less than 50 percent of poverty will receive the same WIC benefits as a participating child in a family with income 185 percent of poverty (or even 300 percent of poverty due to participation in some States' Medicaid program). In contrast, food stamp benefits are reduced by 30 cents for every dollar of income net of program deductions, and there are different subsidy levels for meals served in the National School Lunch Program and the School Breakfast Program depending on the child's household income.

A report by the U.S. General Accounting Office (1985) stated that WIC program officials generally considered income to be an unreliable indicator of vulnerability. With the exception of the Commodity Supplemental Food Program, participation in WIC does not preclude an individual from participating in other food assistance programs, such as food stamps. Therefore, the child at 50 percent of poverty may be able to receive food stamps in addition to WIC benefits, while the child at 185 percent of poverty would not be eligible for food stamps. The report further stated that many WIC policy officials believed that individuals whose family incomes are too high to be eligible for assistance from other programs may have greater economic need and nutritional risk than individuals with lower incomes but who qualify for other assistance programs.

In their book *Rethinking WIC*, Besharov and Germanis (2001) state that "WIC's positive effects are probably concentrated among its most disadvantaged recipients" and that, "instead of adding more people to the rolls, it might make sense to change WIC's rules to allow local agencies to provide more food benefits and educational services to poorer families who palpably need more aid than those at higher incomes."[64] Because of the lack of data on the issue, however, little is known about the degree to which WIC benefits accrue to the most disadvantaged, such as those at the lowest income, the most nutritionally at risk, the youngest children, etc. Increasing benefits or services to some WIC participants also raises regulatory and budgetary questions. WIC regulations currently limit the types and amounts of foods that can be provided to participants (7 CFR 246.10). State and local WIC agencies are prohibited from providing either additional types of food or additional amounts of foods to participants without a change in the regulations. Although WIC regulations do not prohibit local WIC agencies from providing additional *services* to participants, budget constraints would necessitate either reducing other services or cutting back services to other WIC recipients in order to do so. (See the section on "Effectiveness of WIC's Nutrition Education Program," p. 62, for an expanded discussion on the implications of enhancing nutrition education in WIC.)

Economic Factors Could Impact Future WIC Caseloads

WIC funding in recent years (up to FY 2008) has been sufficient to provide services to all eligible people seeking to participate, and participation levels continued to increase. The program is likely to face increased demand for program services in the upcoming years. If the current recession continues, the number of people eligible for the program may increase, resulting in more applicants and/or participants staying in the program longer (for example, more infants participating in WIC as children).[65] At the same time, costs per participant will also increase if several economic trends continue (such as, increasing infant formula costs and rising food prices) or if the revisions to the WIC food packages raise the total cost of packages (see the sections on "Potential Impacts of the Revised WIC Food Packages," p. 44, "Food Prices and WIC," p. 48, and "Infant Formula Costs," p. 51, for more information). Increases in the number of applicants and in per person program costs will increase budgetary pressure on the program. Congressional appropriations will have to increase to serve all eligible applicants or the seven-point priority system may once again be needed to allocate program slots among applicants on waiting lists.

Federal Funding and State Incentives

As mentioned earlier, WIC is 100 percent federally funded (i.e., State matching funds are not required).[66] This differentiates WIC from the other large food assistance programs that require States to share at least some expenses. For example, States share approximately half of all administrative expenses in the Food Stamp Program (7 CFR 277.4), and the average cost of producing school meals exceeds Federal subsidies for the meals (Bartlett et al., 2008). Other major assistance programs, such as Medicaid and TANF, also receive substantial State and local funding, in addition to Federal funding (Isaacs, 2008). WIC's unique status, in which States are not required to share the program's expenses, may be a factor in the increasing number of WIC participants over time as well as the proliferation of WIC-only stores in the early 2000s.

Moral Hazard and the Expansion in WIC Caseloads

As seen previously, participation in the WIC program has grown dramatically over time, fueled largely by funding increases from Congress and savings from cost-containment practices. In fact, except for a 3-year period from 1998 to 2000 (when participant numbers fell 1-2 percent each year), the number of WIC participants has grown each year since its establishment in 1974. Some believe that WIC's unique financial status, whereby the program is funded in full by the Federal Government but operated by State and local WIC agencies, has contributed to this almost continual expansion of participants. Since States bear little of the costs associated with more participants in their WIC programs, they have little incentive to curtail expanding WIC caseloads. Besharov and Call (2009) refer to the separation of determining WIC eligibility from paying WIC program costs as an example of a "moral hazard," whereby a party insulated from risk (or costs) may behave differently than if it were fully exposed to the risk (or costs). Since States and local WIC agencies bear little of the costs associated with expanding their WIC programs, they have little incentive to restrict WIC enrollment.[67]

In contrast, only 46 of the 90 WIC State agencies participate in the WIC Farmers' Market Nutrition Program (FMNP), which requires State funding contributions.[68] Federal funds support 100 percent of FMNP food costs, but only 70 percent of the administrative costs (i.e., States operating the FMNP must contribute at least 30 percent of the total administrative cost of the program). WIC also differs from the Food Stamp Program, where States share approximately half of all administrative expenses, but Federal funding is also tied to performance (e.g., State agencies' federally funded share of Food Stamp Program administrative costs can increase if the State has payment error rates below specified levels (7 CFR 275.23)).

"Orphan Program" and WIC-only Stores

The proliferation of WIC-only stores is another consequence of State's insulation from WIC program costs. WIC-only stores—vendors that derive all or nearly all of their annual food sales revenue from WIC food instruments—came about because entrepreneurs recognized the profit-making potential of targeting WIC participants (see the section on "2000 to the Present: Recent Developments," p. 20, for an expanded discussion on WIC-only stores). Since transaction of the WIC food instrument provides foods to the WIC participant without any payment from personal funds, WIC participants are not sensitive to a particular store's price for the item. As a result, WIC-only stores have little economic incentive to keep prices low.[69]

WIC-only stores competed for WIC customers using nonprice factors, such as convenience and increased customer services. For example, many WIC-only stores were located in close proximity to WIC clinics and some provided free transportation to and from the store (Neuberger and Greenstein, 2004). A study by the U.S. Government Accountability Office (GAO) found that WIC-only vendors often gathered the food items listed on the food instrument for WIC participants from food maintained behind a counter, eliminating participants' need to search store aisles and shelves for the specified food type, brand, and size (U.S. Government Accountability Office, 2006b). Shopping at WIC-only vendors is also likely to reduce the stigma associated with using Government checks to purchase food in regular grocery stores. In the past, WIC-only vendors also gave away incentive items to attract customers, including strollers, diapers, gift certificates, and even cash (U.S. Government Accountability Office, 2006b).[70]

WIC-only stores proved to be popular with WIC participants and, beginning around 2000, the number of WIC-only stores increased rapidly (U.S. Government Accountability Office, 2006b). From 1999 to 2004, the number of WIC-only stores almost tripled (Figure 14). Although WIC-only stores accounted for only 2 percent of all WIC vendors in 2002, they accounted for 9 percent of all WIC redemptions that year (Neuberger and Greenstein, 2004). In California, the State with the largest number of WIC participants, WIC-only stores accounted for about 40 percent of WIC redemptions in FY 2004. WIC-only stores in California have been estimated to increase WIC food costs by about $33 million per year (Neuberger and Greenstein, 2004).

WIC's status as an "orphan program" at the State legislative level may be one factor responsible for the rapid increase in WIC-only stores.[71] Because States are not required to match Federal funds, State government officials have little financial stake—and therefore little interest—in WIC operations. As a result, State WIC administrators may have difficulty instituting vendor cost-containment measures through State law and regulations. Although WIC State agencies have considerable latitude in the design and operation of their vendor management practices, including the authorization of WIC vendors, California illustrates the difficulty that State WIC administrators may have instituting vendor cost-containment measures through State law and regulations (California WIC Association, 2005). In the early 2000s, the California WIC agency attempted to enact State legislation that would have ensured that WIC-only stores in California would not be reimbursed for higher food prices than regular price-competitive stores. The owners of WIC-only stores responded by hiring lobbyists to fight the proposed legislation. With no State funds at stake, the California WIC agency had difficulty garnering the political support needed to overcome the lobbying effort, and the agency's attempt to enact State legislation was defeated (Neuberger and Greenstein, 2004).

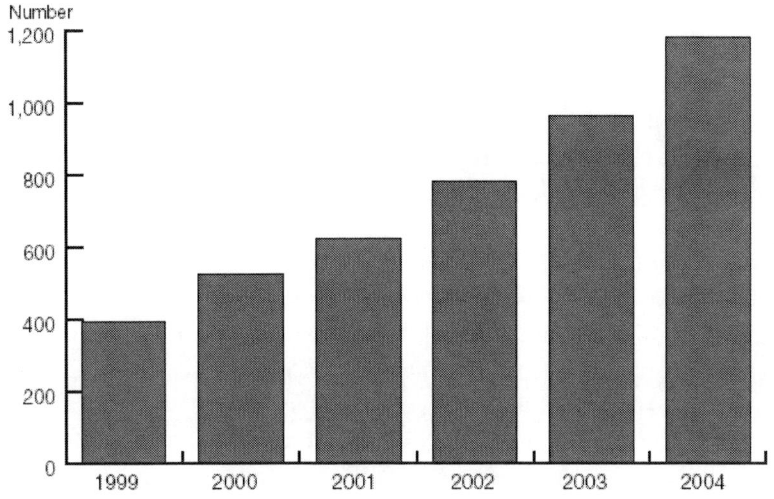

Source: U.S. Government Accountability Office, 2006b.

Figure 14. National total of WIC-only vendors, FY 1999-2004

When the WIC State agencies were unable to address the growth of WIC-only stores and increased food costs to WIC, the Federal Government intervened and enacted legislation to stop the growth of these stores (see box, "Federal Legislation Affects WIC-Only Stores," p. 40).[72]

Tradeoffs and Preferences

Because States are not required to provide funds for WIC, they experience few negative consequences when the program expands. They do, however, face tradeoffs with regard to the authorization of WIC-only stores. In California, State interest in supporting WIC-only store owners—and thereby promoting small businesses—overrode concerns that higher cost WIC-only stores might reduce the number of low-income residents served by WIC.[73] Congress also faces tradeoffs when it comes to the WIC program. Because WIC is a discretionary program, it has to compete with other discretionary programs for congressional appropriations. The annual increases in congressional appropriations for WIC, which in recent years have allowed every eligible person who applies for WIC to participate, suggests that Congress has revealed its preference for expanding WIC.

Funding for Nutrition Services and Administration (NSA)

WIC State agencies receive Federal funding under two separate grants: (1) food grants, which cover the cost of the supplemental foods; and (2) Nutrition Services and Administration (NSA) grants, which cover not only the costs of administering the program (certifying participants, voucher issuance and redemptions, vendor management, and cost containment) but also the costs associated with providing key services (nutrition education, breastfeeding promotion and support, and preventative and coordination services, such as health care and immunization referrals).[74] Food and NSA grants are allocated to WIC State agencies through a formula based on caseload, infl ation, and poverty indices.[75] In FY 2008, WIC grants to States totaled approximately $6.2 billion, $4.5 billion of which went to food and $1.7 billion went to NSA (USDA, 2008b). In recent years, NSA funding has been the subject of considerable confl ict.

NSA Funding Changes from Fixed Percentage to per Participant Basis

Prior to 1989, NSA grants to WIC State agencies were allocated as a fixed percentage (20 percent) of the total WIC grants to States. Fixed-percentage allocations discouraged WIC State agencies from developing cost-containment measures to reduce WIC food costs, since WIC State agencies that lowered their food costs and used the savings to serve more eligible individuals could not receive additional NSA funds to cover the additional participants. This resulted in a reduction in the per participant NSA grant. To correct for this disincentive to reduce food costs, the methodology used to distribute WIC funds between food and NSA was changed by P.L. 101-147 in 1989 to allocate NSA costs on a per participant basis. That is, per person NSA funding at the national level is held constant over time, except for an adjustment for infl ation.[76] Under this system, WIC State agencies that serve more eligible individuals through cost-containment savings are not penalized with a decrease in their per participant NSA funds.

Federal Legislation Affects WIC-only Stores

The Child Nutrition and WIC Reauthorization Act of 2004 (P.L. 108-265) includes several vendor cost-containment provisions in response to the rapid increase in the number of WIC-only stores. State agencies must establish peer groups to determine the competitive-price criteria and maximum allowable reimbursement levels applicable to each peer group. Vendors are assigned to peer groups based on characteristics such as geographic location, number of cash registers, WIC sales volume, and type of ownership (sole proprietorship, corporate, or partnership), and other criteria, indicating that all of the vendors in a peer group would be expected to have similar prices. State agencies must use the competitive-price criteria to evaluate the prices a vendor applicant charges for supplemental foods as compared with those charged by other vendor applicants and authorized vendors and must authorize vendors selected from those that offer competitive prices.

P.L. 108-265 mandated special requirements to contain the costs of "above-50-percent vendors" (i.e., vendors that derive more than 50 percent of their annual food sales revenue from WIC food instruments). State agencies must ensure that the prices of above-50-percent vendors do not infl ate the competitive-price criteria and allowable reimbursement levels for the peer groups or result in higher total food costs if program participants transact their food instruments at above-50-percent vendors rather than at other vendors. The new law also prohibits the authorization of payments to above-50-percent vendors who provide incentive items or other free merchandise to program participants, unless the incentives are of nominal value or were obtained at no cost.

P.L. 108-447, which contained the FY 2005 appropriations for WIC, and P.L. 109-97, which contained the FY 2006 appropriations for WIC, prohibited the authorization of new above-50-percent vendors with the exception of stores needed to ensure participant access to program bene-fits. This prohibition was not continued in succeeding years because P.L. 108-265 required FNS certification of a State agency's vendor cost-containment system as a condition for authorizing above-50-percent vendors; these certifications were completed by the end of FY 2006.

NSAs Increasing Share of Program Funding—A Sign of Program Inefficiency or Efficiency?

As intended by the 1989 legislation, per participant NSA grants have remained constant in infl ation-adjustment terms—that is, they have increased by the full rate of infl ation (58 percent between 1989 and 2006). In recent years, the administration has proposed capping the per participant NSA grant. The President's proposed budget for FY 2006, which was rejected by Congress, requested that NSA be capped at 25 percent of total WIC grants to States. Subsequent budgets, which have also been rejected by Congress, also included proposals to cap NSA. In FY 2009, the President's budget proposed capping the average per participant NSA grant at the FY 2007 level ($14.97) for an estimated savings of $145 million in FY 2009 (USDA, 2008e).[77] The rationale is that the cap would encourage WIC State agencies "to strive for administrative efficiency and allow for a greater proportion of appropriated funds to be used for food benefits," which would enable the program to serve more participants (Johner, 2008).

The National WIC Association opposes the cap, which they believe will erode benefits and services for participants and "irreparably damage effective State food and vendor cost containment measures" (National WIC Association, 2008). The Center on Budget and Policy Priorities (CBPP) argues that the increase in the NSA share of program funding simply refl ects the success of the current system in reducing WIC food costs (Neuberger and Greenstein, 2006). Between 1989 and 2006, WIC per participant food costs increased by 25 percent—less than half the 53-percent increase in grocery store food costs as measured by the Consumer Price Index (CPI) for food at home. The smaller growth in per participant food grants (25 percent), relative to per participant NSA grants (58 percent), explains the increase in the NSA share of total WIC grants to States. Rather than indicating program inefficiencies, the CBPP argues that the increase in NSA share indicates program efficiencies in reducing food costs.

The view that increasing NSA share is not a sign of administrative inefficiencies, but a sign of the success and increased efficiency of WIC's cost-containment measures, is supported by a GAO study. The study shows that, when total program costs are taken into account—when the infant formula rebate funds are added to Federal program costs—NSA costs remained constant at roughly 20 percent of total program costs between 1988 and 1999 (the most recent year for which data were available at the time of the GAO study) (U.S. General Accounting Office, 2001b). More recent data indicate that NSA costs as a percentage of total program costs plus rebates have continued at about 20 percent through FY 2007

(Figure 15). The CBPP points out that infant formula rebates have leveled off in recent years and the share of WIC funds allocated for NSA has plateaued, remaining fairly constant at about 27 percent excluding rebates (Neuberger and Greenstein, 2006).

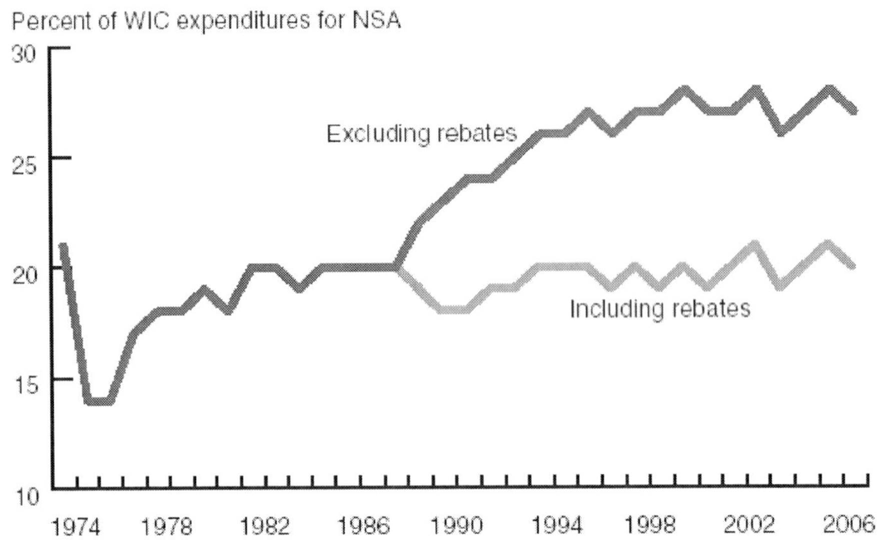

NSA=Nutrition Services and Administration.
Note: Update of chart in U.S. General Accounting Office, 2001b.
Source: Economic Research Service analysis of USDA, Food and Nutrition Service data.

Figure 15. Percent of WIC expenditures for NSA, including and excluding infant formula rebates, FY 1974-2007

The GAO study also describes a number of challenges that raise the cost to WIC of delivering nutrition services (U.S. General Accounting Office, 2001b). For example:

- Since the late 1980s, WIC program staff have been required to perform additional administrative and service delivery tasks—such as cost-containment measures, breastfeeding promotion, screening and referring children for immunizations, and controlling program abuse—with no additional funding or reimbursement and little reduction in other activities.[78]
- The rapid growth since 1991 in the percentage of Medicaid beneficiaries who are enrolled in managed care and welfare reform's elimination of TANF, Food Stamp, and Medicaid benefits for many individuals have made it more difficult for WIC agencies to identify eligible individuals and coordinate services with the participants' health care providers.[79] As a result, WIC staff spend more time collecting and reviewing documents to determine eligibility and in outreach and coordination efforts.
- The greater prevalence of obesity and related diseases (such as gestational diabetes and noninsulin dependent diabetes) has increased the complexity of nutrition education issues. It takes considerably more than WIC's typical two short sessions to deliver effective, obesity-related counseling. It may also require greater skills and knowledge by the person providing the nutrition education. Yet, many agencies

report a shortage of professional staff, partly as a result of noncompetitive salaries and/or benefits.

- The greater ethnic diversity of WIC's participants increases the complexity of providing culturally relevant nutrition education, leading many agencies to develop materials in multiple languages. Many agencies also pay for interpreter services. All of these services raise the cost of delivering an effective program.
- Welfare reform's emphasis on participant work has intensified the pressure on WIC agencies to offer WIC services outside of normal working hours. Improving access, which may involve offering evening or weekend hours, can result in higher costs to the WIC program.
- State budget cuts have resulted in reductions in State and local in-kind services, such as shared rent and utilities.

According to the GAO report, 56 percent of WIC State agency automated management information systems (MIS) were not capable of performing or efficiently performing one or more of 19 program automation tasks essential for efficient program operations. The cost of bringing WIC's essential program tasks up to standard over 6 years was estimated by USDA at between $147 million and $267 million (U.S. General Accounting Office, 2001b).[80] Since States must meet their MIS needs almost entirely from their Federal NSA grants, GAO's finding suggests that NSA funding is not just insufficient, but may lead to both administrative and outcome inefficiencies.[81, 82] For example, no data are collected on health referrals, which makes it difficult to determine referral effectiveness or its role in participants' health outcomes.

CBPP argues that placing a cap on NSA funds is synonymous with ignoring the lessons policymakers learned in the 1980s, undermining what may be the most effective cost-containment practices instituted by any Federal health-related program. Because of the likely deleterious effects on WIC cost containment, an NSA cap could cost the Federal Government significant sums over time (Neuberger and Greenstein, 2006). A cap on NSA could also increase administrative inefficiencies by hampering WIC State agencies' efforts to update their MIS and further delay efforts to convert from paper food instruments to an EBT system.[83] Lack of funds could also force WIC State agencies to cut costs and make changes in service delivery, with potentially negative impact on the quality of WIC services and participant outcomes.

NSA Cap Could Impact Implementation of the Revised Food Packages

A cap on NSA in FY 2009 may hinder WIC State agencies' efforts to implement the revised food packages (for additional details on the revised WIC food packages, see the section on "Potential Impacts of the Revised WIC Food Packages," p. 44). The changes refl ect the most significant revisions to the WIC food packages since the program's inception and require that all WIC State agencies begin implementing the revised food packages by October 1, 2009. In order to be ready to implement the interim final rule, WIC State agencies must undertake a number of complex and time-consuming activities that will likely increase NSA-related costs, including:

- For the new foods, identify specific brands of foods that meet federally mandated nutritional profiles and are widely available within the State.
- For brands that do not meet federally mandated nutritional profiles or are not widely available within the State, meet with manufacturers regarding their interest and ability to bring their products into compliance.
- Conduct price surveys on all brands and package sizes of eligible foods that meet federally mandated nutritional profiles and are widely available within the State, deciding which specific foods, brands, and package sizes, to include on the State food list.
- Modify the State's MIS (older systems may require extensive upgrades) and incorporate the ability to track the new cash voucher for fruits and vegetables.
- Program hardware to print the new cash vouchers for fruits and vegetables.
- Meet with authorized retailers to ensure that all allowable foods are available at the time of implementation.
- Provide both WIC program staff and authorized retailers with timely training on the revised food package foods.
- Identify what additional nutrition education and breastfeeding promotion and support efforts will be needed to support the food package changes.

No State-Matching Requirements for NSA

Because WIC has no State-matching requirement, WIC State agencies rely almost entirely on Federal grants to cover NSA costs. Although some State governments voluntarily provide their WIC State agency with additional NSA funds, both the number of States providing additional funds and the amount they contribute have been declining. For example, in FY 1992, 18 States appropriated $91 million for WIC, while in 2001, 13 States made only $45 million available (U.S. General Accounting Office, 2001b). Similarly, both monetary and in-kind contributions (such as office space) by local governments and nonprofit organizations have declined, increasing WIC State and local agencies' dependence on Federal funding to cover NSA costs (U.S. General Accounting Office, 2001b).

Higher per participant NSA amounts may enhance WIC services and administrative efficiencies, helping the program meet its responsibility as an adjunct to health care and improving program outcomes. There are no guarantees, however, that additional resources would be spent efficiently or improve outcomes. Higher NSA amounts (for a given appropriation) reduce resources available for food benefits. It is also difficult to justify additional NSA funds when there is no information about how much it costs to provide essential services and/or the cost-effectiveness of nutrition services (for more information on program effectiveness, see the section on "Effectiveness of WIC's Nutrition Education Program," p. 62).

Potential Impacts of the Revised WIC Food Packages

On December 6, 2007, USDA published an Interim Final Rule revising the WIC food packages (72 *Federal Register* 68965-69032).[84] These rule changes represent the most significant revisions to the WIC program since its inception in the early 1970s (see box, "Summary of Major Revisions to the WIC Food Packages," p. 45).

SUMMARY OF MAJOR REVISIONS TO THE WIC FOOD PACKAGES

- Addition of fruits and vegetables (as commercial baby foods for older infants and as cash-value vouchers for children and women).
- More whole-grain foods—at least half of the cereals in a State's list of approved WIC foods must be whole grain. New whole-grain products are allowed, including breads, brown rice, tortillas, and bulgur.
- Addition of baby food meats for fully breastfed older infants.
- Greater variety, such as soy beverages and tofu as substitutes for milk for women.
- Less milk, cheese, eggs, and juice. New constraints on choices include a reduced amount of cheese that may be substituted for fl uid milk; no whole milk except for 1-year-old children or with medical documentation for other participant categories; no juice for infants.
- Delayed provision of complementary infant foods from 4 to 6 months (only infant formula will be provided until the infant is 6 months old).
- Less infant formula for partially breastfed infants and for older infants (6-11 months) and more infant formula for fully formula fed infants ages 4-5 months (to compensate for the elimination of complementary infant foods for this age group).

See table 3 for more information on the specific changes to the WIC food packages.

The WIC food package revisions were designed to bring about positive changes in participants' behaviors and outcomes, while minimizing vendor burden and maintaining cost neutrality. There are a number of issues, however, that might infl uence whether the revised food packages achieve their desired objectives. There are also some questions regarding potential impacts of the revised food packages on food manufacturers and on non-WIC consumers.

Potential Impact on Program Participants

Participation Effects—The food package revisions may increase food package desirability, thereby attracting new families to the program. Many people eligible for WIC do not participate in the program. For example, in 2003, only about 45 percent of all eligible children participated in WIC compared with 83 percent of all eligible infants (see Figure 13). By offering a greater variety of foods to choose from—including the addition of fruits and vegetables—the revised food packages are more likely to accommodate individual and culturally based preferences, providing more incentives for families to apply for WIC. An increase in applications could lead to an increase in participation, assuming that program funds are sufficient to enroll new applicants.[85]

Consumption Effects—Compared with the old food packages, the revised packages are estimated to provide greater amounts of nearly all the nutrients identified by the IOM as lacking in the diets of the WIC-eligible population, such as iron, fiber, and vitamin E

(Institute of Medicine, 2005). The revised food packages for women and children also provide less saturated fat, cholesterol, total fat, and sodium than the old packages. One of the most significant changes is the addition of fruits and vegetables to most food packages.[86] Data from fruit and vegetable voucher demonstration projects in California and New York indicate that the vouchers increased WIC participants' *purchases* of fruits and vegetables (Herman et al., 2006; Klein, 2008).[87] The demonstration project in California also shows an increase in *consumption* of fruits and vegetables (Herman et al., 2008).

The impact of the revised food packages on fruit and vegetable consumption is likely to vary depending on how WIC State agencies choose to operationalize the revised food packages. For example, WIC State agencies have the fl exibility to determine what combination of canned, frozen, and fresh forms of fruits and vegetables they will allow; whether to allow participants to redeem their vouchers at farmers' markets; what denomination to use for each voucher; the types of nutrition education provided to participants; and the minimum stocking requirements for authorized stores.[88]

The addition of new substitutes for milk—such as calcium-set tofu and calcium-fortified soy beverages—in the packages for women may increase their calcium intake. Similarly, the addition of whole-wheat bread and other whole-grain products is anticipated to increase consumption of whole grains and fiber. The impact of these changes will depend on the uptake of new foods by participants and, to a large extent, on the availability of some of the new foods.

On the other hand, the reduced amounts of milk, eggs, and juice and the elimination of whole milk from the food packages for women and children age 2 and older could reduce consumption of those foods and potentially increase negative consumption substitutions. For example, some participants may replace some of the "shortfall" in WIC juice with fruit drinks or other sweetened beverages. Participants who do not adapt to the taste of lower fat milks may choose to drink less milk.

Health Outcomes—The addition of fruits and vegetables and the emphasis on whole grains are consistent with the *Dietary Guidelines'* recommendations for food patterns that may contribute to a healthy weight, potentially improving the proportion of WIC participants with healthy weight (U.S. Department of Health and Human Services and U.S. Department of Agriculture, 2005). In addition, the revised food packages were designed to encourage breastfeeding, which may also contribute to a reduced risk of overweight in children. (For more information on the impact on obesity and breastfeeding, see the sections on "WIC and Childhood Obesity," p. 64, and "WIC and Breastfeeding Rates," p. 66.)

Potential Impact on WIC Vendors and Farmers

Implementation of the revised WIC food packages will impact WIC-authorized vendors in a variety of ways. Vendors will be required to stock at least two varieties of fruits, two varieties of vegetables, and one whole-grain cereal.[89] Thus, some small vendors may have to expand their current stock of foods. Vendors will also have to reprogram their store computers to accept WIC transactions using the standard food instrument as well as the new cash-value voucher for fruits and vegetables.

Vendors will need to provide employee training on the new requirements and may also consider whether they need to provide additional assistance to WIC shoppers (i.e., determining the cost of unpackaged produce selections or identifying the specific types of foods eligible for the program, like whole-grain breads and tortillas). The additional requirements and responsibilities associated with the revised food packages could lead some vendors—small vendors, in particular—to decide not to participate in the program. On the other hand, a pilot demonstration project in New York State showed that providing WIC participants with cash vouchers for fruits and vegetables increased store sales, not just for fruits and vegetables but overall, with little vendor burden other than staff training (Klein, 2008). The pilot significantly increased store sales, even though stores did not have to increase payroll or bring in a new product line and required virtually no operational changes. By the end of the pilot program, participating stores averaged 12-14 voucher transactions per day, with fresh fruits and vegetables (averaging 40 percent gross margin) accounting for 71 percent of sales. Canned fruits and vegetables accounted for 19 percent of sales, and frozen products accounted for the remaining 10 percent. For those stores that were tracked, the produce department averaged a 4.7-percent increase in sales. Furthermore, after the pilot ended, produce sales remained higher than before the pilot began.[90]

The new fruit and vegetable cash-value vouchers could also lead to increased sales opportunities for some fruit and vegetable farmers if their WIC State agency chooses to allow participants to redeem vouchers at farmers' markets.

Potential Impact on Food Manufacturers

The interim final rule expanded the list of foods allowed by the WIC program to increase the cultural acceptability of the food packages and the variety of foods from which participants could choose. The inclusion of these foods (including fruits and vegetables, soy-based beverages, tofu, whole-grain products, and baby foods) in the WIC food packages may result in increased sales of these products. Conversely, the revised food packages reduce the amounts of some food allowances, particularly milk, eggs, and juice, that could result in a decrease in their sales.

Several of the new foods must meet strict nutritional standards and size requirements that may not be commonly available. For example, the revised food packages established a maximum allowance of 2 pounds of whole-wheat bread or other whole-grain options for children in Food Packages III and IV and 1 pound of whole-wheat bread or other whole-grain options for women in Food Packages III, V, and VII. Bread, however, is not typically sold in either 1- or 2-pound loaves (typical sizes are 18 or 24 ounces).[91] Similarly, none of the soy beverages currently available in markets meet the required nutritional standards. WIC requirements have infl uenced manufacturers' behavior in the past, and manufacturers may be willing to redesign their processing lines to produce the WIC-specified size of container or reformulate their products to meet WIC requirements.[92] Such changes are more likely to occur if they are fairly simple and inexpensive, the reformulation does not adversely affect the taste or appearance of the product, and/or the increased demand from the WIC market justifies the cost.[93]

Potential Impact on Non-WIC Consumers

Increased demand for the new foods from the WIC program may increase food prices, affecting non-WIC consumers.[94] This increased demand may be particularly relevant for baby food fruits and vegetables because nearly half of all infants in the United States participate in the WIC program and the number of baby food manufacturers is limited. It may also be relevant if some of the new foods have to be reformulated to meet the program's requirements and have few manufacturers—such as whole-wheat breads sold in 1- and 2-pound packages and soy beverages. WIC's definition of a particular package size may increase opportunities for stores and manufacturers to price discriminate between WIC and non-WIC customers.

State-Level Food Costs

The food package revisions were required to be cost-neutral at the national level so the program could continue to serve the same number of eligible applicants. Thus, in order for a new food to be added to the package, something had to be deleted or reduced. Cost-neutrality estimates were based on assumptions about the take-up rates of the various foods among WIC participants. For example, the interim final rule assumed that about 3 percent of WIC women would choose tofu and that fruit and vegetable vouchers would be redeemed at a rate of 87.5 percent.[95] States that experience a higher-than-estimated demand for the higher cost food alternative (i.e., a take-up rate greater than 3 percent for tofu) are likely to see an increase in food costs. Some WIC State agencies may implement or increase cost-containment practices to offset anticipated price increases. Since WIC State agencies retain the right to exclude particular products from their food packages, some WIC State agencies may choose not to include some of the higher cost alternatives.

Food Prices and WIC

Because food accounts for almost three-quarters of total WIC costs, changes in food prices have important implications for program funding and the number of participants who can be served. Variation in food prices across geographic areas also raises issues of equity.

Rising Food Prices

Overall, prices of food at home rose 6.4 percent in 2008 compared with an average 2.4 percent per year for the previous 10 years (Figure 16). The increase in 2008 prices represents the largest single-year increase since 1990. Rising commodity prices, led by corn, is one of the main factors impacting retail food-price infl ation (Leibtag, 2008).

The percentage increase in food prices varies by food item. In 2008, the price of some items in the WIC food packages, such as eggs (up 14.0 percent), cereals and bakery products (up 10.2 percent), and dairy products (up 8.0 percent), increased by more than the average for all items (table 7).

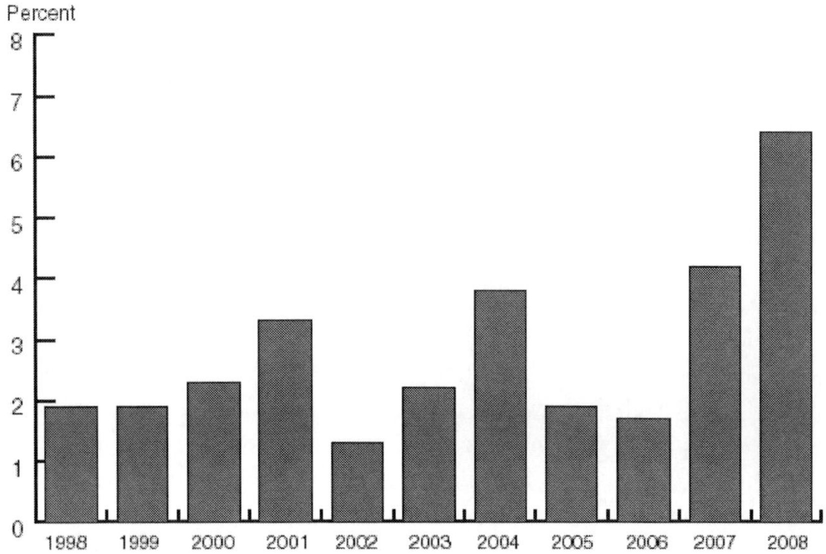

Source: Economic Research Service calculations using Bureau of Labor Statistics' Consumer Price Index data for food at home.

Figure 16. Change in prices for food at home, 1998-2008

Table 7. Change in food prices for selected items, 2008

Food	Annual change
	Percent
All food	5.5
Food at home	6.4
Dairy products	8.0
Eggs	14.0
Cereals and bakery products	10.2
Fruits and vegetables	6.2
Fresh	5.2
Processed	9.5

Source: USDA, 2009.

Higher food prices can strain the WIC State agencies' ability to serve all eligible program applicants. As a discretionary grant program, the number of participants that can be served each year depends upon annual appropriations from Congress and the cost of operating the program. WIC regulations require that the authorized maximum monthly allowances of all WIC foods be made available to participants if medically and nutritionally warranted (7 CFR 246.10). As a result, WIC State agencies are prohibited from reducing the amounts of food offered to participants in order to reduce food costs. However, WIC State agencies can implement cost-containment practices to stretch their food dollars. In addition to negotiating rebate contracts with manufacturers of infant formula, other cost-containment practices used by some WIC State agencies include limiting authorized vendors to outlets with lower food prices; limiting approved brands, package sizes, forms, or prices (e.g., requiring purchase of least-cost items or requiring the purchase of store brands or private labels); and negotiating rebates with food manufacturers or suppliers (e.g., rebate contracts with manufacturers of infant cereal) (Kirlin, et al., 2003). Absent the implementation of further cost-containment practices by WIC State agencies, an increase in food prices will lead to higher WIC food costs and fewer people will be able to participate in the program without increased congressional appropriations.

Unlike the regular quantity-based WIC food vouchers that entitle participants to a specific amount of WIC-approved food, the new fruit and vegetable vouchers provided in the recent WIC food package revisions have a fixed monthly cash value ($6 for children, $10 for fully breastfeeding women, and $8 for all other women). Thus, it might appear that these vouchers would be immune (from a cost perspective to WIC) from price increases for fruits and vegetables. These vouchers, however, are adjusted annually for infl ation, so participants do not lose value (in terms of the amount of food they can purchase) if food prices increase.[96] Therefore, an increase in fruit and vegetable prices will result in an increase in the cost of the fruit and vegetable vouchers, further stressing WIC State agency resources.

Geographic Variation in Food Prices

Another issue relates to the geographic variation in food prices. To measure differences in prices across States, an ERS study simulated the average food costs for specific quantities of nine WIC-authorized foods in 17 States, using supermarket scanner data on food prices from 1997 to 1999 (Davis and Leibtag, 2005). Average monthly food costs per participant varied markedly across States, ranging from a low of $29 in Texas to a high of $37 in Tennessee. Variation in food costs across States may result from differences in cost-containment practices, differences in food prices, as well as differences in the proportion of participants receiving food packages (i.e., WIC caseload composition). Since each category of WIC enrollees (women, infants, or children) qualifies for food packages that differ in cost, variation in overall average food costs can arise as the mix of enrollees (composition of participants) differs across States. The study also found that variation in food prices across the Nation for the same food group plays an important role in the differing costs of WIC food packages from State to State. Simulated average monthly food costs suggest that States with higher-than-average WIC costs usually have higher-than-average food prices. Similarly, States with lower-than-average WIC costs generally have lower-than-average food prices. The study also found that interstate variation in WIC participant caseload composition also contributes to variations in average monthly food costs across States, although to a lesser degree than the interstate variation in food prices. In addition, cost-containment practices by WIC State agencies provide different levels of cost savings in different States.

These results raise questions about program equity across States. Prior to the 2007 revisions to the WIC food packages, a WIC participant in one State could receive the same amount of food as a participant in either a different part of the State or in a different State altogether. The recent revisions included the introduction of cash-value vouchers for fruits and vegetables for children and women.[97] Because of price differences both *across and within States*, participants in States with relatively high fruit and vegetable prices will not be able to purchase as much as participants in other States or their fruit and vegetable choices may be limited to lower priced products.

Infant Formula Costs

WIC's most effective cost-containment measure is the use of infant formula rebates. Over half of all infant formula sold in the United States is purchased through the WIC program. Without the rebates, which totaled $1.8 billion in FY 2007, infant formula would be the single most expensive food item provided by WIC (Figure 17). For example, without the rebates offered in FY 2005, infant formula would have cost the program $2.3 billion, or 44 percent of all food costs, compared with the actual $0.6 billion, or 17 percent of all food costs after rebates (USDA, 2007b).[98] The dramatic expansion of the WIC program since the late 1980s is partly due to the savings generated from infant formula rebates. Since 1997, about a quarter of all WIC participants have been supported by infant formula rebates (Figure 18). In recent years, however, some WIC State agencies have reported a marked increase in their per can cost of formula. Because of the large volume of infant formula purchased through WIC, even small increases in the per can cost of infant formula to WIC could have far-reaching negative implications for the program.

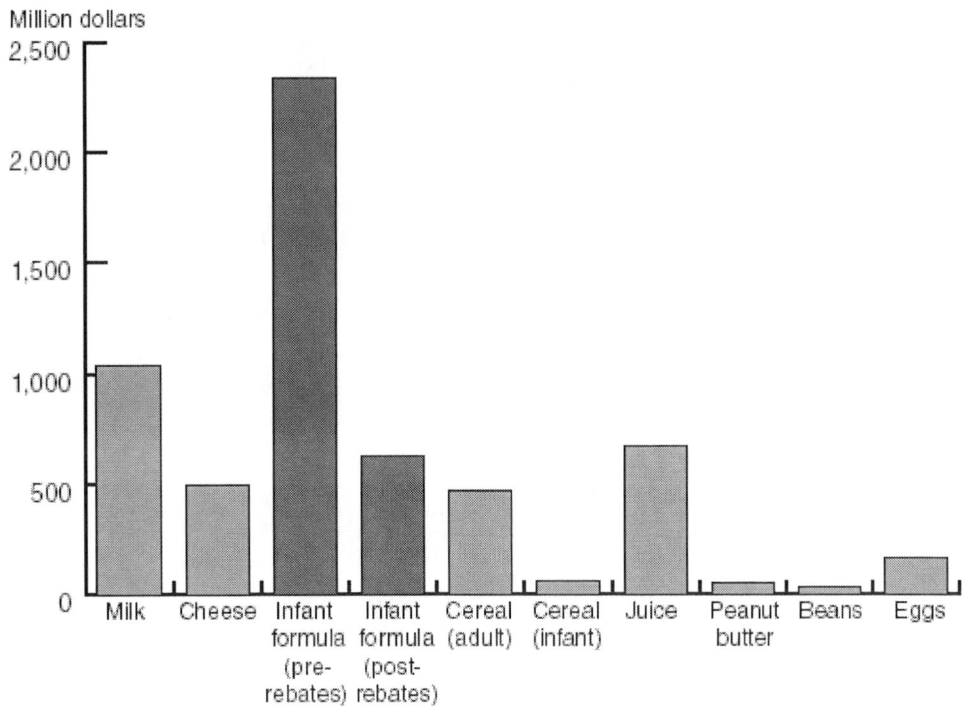

Source: USDA, 2007b.

Figure 17. WIC food costs, by food item, FY 2005

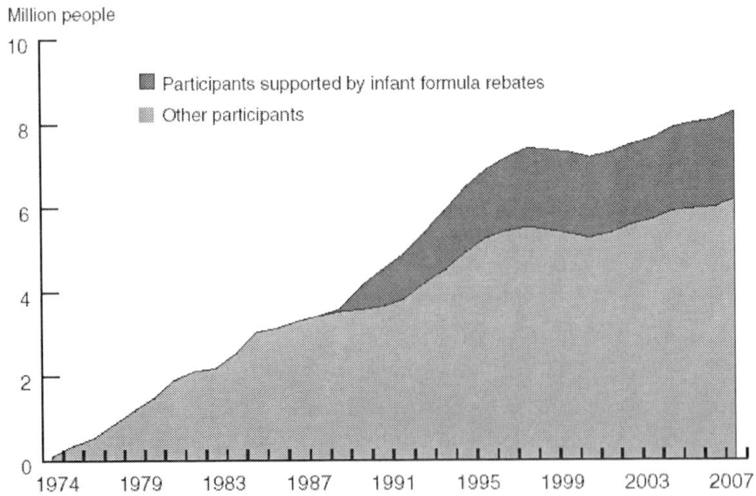

Note: The number of WIC participants supported by infant formula rebates was calculated by multipling the total number of WIC participants by rebates' share of total program expenditures and rebates.

Source: Economic Research Service calculations based on Food and Nutrition Service data.

Figure 18. Average number of WIC participants, FY 1974-2007

Infant Formula Rebate Program

Since 1989, Federal law has required that WIC State agencies enter into cost-containment contracts for the purchase of infant formula.[99] Typically, WIC State agencies obtain substantial discounts in the form of rebates from infant formula manufacturers for each can purchased. In exchange, the manufacturer is given the exclusive right to provide its product to WIC participants in the State. These sole-source contracts are awarded on the basis of competitive bids: The firm offering the lowest *net wholesale price* (equal to the manufacturer's wholesale price minus the rebate) wins the WIC contract. The contract-winning manufacturer is billed by the WIC State agencies for rebates on all infant formula purchased by WIC participants with vouchers at authorized retail outlets. The brand of formula provided by WIC will vary by State depending on which manufacturer holds the contract for that State.[100] Currently, three infant formula manufacturers—Mead Johnson, Abbott, and Nestle—hold rebate contracts in various States. The rebate program has successfully reduced the cost of formula to WIC. The percentage discount rebates (i.e., the amount of the rebate expressed as a percentage of the manufacturer's wholesale price) for contracts awarded from 1999 to 2008 averaged 86 percent. In other words, the infant formula purchased through WIC, on average, cost the program only 14 percent of its wholesale price (plus the amount of the retail markup) (Oliveira and Davis, 2006).[101] Both supply-side and demand-side characteristics of the infant formula market may explain why WIC State agencies receive such large rebates from infant formula manufacturers. On the supply side, the formula market is highly concentrated—a factor often associated with higher profit margins. This could give manufacturers the cushion to offer high rebates. On the demand side, WIC participants purchase over half of all infant formula, ensuring large sales for the contract-winning manufacturer. In addition, manufacturers may realize spillover benefits from their WIC contract: Retailers may devote more shelf space to the WIC contract brand,

and hospitals and/or physicians may be more likely to recommend the WIC-contract brand to their patients, spurring sales to non-WIC consumers.

WIC Infant Formula Has Two Cost Components

Net wholesale price—which is determined by infant formula manufacturers—is only part of the cost that WIC pays for infant formula.[102] Because most WIC participants purchase their WIC foods via the retail food delivery system (i.e., participants purchase WIC foods at full retail price from grocery and other food stores using their WIC vouchers or coupons), WIC also pays for the *retail markup* of the formula.[103] Retail markup is equal to the retail price minus the wholesale price and is determined by retailers (Figure 19).[104]

Retailers play an important role in determining the cost of infant formula to WIC, as they—not the infant formula manufacturers—set the retail price. Although wholesale prices are a major determinant of retail prices, retailers consider additional factors: the cost of transporting the formula from the warehouse to the store, shelf space, overhead, product movement, profit, and other local supply and demand factors.[105] An earlier analysis of retail infant formula prices found that formula identified as the WIC-designated brand increased the retail price of formula, especially in areas with a high percentage of WIC infants (Oliveira et al., 2004). This finding is consistent with economic theory. Winning the WIC contract increases the demand for the contract brand of formula among WIC participants, resulting in an increase in its retail price (WIC recipients do not pay for their WIC formula out of their own pocket, so they are price insensitive). Demand for the contract brand of formula may also increase among non-WIC consumers to the degree that winning the WIC contract results in increased store shelf space and greater product visibility.

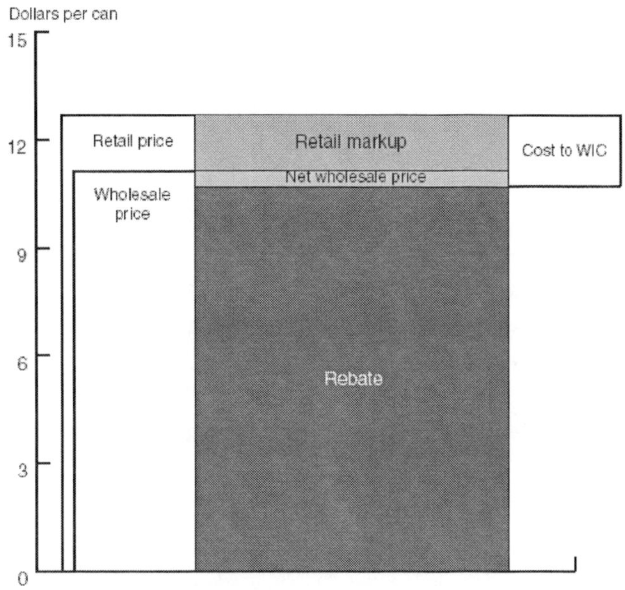

Note: Example based on a 12.9-oz can of Ross Similac with iron (milk-based powder) in the California WIC program during the second quarter of 2004.

Source: Oliveira and Davis, 2006.

Figure 19. Cost components for can of infant formula

Increasing WIC Infant Formula Costs

Results from a recent ERS study that examined trends in WIC infant formula costs from 1998 to 2006 indicate that after adjusting for infl ation, both of the cost components to WIC—net wholesale price and retail markup—have increased in recent years (Oliveira and Davis, 2006).

In most States, the retail markup, and not the net wholesale price, is now the largest component of infant formula costs to WIC (because of the effectiveness of the rebate program, net wholesale prices are low relative to retail markups). All WIC State agencies now offer the DHA- and ARA-supplemented formulas (see box, "DHA/ARA-Supplemented Formulas," p. 55) to their participants, and the percentage retail markup for these formulas exceeds that of the unsupplemented formulas (Oliveira and Davis, 2006). This markup difference is likely because purchasers of the more expensive supplemented formula may be less price sensitive than purchasers of unsupplemented formula.

Real net wholesale prices have been increasing since 2003 (Figure 20). Some of this increase can be attributed to the introduction of DHA- and ARA-supplemented formulas that have higher wholesale prices relative to unsupplemented formulas. So, if the amount of the rebate is held constant, the net wholesale price will be higher. Furthermore, the percentage discount rebates have trended downward. That is, manufacturers are offering lower rebates as a percentage of their wholesale price. The U.S. Government Accountability Office (2006a) estimated that if the average rebate that States received per can in 2004 had fallen from 93 percent of the wholesale price of infant formula to 75 percent of the wholesale price, about 400,000 fewer participants would have been able to participate in WIC.

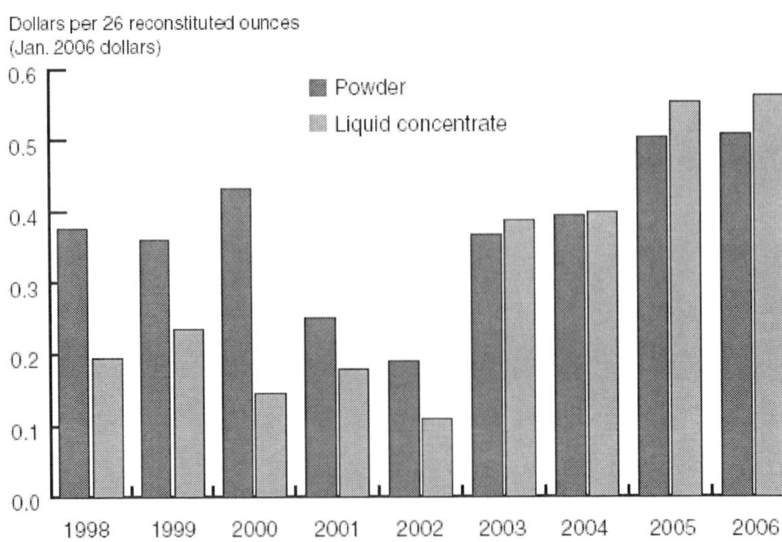

Note: Calculations are based on unweighted data---that is, the net wholesale prices for all States awarding contracts in a particular year are counted the same regardless of the size of their WIC infant population.

Source: Oliveira and Davis, 2006.

Figure 20. Average real net wholesale prices of newly awarded infant formula rebate contracts, 1998-2006

DHA/ARA-Supplemented Formulas

An important development in the domestic infant formula market was the introduction of infant formulas supplemented with the fatty acids docosahexaenoic acid (DHA) and arachidonic acid (ARA) in 2002. While some studies suggest that the addition of these fatty acids to infant formula may improve visual function and the mental development of infants, other studies have not found such a relationship.

Since their introduction, the share of total sales of infant formula attributed to DHA- and ARA-supplemented formulas has increased dramatically. By the second quarter of 2004, supplemented formula accounted for almost two-thirds (64 percent) of total dollar sales of infant formula sold in supermarkets (Oliveira and Davis, 2006). Both the wholesale and retail price of supplemented formula is significantly greater than that of unsupplemented formula.

A number of other factors may explain the increase in net wholesale prices, all of which are based on the premise that the size of the rebates offered by formula manufacturers depends on the degree to which winning the WIC contract leads to increased shelf space and/or increased hospital and physicians recommendations, which in turn, lead to increased sales to non-WIC consumers. For example, Neuberger and Greenstein (2004) theorize that the increase in net wholesale price may have been related to the growth in the number of WIC-only stores (which they defined as stores that stock only WIC foods and serve only WIC customers) in the early 2000s. Since shelf space in WIC-only stores does not promote sales to non-WIC customers, as more WIC participants purchase their formula in WIC-only stores, sales of the contract brand of formula to WIC customers in traditional retail food stores decrease. Retail stores may respond by stocking less of the WIC contract brand and/or giving it less shelf space. Infant formula manufacturers may then lower their rebate bids as a result of the reduced opportunity to attract non-WIC customers to their products.

Besharov (2007) links the increase in net wholesale price to the high percentage of infants participating in WIC. He states that, as the percentage of infants in WIC increases beyond some threshold, rebates will decrease since manufacturers will have less to gain from the additional shelf space as the size of the non-WIC market decreases.

A third hypothesis holds that the increase in net wholesale price may be related to the larger retail markups associated with the WIC contract brand of formula. That is, as retail markup for the WIC brand of formula increases, so too does the retail price. Price-sensitive non-WIC consumers will respond by purchasing less of the contract brand, resulting in fewer sales in the non-WIC market. In response, manufacturers will offer lower rebates.

Increasing Breastfeeding Rates in WIC May Reduce Net Wholesale Prices

One possible way to reverse the trend in higher net wholesale prices is to increase the prevalence of breastfeeding among WIC infants. An increase in breastfeeding would reduce the number of WIC formula-fed infants and decrease WIC's demand for infant formula and its infl uence on the infant formula market. Retailers would not be able to take advantage of price-insensitive WIC participants to the degree they can currently if WIC consumers account for a smaller percentage of infant formula sales. Similarly, manufacturers might be more willing to offer high rebates and low net wholesale prices to win the WIC rebate contract and increase its visibility among non-WIC consumers.

One of the objectives of the 2007 WIC food package revisions was to provide stronger incentives for breastfeeding (72 *Federal Register* 68965-69032). For example, fully breastfeeding mothers receive the most variety and largest quantities of food, and fully breastfeeding infants 6 months of age or older receive larger quantities of baby food fruits and vegetables along with baby food meat. In addition, partially breastfeeding infants receive less infant formula than previously. These changes narrow the difference in the market value between the food packages for fully breastfed infants (and their mothers) and the other food packages for infant/mother pairs. The effectiveness of these revisions in increasing breastfeeding and reducing the use of infant formula among WIC infants could reduce the costs of providing infant formula in the WIC program by decreasing both the net wholesale prices and the retail markup of the WIC brand of formula.

However, even if WIC is successful at increasing breastfeeding among program participants and lowering the cost of formula to WIC, *overall* program costs could actually increase due to the higher post-rebate cost of the food packages for fully breastfed infant/mother pairs relative to formula-fed infant/mother pairs. Whether increasing the prevalence of breastfeeding among WIC women would result in an increase or decrease in program costs depends on a number of factors: the ratio of fully formula-fed infants to partially breast fed infants; how long fully breast fed infants are breastfed (e.g., 6 or 12 months); and the impact on infant formula rebates (see the section on "WIC and Breastfeeding Rates," page 66, for an expanded discussion on increasing breastfeeding rates among WIC mothers and the resulting increase in costs to WIC).

Outcome-Based Issues in WIC

Given that WIC was created to safeguard the health of low-income women, infants, and children, an important measure of effectiveness is whether WIC improves the health of program participants, as measured by birth outcomes, nutritional status, and nutrient intake. The effectiveness of WIC's nutrition education program and WIC's impact on childhood obesity and breastfeeding rates are also important measures of effectiveness.

WIC's Effect on the Health of Participants

With regard to its impact on nutrition and health, WIC has been one of the most studied of all Federal food and nutrition assistance programs. Research coverage among the different participant groups—infants; children; and pregnant, breastfeeding, and postpartum women—has been uneven, however, and methodological issues, such as selection bias, simultaneity bias, and the complexity of health outcomes, have made it difficult for researchers to obtain clear estimates of the program's impact (Fox et al., 2004).

Birth Outcomes

Most of the existing research on WIC's impact on nutrition and health has focused on the impact of prenatal WIC participation on birth outcomes. Although pregnant women account for only 11 percent of all WIC participants, WIC research has focused on critical birth outcomes, such as low birthweight, preterm delivery, and infant mortality. Birth outcomes have also been relatively easy to study because they are easily identified and can be observed in the short run.

Most of the studies on birth outcomes reported beneficial effects from WIC participation. In fact, much of the strong congressional support for WIC has been attributed to this research. Two of the most infl uential studies were published in the early 1990s. A study by Devaney et al. (1990), based on 1987-88 data from five States, found that each dollar spent on prenatal WIC services yielded a $1.77 to $3.13 savings in Medicaid costs for newborns and mothers over the first 60 days after birth. The study also found that prenatal WIC participation was associated with increased birthweight, fewer preterm births, and longer gestational age. The U.S. General Accounting Office (1992) statistically combined results from 17 studies conducted between 1971 and 1988 that compared rates of low birthweight among WIC participants and similar nonparticipants and found that prenatal WIC benefits reduced the rate of low birthweight births by 25 percent and reduced the rate of very low birthweight births by 44 percent. GAO concluded that "each Federal dollar invested in WIC benefits returns an estimated $3.50 over 18 years in discounted present value" to Federal, State, local, and private payers. It is largely on the basis of these two birth outcomes studies that WIC is often cited as being one of the most cost-effective food assistance programs in the Nation.[106]

A number of other studies have examined WIC's impact on birth outcomes since the release of the Devaney and GAO publications. Several years ago, ERS commissioned a comprehensive review and synthesis of published research on the impact of USDA's domestic food and nutrition assistance programs, including WIC, on participants' diet and health. The resulting report—the most systematic and thorough assessment to date of research on the topic—summarized what is and what is not known about the nutrition- and health-related impact of WIC (Fox et al., 2004). The review, which examined WIC-related research published from 1978 to 2004, concluded that, even with the pervasive problem of selection bias and other limitations, "taken as a whole, the available body of research provides strong, suggestive evidence that WIC has a positive impact on mean birthweight, the incidence of low birthweight, and several other key birth outcomes, and that these positive effects lead to savings in Medicaid costs."[107] The report further notes that because of the studies' design characteristics, "it is difficult to characterize the relative size of WIC's impact."

Besharov and Germanis (2001), however, have questioned whether the positive effects of prenatal participation in WIC have been overstated. They state that methodological weaknesses in much of the WIC research—including selection bias and simultaneity bias—add uncertainty to the findings (see the box below, "Selection Bias and Simultaneity Bias"). They also state that much of the previous research lacks generalizability because it was based on one or a few States and may not be applicable to other States. The research is also based on studies conducted over a decade ago when the program was considerably different. Changes in the size, composition, and characteristics of the WIC population make it difficult to generalize results from these earlier studies to today's WIC program.

SELECTION BIAS AND SIMULTANEITY BIAS

Issues related to selection bias and simultaneity (or gestational age) bias complicate the interpretation of the research examining WIC's impact on participants' health. WIC research is typically limited to a quasi-experimental design, comparing those who participate in the program with those who do not. A problem exists if WIC participants differ in unobservable ways from eligible nonparticipants and if these unobservable differences infl uence outcomes. Selection bias can either enhance or downplay the effects of WIC participation. For example, it can exaggerate the benefits of WIC when individuals who value health and nutrition are more likely to participate in the program than individuals who are at higher risk and do not see the value of participating. WIC effects can be downplayed in research if those not participating in WIC are at lower health risk than the WIC sample. The potential for selection bias is evident in almost all WIC studies. While researchers attempt to control for it in study design and analysis, it is uncertain how successful they are.

Simultaneity bias may occur because the longer a mother's pregnancy, the more likely she is to have a healthy baby. The longer she is pregnant, however, the more time she has to enroll in WIC and the greater her chance of participating in the program. As a result, it is possible that the positive effects from longer pregnancies, independent of WIC benefits, will be attributed to participation in WIC, thereby exaggerating WIC's impact.

More recently, a debate among researchers about WIC's relative impact on birth outcomes played out in several issues of the *Journal of Policy Analysis and Management* (JPAM). An article by Bitler and Currie (2005), based on a 19-State study of WIC-eligible Medicaid mothers, concluded that WIC participation was associated with improved birth outcomes and that the positive impact of WIC was even larger among more disadvantaged women, such as teens, single high school dropouts, and women who received public assistance the previous year. An article in a later issue by Joyce et al. (2005), however, based on a study of women on Medicaid in New York City from 1988 to 2001, found no relationship between prenatal WIC participation and measures of fetal growth among singletons (i.e., infants who are not part of a multiple birth), although there was a strong association between WIC and preterm births among U.S.-born Black twins.[108] Joyce et al. concluded that the mothers' prenatal participation in WIC had relatively little impact on infant health in New York City during the study period. Furthermore, they claimed that associations between WIC and birth weight are suspect (especially given the modest monetary value of the WIC packages) and questioned whether there is a plausible mechanism for WIC to improve birth outcomes given the lack of evidence from medical literature that prenatal nutritional supplementation has a strong effect on reducing preterm births.

The editor of *JPAM* invited two scholars to "make sense of the seemingly contradictory findings" in the two articles (Pirog, 2005). After reading the papers, Ludwig and Miller (2005) acknowledged that selection bias is an issue and that both WIC research and policy would benefit from a better understanding of the determinants of WIC participation. They offered a "less pessimistic conclusion about WIC's impact on birth outcomes compared with the interpretation offered by Joyce." They concluded that it was possible that WIC's bundle of services could affect preterm birth rates and that even a small impact on birth outcomes from WIC participation could be sufficient for WIC benefits to exceed costs. In a more recent *JPAM* article, Joyce et al. (2008), after attempting to address some of the limitations in previous work by including information on the mothers' timing of WIC enrollment, found modest effects of WIC "but on fewer margins and with less impact than has been claimed by policy analysts and advocates."

Other Outcomes

Other than the research on the effect of WIC on birth outcomes, research on WIC's impact on pregnant women is scarce and relatively dated (Fox et al., 2004). Even fewer studies have looked at WIC's impact on postpartum women. The limited research suggests that postpartum WIC participation may improve the birth outcomes of subsequent pregnancies. The effect of WIC on the health of breastfeeding mothers and their infants has not been studied. (For information on WIC's effect on breastfeeding rates, see the section on "WIC and Breastfeeding Rates," p. 66.)

Another area that has not been studied in depth is the health effect of WIC on children, even though they make up almost half of all WIC participants. Little is known about WIC's effect on the long-term growth and development on both physical and cognitive/psychological scales of children (Fox et al., 2004). It is difficult to link future health outcomes with WIC participation. Assessing WIC's impact on the growth and development of children requires a longitudinal study because a long period may be necessary to detect changes. In the early 1990s, Congress canceled a planned FNS-funded longitudinal study of the long-term developmental effects of WIC on children due primarily to the high costs of the project (Devaney, 1998).

Although results from several studies have suggested that WIC participation increases children's intake of selected nutrients, these studies were conducted using old dietary standards (Recommended Dietary Allowances, or RDAs) and outdated methods to assess nutrient adequacy. A new set of dietary reference standards—Dietary Reference Intakes (DRIs)—has been developed to replace and expand the RDAs and combined with a statistically based methodology for assessing nutrient adequacy and recommended methods for assessing program impact. It is unclear whether previously observed increases in nutrient intake attributed to WIC participation are associated with real "benefits," such as an increased proportion of WIC children with adequate nutrient intakes. Although data tabulations by Cole and Fox (2004) show that nearly all WIC infants and children consume adequate amounts of most nutrients, no research is available yet that measures the impact of WIC on nutrient adequacy.

The strongest evidence of WIC's positive impact on children is in the area of iron-deficiency anemia, a serious health concern. In their review of WIC's impact on nutrition and health, Fox et al. (2004) found that most studies of the relationship between WIC participation and iron status revealed that WIC participation had a positive effect on mean levels of hemoglobin or hematocrit and/or a reduction in the incidence of anemia. WIC may also have had an indirect effect on the iron status of nonparticipants due to the presence of WIC foods on supermarket shelves (Devaney et al., 1997). WIC products, such as infant formula and cereal, are required to be iron-fortified and are consumed by nonparticipants as well as WIC program participants.

Research Challenges

Much of the research on WIC's effect on participants' health is old and predates important changes in WIC, such as participation expansion, racial/ethnic composition changes, and WIC food package revisions. While research on the impact of today's WIC program on participants is necessary to determine the current program's effectiveness, researchers face a number of methodological challenges, in addition to issues of selection bias. For example, many program outcomes develop over a long period and may require measures of both pre- and post-participation in WIC. Studies also need to control for the complex interplay of diet, heredity, and environment that makes determining the specific impact of food and nutrition programs, such as WIC, on long-term outcomes difficult (Fox et al., 2004). Furthermore, a majority of WIC participants also use other assistance programs, such as Medicaid and the Food Stamp Program, making it necessary to ascertain whether observed "impact" is due toWIC or to other programs.

Effectiveness of WIC's Nutrition Education Program

Most of the existing research on WIC has focused on the combined or overall impact of WIC rather than on the effectiveness of specific components. Although WIC's positive effects are usually attributed to the provision of supplemental food, Rossi (1998) claims that they should be viewed as the joint effects of WIC's supplemental foods, nutrition education, and health care referrals. The importance of separating out the effects of WIC's individual components was articulated by Besharov and Germanis (2001) who stated that "increasing WIC's impact is best accomplished with a knowledge of which of its elements seem to have the greatest effect on recipients. That knowledge would help determine whether the intensity of the entire program should be increased or only some element of it, such as the food packages or the nutritional counseling."

WIC's Nutrition Education

Poor diet, along with sedentary lifestyle, is a major cause of morbidity and mortality in the United States. Some of the diseases and conditions linked to poor diet include cardiovascular disease, hypertension, type 2 diabetes, overweight and obesity, iron-deficiency anemia, malnutrition, and some cancers. WIC's nutrition education—a mandatory component of WIC—is designed to improve health status and achieve positive changes in dietary and physical activity habits, emphasizing relationships between nutrition, physical activity, and health (7 CFR 246.2). Federal regulations require that WIC State agencies spend at least a sixth of their NSA expenditures on nutrition education (7 CFR 246.14). Local WIC agencies are required to offer participants or caretakers at least two nutrition education sessions during each 6-month period, although individuals are not required to attend.

A number of factors make evaluating the effect of WIC's nutrition education component difficult. For example, because recipients may receive nutrition education along with supplemental foods and referrals to health care services, it is difficult to separate out the effect of each component. Also, the content of the nutrition education, how it is implemented, and the characteristics of the participants (e.g., literacy level, primary language, nutritional needs) varies both among and within States.[109]

Previous Research

Despite these challenges, a number of attempts have been made to determine the effectiveness of WIC's nutrition education services. A study by the U.S. General Accounting Office (GAO) (2001a) reviewed previous research conducted between 1995 and 2000 on the effectiveness of WIC's nutrition education and referral services.[110] The study found that the research was severely limited by methodological constraints, including the use of outdated and poor-quality data, and concluded that the research provided few, if any, insights into the effectiveness of specific WIC nutrition services.

Since the GAO assessment, several studies have examined the effect of WIC's nutrition education. FNS sponsored a demonstration study of the effectiveness of innovative approaches to nutrition education on prenatal WIC participants. The study incorporated two approaches: a computerized touch-screen video for individual nutrition education and a facilitated group intervention (Randall et al., 2001b). Results showed no increase in nutrition knowledge from the interventions. The study noted, however, that the assessment tool used in the study measured knowledge only, may or may not have affected behavior, and would not detect knowledge in areas not covered by the test.[111]

A more recent ERS-sponsored study found that nutrition education intervention had minimal impact on WIC participants' food purchasing behavior. Bell and Gleason (2007) examined whether WIC clients in Washington State changed their food purchasing behavior after receiving nutrition education encouraging the purchase of 1-percent and skim milk, as well as low-fat cheese, in order to prevent and reduce obesity. Data were collected on food purchases both before and after the nutrition education intervention, and researchers found no significant change in purchasing patterns among the study participants. Focus group participants explained that taste preference, pressure from family members, and historical purchasing patterns infl uenced their choice of milk or cheese more than WIC nutrition education. The results point out the difficulty of changing food consumption behavior.

The lack of research that demonstrates positive effects from WIC's nutrition education services may be, at least in part, the result of low exposure rates of participants to WIC's nutrition education. An FNS-funded study of the nutrition education services offered in six local WIC agencies in the mid-1990s found that large percentages of women failed to attend nutrition education sessions (Fox et al., 1998).[112] A GAO study of six local WIC agencies found that individual nutrition education sessions ranged from an average of only 4 to 17 minutes (U.S. General Accounting Office, 2001b).[113] As Rossi (1998) points out, 15 minutes for nutrition education is "certainly inadequate for all but superficial instruction."

Enhanced Nutrition Education in WIC

While recognizing the limited effectiveness of current nutrition education services, Besharov and Germanis (2001) contend that WIC agencies should be allowed greater programmatic fl exibility to try new, innovative approaches to make WIC more effective, including enhanced nutrition education for some families and requiring WIC participants to attend nutrition education classes.[114] Many of the program enhancements, however, would require increased funding for both services and evaluations. An increase in costs would be problematic since nutrition education is supported by NSA funds that are currently held constant over time (except for infl ation adjustments). The NSA grant in FY 2008 was $15.71 per participant per month and, in addition to nutrition education, also funded breastfeeding support and promotion, health care referrals, and administrative tasks, such as outreach, eligibility determination, voucher issuance, and vendor management. Without increases in the per person NSA grant, higher nutrition education costs would necessitate cutbacks in other services funded by the NSA grants.

WIC and Childhood Obesity

WIC was established in the early 1970s to combat the malnutrition and hunger facing many low-income Americans. Since then, however, the major nutrition problems facing Americans have shifted from underconsumption to overconsumption of calories, leading to an increasing prevalence of obesity and overweight in children. Overweight children are more likely to experience health problems during their youth and also tend to become obese adults. Obesity in adulthood is a known risk factor for a number of chronic diseases, including heart disease, diabetes, stroke, and some forms of cancer. Between 1988-94 and 2003-04, the prevalence of overweight among children ages 2-5 increased from 7.2 percent to 13.9 percent (Centers for Disease Control and Prevention, 2008).[115] As the prevalence of overweight among children increases, questions have been raised as to whether food and nutrition assistance programs, such as WIC, contribute to childhood overweight by providing too much food and encouraging overeating.[116] Understanding the impact of WIC on children's weight status is especially important since, at any point in time, half of all infants and a quarter of all children ages 1-4 in this country participate in WIC.

Previous Research

Research has shown that the proportion of overweight or obese children participating in the WIC program is growing. An FNS-funded study (based on data from 1992, 1994, 1996, and 1998) of overweight among children participating in WIC found that overweight prevalence increased 20 percent over the period, reaching 13.2 percent in 1998 (Cole, 2001). For boys, overweight prevalence increased from 11.6 to 13.9 percent; for girls, overweight prevalence increased from 10.3 to 12.4 percent.

The prevalence of overweight, however, has also increased among non-WIC children. Evidence shows that children who receive WIC have weight similar to eligible nonparticipants, suggesting that the increase in overweight among WIC children is a refl ection of the increase in overweight among the general population of children. One ERS study using 1988-94 data compared WIC children ages 1-4 with income-eligible nonparticipants and higher income children and found no difference between the three groups in the prevalence of risk for being overweight (Lin, 2005).[117] There was also no difference between WIC children and income-eligible children in the prevalence of overweight. WIC children, however, were more likely to be overweight than higher income children. A more recent ERS study using data from two periods (1988-94 and 1999-2002) also suggests that there is little evidence that WIC participation increases the prevalence of overweight in children (Ver Ploeg et al., 2007). The study found that WIC children had BMI and probabilities for overweight similar to those of eligible nonparticipants. This was true for both boys and girls and for both survey periods. Furthermore, the weight status of WIC participants was similar to that of higher income children with one exception: In 1999-2002, higher income boys were less likely to be at risk of overweight and have lower BMI than boys participating in WIC.

Another ERS study found no evidence that participation in WIC contributes to increased caloric intake among low-income children. Oliveira and Chandran (2005) examined the consumption patterns of WIC children with those of three different groups: Eligible nonparticipating children living in non-WIC households, eligible nonparticipating children living in WIC households (i.e., some other household member participated in WIC), and children living in high-income households that made them ineligible for WIC. Participation in WIC was associated with a significant increase in calories consumed from all WIC-allowed foods combined (i.e., low-sugar cereal, 100 percent fruit and/or vegetable juice, eggs, milk, cheese, peanut butter, and dried peas/beans). WIC participants, however, consumed significantly fewer calories from non-WIC foods than the two groups of eligible nonparticipants. Although WIC participants consumed more total calories than children not eligible because their household income was too high, there was no evidence that participation in WIC contributed to increased caloric consumption among children eligible to participate. These results suggest that WIC foods replace non-WIC foods in the diets of children participating in WIC rather than add to their overall food consumption.

Revisions to the WIC Food Packages May Help Reduce the Prevalence of Obesity

Although previous research has not linked WIC participation to overweight and obesity, the high prevalence of overweight and obesity among the WIC population was one reason the IOM Committee to Review the WIC Food Packages recommended changes in the WIC food packages that promote healthy body weight for WIC participants (Institute of Medicine, 2005). Because it is difficult to achieve long-term weight loss, prevention of obesity is critical, and prevention efforts need to begin at an early age. The WIC program provides a natural entry point for early intervention because it reaches a large number of the Nation's infants and children. Furthermore, WIC targets overweight individuals for participation in the program. Overweight is one of the anthropometric nutritional risk criteria used for determining program eligibility. For a given participant category (i.e., infant, child, pregnant women, etc.), the highest priority is given to people demonstrating medically based nutritional risks, including anthropometric risks such as overweight (see table 4).[118]

Among the revisions to the WIC food packages, changes that may have a positive effect on preventing/reducing overweight among participants include:

- The addition of cash-value vouchers for fruits and vegetables.
- The elimination of juice from the infant food packages and reductions in the quantities of juice for children and women.
- Reductions in the quantities of milk and cheese for children and women.
- Reductions in the quantities of eggs for children and women.
- Authorization of only milk with 2 percent or lower fat content for women and children age 2 and older.
- The addition of whole-wheat or whole-grain products for children and pregnant and breastfeeding women, allowing substitutions of other whole-grain foods for bread, and requiring that at least half of WIC cereals be whole grain.

- A delay in the introduction of complementary foods to infants by 2 months (from child's 4th month to their 6th month).
- Additional incentives to support long-term breastfeeding.

WIC State agencies are required to implement the new food package provisions no later than October 1, 2009.

WIC and Breastfeeding Rates

Breastfeeding is widely acknowledged to be the best feeding method for most infants. Breastfeeding provides a range of benefits for infants' health, growth, immunity, and development and has also been shown to improve maternal health (U.S. Department of Health and Human Services, 2000). Breastfeeding also provides significant economic benefits, reducing health care costs and other costs.[119] The American Academy of Pediatrics (AAP) recommends that mothers exclusively breastfeed their infants for the first 6 months of life, with continuation of breastfeeding through 12 months and beyond as other foods are introduced (American Academy of Pediatrics, 2005). Although WIC promotes breastfeeding to all its pregnant women (unless medically contraindicated), low breastfeeding rates among WIC participants have raised questions about WIC's effects on breastfeeding.

WIC Participation Is Associated with Lower Breastfeeding Rates

Historically, both breastfeeding initiation rates (as measured by breastfeeding in the hospital) and breastfeeding rates at 6 months postpartum have been lower among WIC women than among non-WIC women (Figure 21).[120] In 2003, 76.1 percent of non-WIC women initiated breastfeeding compared with only 54 percent of WIC women (Ryan and Zhou, 2006).[121] The disparity in breastfeeding rates by WIC status remains pronounced at 6 months of age, with non-WIC women still more likely to breastfeed than WIC women (42.7 percent compared with 21 percent). Breastfeeding rates, both in-hospital and at 6 months, were significantly higher for non-WIC women across a variety of demographic characteristics, including mother's race/ethnicity, age, education, employment status, and census region (Ryan and Zhou, 2006).

Lower breastfeeding rates among WIC women do not necessarily mean that WIC decreases the likelihood of breastfeeding. Studies of WIC are typically complicated by selection issues (i.e., mothers who choose to participate in WIC are likely to be different than mothers who do not participate). One might expect that the provision of free infant formula would make the program more attractive to mothers who choose not to breastfeed and who might not have breastfed even in the absence of the program. In addition, mothers in lower socioeconomic groups, including women who are Black, poor, and less educated—that is, women who are more likely to participate in WIC—have traditionally been less likely to breastfeed their children (Li and Grummer-Strawn, 2002). Breastfeeding may also be a challenge after the mother returns to work or school, especially for low-income women who tend to work in environments that do not allow for breaks to pump breastmilk and do not provide refrigerated storage facilities for the milk. A review of published research on the impact of WIC on breastfeeding found no solid evidence that WIC had an impact on initiation and/or duration of breastfeeding (Fox et al., 2004). Although most of the reviewed studies were completed prior to the expansion of breastfeeding promotion efforts in WIC, more recent studies also provide conflicting results.[122]

WIC's Breastfeeding Promotion Efforts

Breastfeeding women have been a focus of WIC since the program's inception. The legislation first authorizing WIC as a pilot program in 1972 (P.L. 92-433) specifically identified "lactating women," pregnant women, and infants as the program's target groups and excluded nonbreastfeeding postpartum women. The 1975 legislation that established WIC as a permanent program (P.L. 94-105) made breastfeeding women eligible to participate up to 1 year after birth. The legislation also extended categorical eligibility to nonbreastfeeding postpartum women, but only up to 6 months after birth.

Beginning in the late 1980s, WIC instituted a number of changes aimed at increasing breastfeeding rates among participants (USDA, 2008a). For example, in 1989, the Child Nutrition and WIC Reauthorization Act earmarked $8 million per year to promote breastfeeding, authorized the use of NSA funds to purchase breastfeeding aids, such as breast pumps, and required WIC State agencies to designate a breastfeeding coordinator to provide training on breastfeeding promotion and support to local agency staff responsible for breastfeeding. In 1992, an enhanced WIC food package was established for women who exclusively breastfeed their infants. In 1994, the method for determining the amount of funds for WIC breastfeeding promotion and support was revised, and WIC State agencies were required to spend $21 per year (adjusted annually for infl ation) for each pregnant and breastfeeding woman. In 1998, the William F. Goodling Child Nutrition Reauthorization Act (P.L. 105-336) authorized the use of food funds for the purchase or rental of breast pumps for participants.

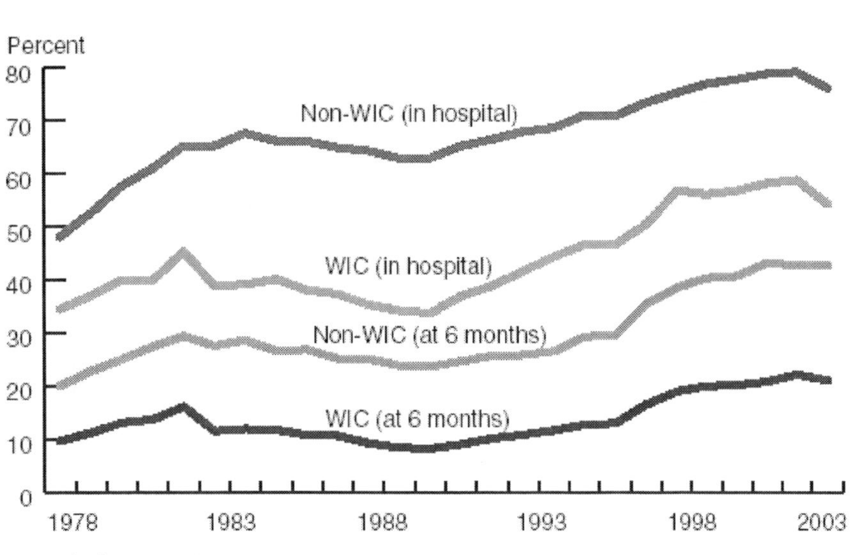

Source: Ryan and Zhou, 2006.

Figure 21.Breastfeeding rates, by WIC status, 1978-2003

Despite these efforts, disparities in breastfeeding rates between WIC and non-WIC women still exist. In fact, the gap in breastfeeding rates at 6 months by WIC status has increased in recent years (Figure 21). Some have questioned whether WIC's breastfeeding promotion and support efforts are sufficient. Ryan and Zhou (2006) estimated that, in 2005, only $34 million, or less than 1 percent of WIC's total budget, excluding rebates, was designated for initiatives to increase breastfeeding among WIC women. Lawrence (2006) claims this amount is too small to be effective. Increasing breastfeeding promotion and support activities, however, may present a challenge to the WIC program, given proposals to freeze funding levels for NSA, which funds breastfeeding promotion (see the section on "Funding for Nutrition Services and Administration (NSA)," p. 39).

Changes to the WIC Food Packages May Increase Breastfeeding Incentives

The lower breastfeeding rates among WIC women have led some to suggest that providing free infant formula to WIC infants discourages breastfeeding. Rossi (1998) states that WIC may be providing "a perverse incentive favoring bottle feeding." Although the *old* food package for breastfeeding women offers the largest quantity of a greater selection of foods, the Institute of Medicine's review of the WIC food packages (2005) estimated that the average value for *1 year of program* benefits for fully formula-feeding infant/ mother pairs ($1,380) and for partially breastfeeding infant/mother pairs ($1,668) is more than twice the value of program benefits for those who breastfeed and whose infants do not receive infant formula from the WIC program ($668) (Figure 22).

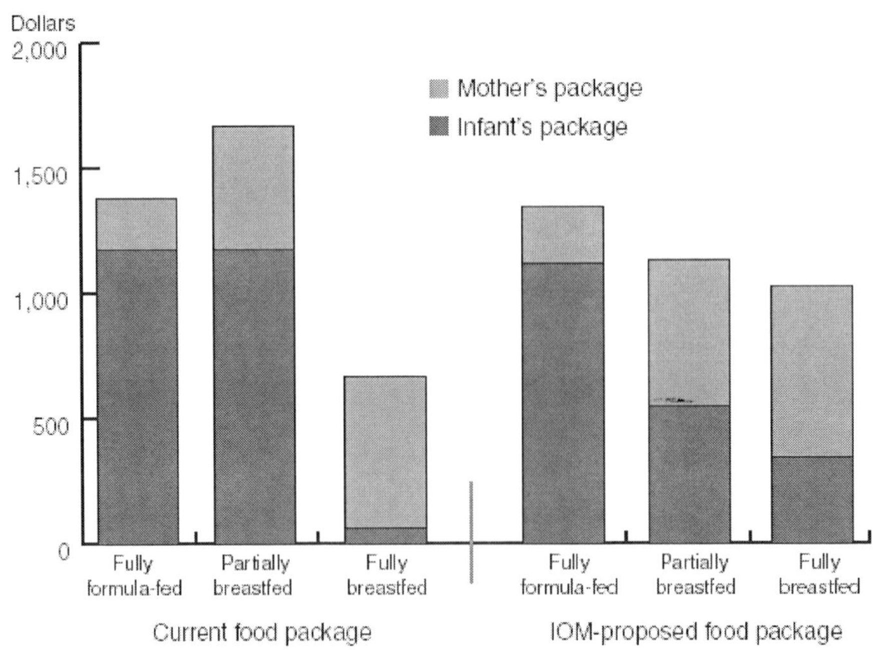

IOM=Institute of Medicine.

Note: The costs for partially and fully breastfed assumed that mothers breastfed for 12 months

Source: Economic Research Service calculations based on Institute of Medicine (2005) data.

Figure 22. Estimated annual market value (pre-rebate) of current and IOM-proposed WIC food packages for infant/mother pairs, 2002

The 2007 revisions to the WIC food packages for infants and all postpartum women were designed to strengthen WIC's breastfeeding promotion efforts and provide additional incentives for mothers to initiate and continue to breastfeed. A three-pronged approach was used (72 *Federal Register* 68965). The revised food packages address the fully breastfeeding woman's higher need for calories, vitamins, and minerals by providing greater quantities of a larger selection of foods. Similarly, the package for fully breastfed older infants is the only one to include baby food meats to meet the infant's need for supplemental sources of iron and zinc (Institute of Medicine, 2005). The revisions attempt to minimize early supplementation with infant formula, which can interfere with the establishment or continuation of breastfeeding. The amount of milk a breastfeeding woman produces depends directly on how often and how long she nurses. Providing supplemental formula to a new breastfeeding mother may interfere with her milk production and success at continued breastfeeding. Thus, the proposed rule initially recommended only two infant feeding options for the infant's first month—either full breastfeeding or full formula-feeding. Concerns were raised, however, that a mother who feels less confident about her ability to breastfeed may choose to either categorize her infant as fully formula fed, thus receiving more formula than necessary for the breastfeeding infant and further compromising successful breastfeeding, or not breastfeed at all. The revised food packages authorize three infant feeding options in the first month after birth:

- Fully formula feeding.
- Fully breastfeeding (with no supplemental formula).
- Partial breastfeeding (a State option), where an infant may receive the equivalent of not more than 104 fluid ounces of reconstituted infant formula. This allows WIC State agencies the option of issuing one can of powder infant formula to the mother upon request.

The revised food packages increase the market value of the food packages for the fully breastfeeding infant/mother pair relative to the fully formula-feeding infant/mother pair, with the objective of increasing the mother's incentive to breastfeed. There is some evidence that attractive food packages for fully breastfeeding mother/infant pairs might increase the mother's incentive to breastfeed (Institute of Medicine, 2005). Under the old food package, the market value of the food packages is nearly twice as large for the formula-feeding infant/mother pair than for the fully breastfeeding infant/mother pair.[123] Under the IOM's proposed food packages (which differ somewhat from the revised food packages), the difference in market value between the formula-feeding and the fully breastfeeding infant/mother packages becomes smaller.

Using 2002 prices, the IOM estimated that the average annual costs to WIC of food benefits for the fully breastfeeding infant/mother pair increases from $668 in the *old* food package to $1,027 in the *proposed* food package (Figure 23).[124] This is about 75 percent of the value of the food package for the fully formula-fed infant/mother pair (which declined slightly in monetary value from $1,380 to $1,345).

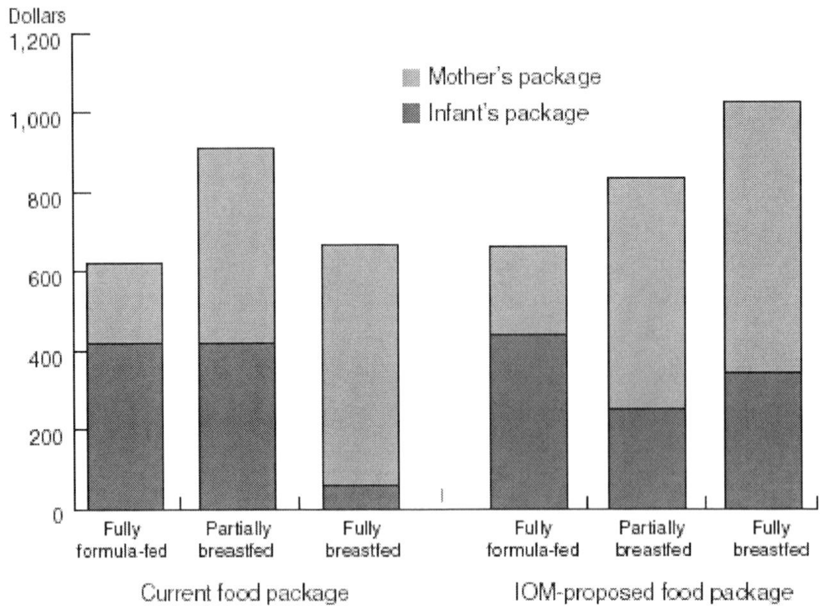

IOM=Institute of Medicine.

Note: The costs for partially and fully breastfed assumed that mothers breastfed for 12 months Source: Economic Research Service calculations based on Institute of Medicine (2005) data.

Figure 23. Estimated annual cost to WIC (post-rebate) of the current and IOM-proposed WIC food packages for infant/mother pairs, FY 2002

The revised food packages affect partially breastfed infant/mother pairs the most.[125] Whereas partially breastfed infants may currently receive up to the full amount of infant formula as fully formula-feeding infants, under the revised food package, they would receive only about half the infant formula. Although the objective is to encourage mothers to increase both duration and intensity of partial breastfeeding, there are concerns that some women may choose, instead, to breastfeed even less—or not at all—to qualify for the full amount of infant formula in the fully formula-feeding package.

There is a large degree of interest in how these package changes will affect a mother's breastfeeding decisions and practices. FNS is requesting approval from the Office of Management and Budget to collect information needed to evaluate the impact of the interim final rule on food package choices and breastfeeding outcomes for postpartum women who participate in WIC (73 *Federal Register* 34702-34703).

Breastfeeding Could Increase WIC Costs

While breastfeeding is cost effective from both the individual's and society's perspective, increasing WIC participants' breastfeeding rates could raise program costs, depending on the duration and intensity of breastfeeding. Increased breastfeeding rates could affect the level of infant formula rebates, which considerably lower the cost of buying infant formula. Using 2002 prices, the IOM estimated that the market value of the *proposed* food package was about 25 percent higher for the fully formula-feeding infant/ mother pair than for the fully breastfeeding infant/mother pair ($1,345 compared with $1,027) if infants breastfeed for 12 months. After rebates, the cost to WIC of offering the fully formula-feeding food packages is about half ($663) (Figure 23). Rebates have no effect on WIC's costs for offering the fully breastfeeding package, which would still cost the program $1,027 for a year of benefits. Thus, after rebates, each breastfeeding infant/mother pair costs the program $364 more per year than a fully formula-feeding infant/mother pair. Similarly, after rebates, each partially breastfeeding infant/mother pair would cost the program $173 more per year than a fully formula-feeding infant/mother pair.

On the other hand, if mothers breastfeed for only 6 months (a more likely scenario, considering that only about 40 percent of all women in the United States still breastfeed at 6 months), the program would save approximately $66 per fully breastfeeding infant/mother pair and $48 per partially breastfeeding infant/mother pair compared with a fully formula-feeding infant/mother pair under the proposed food packages.[126] Given the similarities between the proposed and revised food packages, the cost estimates presented here are not likely to be very different for the revised food packages. Thus, the extent to which the revised food packages increase the prevalence and duration of breastfeeding among WIC mothers could have a significant impact on program costs.

FUTURE RESEARCH DIRECTIONS

Since its inception as a small pilot program in the early 1970s, WIC has grown to become one of the cornerstones of the Nation's food and nutrition safety net for low-income children and women. During its 35-year existence, a number of legislative acts and new regulations helped shape the program. Now, over 8 million people participate in the program each month, including almost half of all infants and a quarter of all children ages 1-4. Expenditures for WIC total over $6 billion per year, or 10 percent of total Federal Government expenditures for food and nutrition assistance.

Numerous issues are associated with a program of WIC's size and complexity. Addressing these issues is essential for several reasons: (1) WIC is one of the larger food assistance programs in terms of Federal expenditures, and the program must operate efficiently to protect taxpayers' investment; and (2) WIC serves as an entry point for early nutrition and health care intervention for a large number of the Nation's infants and children, so it is important that the program operate as effectively as possible.

This report has identified and framed some of the important economic issues surrounding WIC and suggested valuable areas of research. For example, WIC participation has expanded dramatically and more research is needed on the distributional effects of WIC participation to determine if society would be better served by an expanding program or by targeting more benefits to fewer, more needy families.

Major changes were made to the WIC food packages in 2007, and WIC State agencies are required to implement the revisions by October 1, 2009. Research will be needed to examine the impact of these changes on participants. For example, will the revised food packages affect participation and/or consumption and, if so, will some participant categories be more affected than others? Research will also be needed to examine how the revisions impact WIC vendors, food manufacturers, and non-WIC consumers.

The revised food packages increase breastfeeding incentives and promote healthy body weight for WIC participants. It is important to determine what impact the revisions will have on overweight and obesity among WIC children and the prevalence of breastfeeding among WIC mothers. Whether the revised food packages increase the prevalence and the duration of breastfeeding among WIC infant/mother pairs could have a significant impact on program costs.

Because of the volume of infant formula provided through WIC, increased costs of infant formula provided through WIC have a potentially large impact on WIC program costs. Therefore, the trends in infant formula rebates and retail markup of WIC formula brands need to be monitored.

Although considerable research has focused on WIC's impact on birth outcomes (with some contradictory findings), research on other program outcomes and participation groups is more limited. Furthermore, much of the research is fairly old, capturing a program that is considerably different from the current program. For example, much of the existing research predates important changes in WIC, such as the expansion in participation, changes in the racial/ethnic composition of participants, and revisions in the WIC food packages. More research, refl ecting the current program, is needed to fill the gaps with respect to WIC's impact on the different participant groups.

NSA funds, covering both administrative and key services, currently account for over a quarter of total program costs. Little is known, however, about how NSA funds are used. Better data are needed to determine how spending allocations on key services and administration impact the program's effectiveness.

WIC State agencies are required to spend at least a sixth of their NSA expenditures on nutrition education. Little is known, however, about the effectiveness of WIC's nutrition education. More research is needed on the types of education provided and their outcomes.

A number of economic factors could have a potentially large impact on WIC in the near future. Worsening economic conditions in this country and an increasing number of births could increase the demand for WIC services. At the same time, the program could be facing greater financial pressure from higher food prices and increased infant formula costs, in addition to the possibility of increased costs associated with WIC food package revisions. As a result, WIC may come under more scrutiny. Further investment in research that addresses these issues is needed.

Appendix: Methodology for Estimating WIC Participants as a Percent of U.S. Population Subgroups

Figure 12 illustrates the percentage of various U.S. population subgroups estimated to participate in WIC. A number of calculations were required to develop the estimates.

Infants

The percentage of infants participating in the program was estimated by dividing the average number of infants participating in WIC per month in calendar 2006 (2,093,967 from USDA, 2007a) by the estimated number of births in the United States in 2006 (4,265,996, from Hamilton et al., 2007).

Children

The percentage of children participating in the program was estimated by dividing the average number of children participating in WIC in calendar 2006 (3,987,749 from USDA, 2007a) by the estimated number of children under age 5 as of July, 1, 2006 (20,417,636 from U.S. Census Bureau, 2007) after subtracting the number of infants born in the United States in 2006 (4,265,996 from Hamilton et al., 2007).

Pregnant Women

The percentage of pregnant women participating in the program was estimated by multiplying the average number of women participating in WIC in calendar 2006 (2,043,836 from USDA, 2007a) by the share of pregnant women in WIC in April 2006 (.447 from Bartlett et al., 2007) and dividing it by the number of births in 2006 (4,265,996 from Hamilton et al., 2007) times .75 (since women are pregnant 9 months).

Postpartum Women

The percentage of postpartum women participating in the program was estimated by multiplying the average number of women participating in WIC in calendar 2006 (2,043,836 from USDA, 2007a) by the share of breastfeeding or postpartum women in WIC in April 2006 (.553 from Bartlet et al., 2007) and dividing it by the number of births in 2006 (4,265,996 from Hamilton et al., 2007) which served as the proxy for the number of postpartum women in 2006. Note that the denominator consists of all postpartum women (up to 1 year after birth) in the United States while the numerator consists of all breastfeeding women (up to 1 year after birth) in WIC and all postpartum women in WIC (up to 6 months after birth).

References

Abrams, B. (1993). "Preventing Low Birth Weight: Does WIC Work? A Review of the Special Supplemental Food Program for Women, Infants, and Children," *Annals New York Academy of Sciences* Vol. *678*. March.

American Academy of Pediatrics. (2005). "Policy Statement: Breastfeeding and the Use of Human Milk," *Pediatrics* Vol. *115*, No. 2. February.

Ball, T. & Wright, A. (1999). "Health Care Costs of Formula-Feeding in the First Year of Life," *Pediatrics* Vol. *103*, No. 4. April

Bartlett, S., Bobronnikov, E. & Mendelson, M. (2007). *WIC Participant and Program Characteristics 2006*, Report No. WIC-06-PC, U.S. Department of Agriculture, Food and Nutrition Service, Special Nutrition Programs. December.

Bartlett, S., Brown-Lyons, M., Moore, D. & Estacion, A. (2000). *WIC Participant and Program Characteristics 1998*, No. WIC-00-PC, U.S. Department of Agriculture, Food and Nutrition Service, Special Nutrition Programs, May.

Bartlett, S., Glantz, C. & Logan, F. (2008). *School Lunch and Breakfast Cost Study – II: Final Report,* Report No. CN-08-MCII, U.S. Department of Agriculture, Food and Nutrition Service, Special Nutrition Programs, April.

Bell, L. & Gleason, S. (2007). *Using Point-of-Purchase Data To Evaluate Local WIC Nutrition Education Interventions: Feasibility Study*, Contractor and Cooperator Report No. 26, U.S. Department of Agriculture, Economic Research Service, January.

Bell, L., Ledsky, R., Silva, S. & Anthony, J. (2007). *An Assessment of the Impact of Medicaid Managed Care on WIC Program Coordination With Primary Care Services*, Contractor and Cooperator Report No. 33, U.S. Department of Agriculture, Economic Research Service, September.

Besharov, D. (2007). "Emerging Issues and Recent Findings," presentation at the Annual Food Assistance and Nutrition Research Conference at Economic Research Service, December 6.

Besharov, D. & Call, D. (2009). *The Expansion of WIC Eligibility and Enrollment, Good Intentions, Uncontrolled Local Discretion, and Compliant Federal Officials,* AEI working paper, March 5.

Besharov, D. (2002). *We're Feeding the Poor as if They're Starving*, AEI Print Index No. 14723, American Enterprise Institute for Public Policy Research, December.

Besharov, D. & Germanis, P. (2001). *Rethinking WIC: An Evaluation of the Women, Infants, and Children Program*, The American Enterprise Institute (AEI) Press.

Bitler, M. & Winter, J. (2005). Currie, "Does WIC Work? The Effects of WIC on Pregnancy and Birth Outcomes," *Journal of Policy Analysis and Management* Vol. 24, No. 1.

Burger, A. (2008). "The Costs of Not Doing WIC EBT: A "Through the Looking Glass" Perspective on WIC's Painstaking Migration From Paper to Plastic," presentation at the Annual Food Assistance and Nutrition Research Conference, *"Emerging Issues and Recent Findings,"* at Economic Research Service, December 4.

Burstein, N. (2001). "An Incremental Approach to Testing WIC's Effi cacy," commentary in *Rethinking WIC: An Evaluation of the Women, Infants, and Children Program* by Besharov, D., and P. Germanis, The American Enterprise Institute (AEI) Press.

California WIC Association. (2005). *Cost Containment of High-Priced Stores in the California WIC Program*, November.

California WIC Association & UC Davis Human Lactation Center. (2007). *A Policy Update on California Breastfeeding and Hospital Performance*, November

Centers for Disease Control & Prevention, U.S. Department of Health and Human Services. *Prevalence of Overweight Among Children and Adolescents: United States, 2003-2004*, accessed on March 13, 2008 at http://www.cdc.gov/nchs/products/pubs/pubd/hestats/overweight/over-wght_child_03.htm.

Chatterji, P. & Brooks-Gunn, J. (2004). "WIC Participation, Breastfeeding Practices, and Well-Child Care Among Unmarried, Low-Income Mothers," *American Journal of Public Health* Vol. *94*, No. 8.

Cole, N. (2001). *The Prevalence of Overweight Among WIC Children*, Report No. WIC-01-PCM, U.S. Department of Agriculture, Food and Nutrition Service, Special Nutrition Programs, July.

Cole, N. & Fox, M. (2004). *Nutrition and Health Characteristics of Low-Income Populations: Volume II, WIC Participants and Nonparticipants*, E-FAN-04-014-2, U.S. Department of Agriculture, Economic Research Service, December.

Davis, D. & Leibtag, E. (2005). *Interstate Variation in WIC Food Package Costs: The Role of Food Prices, Caseload Composition, and Cost-Containment Practices*, Food Assistance and Nutrition Research Report No. 41, U.S. Department of Agriculture, Economic Research Service, January.

Devaney, B. (1998). "Commentary," *Feeding the Poor: Assessing Federal Food Aid*, P. Rossi (ed.), Washington, DC: American Enterprise Institute.

Devaney, B., Bilheimer, L. & Schore, J. (1990). *The Savings in Medicaid Costs for Newborns and Their Mothers from Prenatal WIC Participation in the WIC Program: Volume 1*, U.S. Department of Agriculture, Food and Nutrition Service, October.

Devaney, B., Ellwood, M. & Love, J. (1997). "Programs that Mitigate the Effects of Poverty on Children," *The Future of Children* Vol. *7*, No. 2, Summer/ Fall.

Food Research & Action Center (FRAC), (2005). *WIC in the States: Thirty-One years of Building a Healthier America.*

Fox, M., Burstein, N., Golay, J. & Price, C. (1998). *WIC Nutrition Education Assessment Study; Final Report*, prepared by Abt Associates Inc. for U.S. Department of Agriculture, Food and Nutrition Service, September.

Fox, M., Hamilton W. & Lin, B. (2004). *Effects of Food Assistance and Nutrition and Health: Volume 3, Literature Review*, Food Assistance and Nutrition Research Report No. 19-3, U.S. Department of Agriculture, Economic Research Service, October.

Fox, H., McManus, M. & Schmidt, H., (2003). *WIC Reauthorization: Opportunities for Improving the Nutritional Status of Women, Infants, and Children*, NHPF Background Paper, National Health Policy Forum, August 14.

Greenstein, B. (2008). "Budgetary Challenges, Budget Pressures, and WIC," presented at the National WIC Association's 18th Annual Leadership Conference in Washington, DC, March 9-10. Available at http:// www.nwica.org/.

Hamilton, B., Martin, J. & Ventura, J. (2007). *Births: Preliminary Data for 2006, National Vital Statistics Reports*, Vol. *56,* No. 7, National Center for Health Statistics, December.

Herman, D. (2004). *"Are Economic Incentives Useful for Improving Dietary Quality among WIC Participants and Their Families?"* presentation at a public forum on Impact of Changes in the WIC Food Packages, Committee to Review the WIC Food Packages, Institute of Medicine, Los Angeles, CA, July 22.

Herman, D., Harrison, G., Afifi A. & Jenks, E. (2008). "Effect of a Targeted Subsidy on Intake of Fruits and Vegetables among Low-Income Women in the Special Supplemental Nutrition Program for Women, Infants, and Children," *American Journal of Public Health* Vol. *98*, No. 98., January.

Herman, D., Harrison G. & Jenks, E. (2006). "Choices Made by Low-Income Women Provided with an Economic Supplement for Fresh Fruit and Vegetable Purchase," *Journal of the American Dietetic Association* Vol. *106*, Issue 5., May.

Institute of Medicine. (1996). *WIC Nutritional Risk Criteria: A Scientifi c Assessment*, Washington, DC: National Academy Press.

Institute of Medicine, Food & Nutrition Board. (2002). *Dietary Risk Assessment in the WIC Program*, National Academy Press.

Institute of Medicine. (2005). *WIC Food Packages: Time for a Change*, Committee to Review the WIC Food Packages, Food and Nutrition Board, Washington, DC: The National Academies Press.

Isaacs, J. (2008). *The Costs of Benefi t Delivery in the Food Stamp Program: Lessons From a Cross-Program Analysis*, Contractor and Cooperator Report No. 39, U.S. Department of Agriculture, Economic Research Service, March.

Jacknowitz, A., Novillo D. & Tiehen, L. (2007). "Special Supplemental Nutrition Program for Women, Infants, and Children and Infant Feeding Practices," *Pediatrics* Vol. *119*, Issue 2., February.

Johner, N. (2008). *Statement of Nancy Montanez Johner, Statement of the Under Secretary for Food, Nutrition*, and Consumer Services Before the Subcommittee on Agriculture, Rural Development, Food and Drug Administration and Related Agencies, March 13. Available at http://www.fns.usda.gov/cga/Speeches/CT031308.html.

Joyce, T., Gibson, D. & Colman, S. "The Changing Association between Prenatal Participation in WIC and Birth Outcomes in New York City," *Journal of Policy Analysis and Management* Fall (2005). Vol. *24*, No. 4.

Joyce, T., Racine, A. & Yunzal-Butler, C. (2008). "Reassessing the WIC Effect: Evidence from the Pregnancy Nutrition Surveillance System," *Journal of Policy Analysis and Management* Vol. *27*, No. 2. Spring.

Kirlin, J., Cole, N. & Logan, C. (2003). *Assessment of WIC Cost-Containment Practices: Final Report*, E-FAN-03-005, U.S. Department of Agriculture, Economic Research Service, February.

Klein, M. (2008). "*NY State WIC Pilot Vegetable and Fruit Program,*" presented at the National WIC Association's 18th Annual Leadership Conference in Washington, DC, March 9-10. Accessed on July 18, 2008 at http:// www.nwica.org/.

Ku, L., Cohen, B. & Pindus, N. (1994). *Full Funding for WIC: A Policy Review*, Washington, DC: The Urban Institute.

Lawrence, R. (2006). "Lower Breastfeeding Rates Among Supplemental Nutrition Program for Women, Infants, and Children Participants: A Call for Action," *Pediatrics* Vol. *117*, No. 4., April.

Leibtag, E. "Retail Food Price Outlook: 2008," presented at USDA's 2008 Agricultural Outlook Forum in Washington, DC, February 21, 2008. Accessed on May 9, 2008 at http://www.usda.gov/oce/ forum/2008Speeches/PDFPPT/Leibtag.pdf.

Leonard, R., (1994). "Recalling WIC's Program's 1960s Humble Beginnings," *Nutrition Week* Vol. *24*, No. 15., April 22.

Li, R. & Grummer-Strawn, L. (2002)."Racial and Ethnic Disparities in Breastfeeding among United States Infants: Third National Health and Nutrition Examination Survey, 1988-1994," *Birth* Vol. *29*., Issue 4, December.

Lin, B-H. (2005). *Nutrition and Health Characteristics of Low-Income Populations: Body Weight Status*, Agriculture Information Bulletin No. 796-3, U.S. Department of Agriculture, Economic Research Service. February.

Ludwig, J. & Miller, M. (2005). "Interpreting the WIC Debate," *Journal of Policy Analysis and Management* Vol. *24*, No. 4., Fall.

Macro International. (1995). *The WIC Dynamics Study, Volume 1, Final Report*, prepared for U.S. Department of Agriculture, Food and Consumer Service, February.

Martin J., Hamilton, B., Sutton, P., Ventura, S., Menacker, F., Kirmeyer S. & Munson, M. (2007). *Births: Final Data for 2005, National Vital Statistics Reports*, Vol. *56* No. 6, National Center for Health Statistics.

National Bureau of Economic Research, Business Cycle Dating Committee. (2008). *Determination of the December 2007 Peak in Economic Activity* announcement, December 11. Available at http://www.nber.org/ cycles/dec2008.html.

National WIC Association. (2008). *2008 Legislative Agenda*. February

Neuberger, Z. & Greenstein, R. (2006). *WIC Budget Proposal Would Discourage Cost Containment and Represents Unsound Policy*, Center on Budget and Policy Priorities, revise, April.

Neuberger, Z. & Greenstein, R. (2004). *WIC-Only Stores and Competitive Pricing in the WIC Program*, Center on Budget and Policy Priorities, May.

Oliveira, V. & Chandran, R. (2004). *Children's Consumption of WIC-Approved Foods*, Food Assistance and Nutrition Research Report No. 44, U.S. Department of Agriculture, Economic Research Service, May.

Oliveira, V. & Davis, D. (2006). *Recent Trends and Economic Issues in the WIC Infant Formula Rebate Program*, Economic Research Report No. 22, U.S. Department of Agriculture, Economic Research Service, August.

Oliveira, V., Prell, M., Smallwood, D. & Frazão, E. (2004). *WIC and the Retail Price of Infant Formula*, Food Assistance and Nutrition Research Report No. 39, U.S. Department of Agriculture, Economic Research Service, June.

Oliveira, V., Racine, E., Olmsted, J. & Ghelfi, L. (2002). *The WIC Program: Background, Trends, and Issues*, Food Assistance and Nutrition Research Report No. 27, U.S. Department of Agriculture, Economic Research Service, September.

Owen, A. & Owen. G. (1997). "Twenty Years of WIC: A Review of Some Effects of the Program," *Journal of the American Dietetic Association* Vol. *97*, No. 7., July.

Pirog, M. (2005) "Notes from the Editor," *Journal of Policy Analysis and Management* Vol. *24*, No. 4., Fall.

Randall, B., Sprague, K., Connell, D. & Golay. J. (2001a). *WIC Nutrition Education Demonstration Study: Child Intervention*, Report No. CN-01-WICNECI, U.S. Department of Agriculture, Food and Nutrition Service, Special Nutrition Programs., March.

Randall, B., Sprague, K., Connell, D. & Golay. J. (2001b). *WIC Nutrition Education Demonstration Study: Prenatal Intervention*, Report No. CN-01-WICNEPI, U.S. Department of Agriculture, Food and Nutrition Service, Special Nutrition Programs., March.

Riordan, J. (1997). "The Cost of Not Breastfeeding: a Commentary," *Journal of Human Lactation* Vol. *13*, No. 2, June.

Rossi, P.H. (1998). *Feeding the Poor: Assessing Federal Food Aid*, Washington, DC: The American Enterprise Institute.

Ryan, A. & Zhou, W. (2006). "Lower Breastfeeding Rates Persist Among the Special Supplemental Nutrition Program for Women, Infants, and Children Participants, 1978–2003," *Pediatrics* Vol. *117*, No. 4., April.

Schwartz, J., Guilkey, D., Akin, J. & Popkin, B. (1992). *The WIC Breastfeeding Report: The Relationship of WIC Program Participation to the Initiation and Duration of*

Breastfeeding, prepared by the Research Triangle Institute for U.S. Department of Agriculture, Food and Nutrition Service., September.

Tejada-Vera, B. & Sutton. P. (2008). *Births, Marriages, Divorces, and Deaths: Provisional Data for 2007*, National Vital Statistics Reports; Vol. 56, No. 21, National Center for Health Statistics.

Thiel, K. (2008). "*Estimating the Impact of Adjunctive Eligibility for WIC*," presented at the National WIC Association's 18th Annual Leadership Conference in Washington, DC on March 9-10. Available at http:// www.nwica.org/.

U.S. Census Bureau, Population Division., (2007). *Table 1: Annual Estimates of the Population by Five-Year Age Groups and Sex for the United States: April 1, 2000 to July 1, 2006,* NC-EST2006-01, www.census.gov/popest/ national/asrh/NC-EST2006/NC-EST2006-01.xls., released on May, 17.

USDA, Economic Research Service. (2009). *Food CPI, Prices, and Expenditures: CPI for Food Forecasts,* http://www.ers.usda.gov/Briefi ng/CPIFoodAndExpenditures/ Data/cpiforecasts.htm.. Accessed on January, 28.

USDA, Food and Nutrition Service. (1991). *Cost-Effectiveness of Infant Formula Rebate Systems in the Special Supplemental Food Program for Women, Infants, and Children (WIC)*, May.

USDA, Food and Nutrition Service. (1998). Final WIC Policy Memorandum 98-9, Revision 1, Nutritional Risk Criteria, December.

USDA, Food and Nutrition Service. (1999). *History of WIC, 1974-1999, 25th Anniversary: Activities Which Led to WIC's Establishment.*

USDA, Food and Nutrition Service., (2008a). *Legislative History of Breastfeeding Promotion Requirements in WIC*, http://www.fns.usda.gov/wic/ Breastfeeding/bfl egishistory.HTM. Accessed on April 7.

USDA, Food and Nutrition Service. (2007a). *Program Information Report (Keydata), U.S. Summary, FY 2006-FY 2007, September 2007*, November.

USDA, Food and Nutrition Service. (2008b). *Program Information Report (Keydata): U.S. Summary, FY 2007-FY 2008, September 2008*, November.

USDA, Food and Nutrition Service. (2007b). *WIC Food Package Costs and Rebates Summary: Fiscal Year 2005*, September.

USDA, Food and Nutrition Service. (2006). *WIC Program Coverage: How Many Eligible Individuals Participated in the Special Supplemental Nutrition Program for Women, Infants, and Children (WIC): 1994 to 2003?.*

USDA, Food and Nutrition Service, Supplemental Food Programs Division. (2008c). *The Integrity Profi le (TIP) Report, Fiscal Year 2005.* Accessed on November 20, 2008 at http://www.fns.usda.gov/wic/tip/tipreport2005.htm.

USDA, Food & Nutrition Service, Supplemental Food Programs Division. (2001). WIC Policy Memorandum 98-9, Revision 5, Nutritional Risk Criteria, March, 23.

USDA, Office of Budget & Program Analysis. (2008d). *2009 USDA Budget Explanatory Notes for Committee on Appropriations*, section on Food, Nutrition, and Consumer Services.

USDA, Office of Budget & Program Analysis. (2008e). *FY 2009 Budget Summary and Annual Performance Plan*, U.S. Department of Agriculture.

U.S. Department of Health & Human Services. (2000). *Healthy People 2010, 2nd ed., With Understanding and Improving Health and Objectives for Improving Health,* 2 vols., Washington, DC: U.S. Government Printing Office. November.

U.S. Department of Health, Human Services & U.S. Department of Agriculture. (2005). *Dietary Guidelines for Americans, 2005*, 6th Edition, Washington, DC: U.S. Government Printing Office, January.

U.S. General Accounting Office. (1993). *Breastfeeding: WIC's Efforts to Promote Breastfeeding Have Increased*, GAO/HRD-94-13. December.

U.S. General Accounting Office. (1992). *Early Intervention: Federal Investments Like WIC Can Produce Savings*, GAO/HRD-92-18.

U.S. General Accounting Office. (2000). *Food Assistance: Financial Information on WIC Nutrition Services and Administrative Costs*, GAO/RCED-00-66, March.

U.S. Government Accountability Office (2006)a. *Food Assistance: FNS Could Take Additional Steps to Contain WIC Formula Costs*, GAO-06-380, March.

U.S. General Accounting Office. (2001)a. *Food Assistance: Research Provides Limited Information on the Effectiveness of Specifi c WIC Nutrition Services*, GAO-01-442, March.

U.S. General Accounting Office. (2001)b. *Food Assistance: WIC Faces Challenges in Providing Nutrition Services*, GAO-02-142. December.

U.S. General Accounting Office. (1998). *Information on WIC Sole-Source Rebates and Infant Formula Prices*, GAO/RCED-98-146, May.

U.S. General Accounting Office. (1985). *Need to Foster Optimal Use of Resources in the Special Supplemental Food Program for Women, Infants, and Children (WIC)*, GAO/RCED-85-105, September.

U.S. General Accounting Office. (2004).*Nutrition Education: USDA Provides Services through Multiple Programs, but Stronger Linkages among Efforts Are Needed*, GAO-04-528, April.

U.S. General Accounting Office. (1979). *The Special Supplemental Food Program for Women, Infants, and Children (WIC)—How Can It Work Better?* report by the Comptroller General, CED-79-55, February.

U.S. Government Accountability Office. (2006b). *WIC Program: More Detailed Price and Quantity Data Could Enhance Agriculture's Assessment of WIC Program Expenditures*, GAO-06-664, July.

Ver Ploeg, M., Mancino, L. & Lin. B-H. (2007). *Food and Nutrition Assistance Programs and Obesity: 1976-2002*, Economic Research Report No. 48, U.S. Department of Agriculture, Economic Research Service, September.

Weimer, J. (2001). *The Economic Benefits of Breastfeeding: A Review and Analysis*, Food Assistance and Nutrition Research Report No. 13, U.S. Department of Agriculture, Economic Research Service, March.

Whitaker, R. (2004). "Predicting Preschooler Obesity at Birth: The Role of Maternal Obesity in Early Pregnancy," *Pediatrics* Vol. *114*, No. 1, July.

White House Conference on Food, Nutrition and Health. Final Report, (1970). Summary and full report are available at www.nns.nih.gov/1969/confer-ence.htm.

Williams, R., Lessler, J., Wheeless, S. & Wildfire, J. (1990). Study of WIC Participant and Program Characteristics, 1988, Final Report, Volume 1: Summary of Findings, April.

End Notes

[1] The 2008 Farm Bill changed the name of the Food Stamp Program to the Supplemental Nutrition Assistance Program (SNAP) effective October 1, 2008. This report continues to use the older name because most of the references to the program cited were prior to the change.

[2] Since that time, important changes to the program have been implemented and new research published, necessitating an updated version of the report.

[3] Breastfeeding is defined as the practice of feeding a mother's breastmilk to her infant(s) at least once a day, on average (7 Code of Federal Regulations (CFR) 246.2).

[4] WIC regulations state that the maximum allowable family gross income (i.e., before taxes are withheld) must not exceed the guidelines for reduced-price school meals, which are 185 percent of the Federal poverty guidelines (7 CFR 246.7). State agencies may set the income guideline equal to State or local guidelines for free or reduced-price health care as long as they are equal to or less than 185 percent of the poverty guideline and not less than 100 percent of the poverty guidelines.

[5] WIC regulations define "family" as a group of related or nonrelated individuals living together as one economic unit. Residents of a homeless facility or an institution shall not be considered as members of a single family (7 CFR 246.7). The regulations leave open the timeframe for determining "current" rate of income.

[6] Applicants are also adjunctively income eligible if they are a member of a family that is certified as eligible to receive assistance under TANF or if they are a member of a family in which a pregnant woman or an infant is certified as eligible to receive assistance under Medicaid (7 CFR 246.7).

[7] WIC State agencies can require tests for anemia for infants younger than 9 months (7 CFR 246.7).

[8] Most States certify breastfeeding women and their infants for 1 year (communication from FNS on November 20, 2008).

[9] For example, overweight participants may be provided food instruments for low-fat rather than whole milk.

[10] See section on "Cost-Containment Measures" for more information on WIC rebates.

[11] The cash-value vouchers set a dollar limit on the amount of food that can be purchased and provide greater fl exibil-ity to participants on the quantity and variety of food they can purchase.

[12] Checks are routed through the banking system from the vendor's bank account to the State agency's account with a contractor bank, while vouchers refer to food instruments that the vendor submits directly to the State agency (USDA, 2008c).

[13] Vermont uses a home delivery system, while Mississippi, parts of Chicago, IL, and two Indian Tribal Organizations State agencies use direct distribution. All other State agencies currently use a retail food delivery system.

[14] The requirement that prevents WIC agencies from issuing more than a 3-month supply of food instruments to a recipient at a single time was first implemented in 1977 to encourage recipients to attend the local WIC clinic more frequently than once every 6 months (the length of the certification period for most WIC participant categories) and thus take part in nutrition education classes (42 *Federal Register* 43206-43220).

[15] EBT is an electronic process that replaces the paper WIC food instrument. It allocates WIC food prescriptions to a participant account, which is accessed electronically during the checkout process at an authorized retailer point of sale, and WIC food benefits are electronically reconciled against the available food balance. As of May 2008, only Wyoming and New Mexico had implemented statewide EBT systems.

[16] State agencies must include at least two criteria for establishing peer groups, one of which must be a measure of geography, such as metropolitan or other statistical areas that form distinct labor and product markets (7 CFR 246.12).

[17] Over 90 percent of WIC vendors were also authorized Food Stamp Program retailers (USDA, 2008c).

[18] An above-50-percent vendor derives more than 50 percent of its annual food sales revenue from WIC food instruments, and a WIC-only vendor is a type of above-50-percent vendor that derives all or nearly all of its annual food sales revenue from WIC food instruments. Pharmacies provide only infant formula, exempt infant formula, and/or WIC-eligible medical foods in exchange for WIC food instruments.

[19] Data provided by FNS on October 3, 2008.

[20] Most of the WIC State agencies retain a portion of the funds from USDA to cover costs incurred for State-level program operations. In addition, some State agencies, including most of the ITOs, operate WIC without delegating authority to local agencies (U.S. General Accounting Office, 2000).

[21] It is important to note that the most successful cost-containment strategy used in WIC—the use of infant formula rebates—was initiated by the States.

[22] A few States, however, use their own funds to supplement the Federal grant. For example, in 2001, 13 States contributed about $45 million to WIC (some State-level WIC agencies, ITOs, and local WIC agencies also received in-kind contributions) (U.S. General Accounting Office, 2001b). The General Accounting Office also noted evidence that non-Federal support for NSA has decreased since FY 1992.

[23] Food and NSA grants are allocated to WIC State agencies through a complex funding formula, and a particular State's funding level is not necessarily proportional to the number of WIC-eligible people in that State (7 CFR 246.16).

[24] In contrast, USDA's Food Stamp Program is an entitlement program whereby everyone who meets the eligibility criteria may receive benefits if they so choose.

[25] Savings from rebates for other food products are lower than for infant formula, partly because no other single product accounts for as large a portion of WIC costs as infant formula, but also because the market characteristics of other products make it unlikely that manufacturers would offer large rebates per item (U.S. General Accounting Office, 1998).

[26] The commissary in this program was stocked with USDA commodity foods.

[27] In 1973, the Department chose to call it the Special Supplemental Food Program *for Women, Infants, and Children* (WIC program) to prevent confusion with the supplemental food program being operated as an adjunct of the Food Distribution Program (38 *Federal Register* 18447-18451). In 1994, P.L. 103-448 changed WIC's name to the Special Supplemental *Nutrition* Program for Women, Infants, and Children to emphasize its role as a nutrition program.

[28] Nutrition research in the 1970s identi-fied these nutrients as most likely to be lacking in the diets of low-income women, infants, and children (72 *Federal Register* 68965).

[29] The U.S. General Accounting Office (1979) reported that the proponents of the legislation creating WIC "envisioned that, since participants would be routinely visiting health clinics in connection with obtaining the supplemental food, they would be treated for medical conditions that otherwise would go untreated."

[30] In 1980, Wyoming became the last State to enter the program (USDA, 1999).

[31] The U.S. General Accounting Office (1979) reported that these groups were highly vulnerable because they were in critical periods of growth and development and were susceptible to a variety of potentially harmful nutritional and nutritionally related medical problems. The inclusion of pregnant women was justified primarily by the vulnerability of the developing fetus and the beneficial impact of early WIC intervention. Support and reinforcement of breastfeeding practices, along with the increased nutritional demands associated with lactation, justified the inclusion of breastfeeding women. In the case of infants and young children, the rapid and critical stages of their growth and development and the nutritional demands and health risks they impose justified their inclusion.

[32] It has been suggested that Congress established the age limit at 5 years as a bridge between WIC and other child nutrition programs that begin when the child enters school (U.S. General Accounting Office, 1985).

[33] However, participation in the Commodity Supplemental Food Program disqualifies a person from participating in the WIC program.

[34] To receive the food package for children with special dietary needs, a physician was required to document that the child's condition precluded the use of the conventional food package for children.

[35] The current guideline for free school meals is household income at or below 130 percent of the Federal poverty guidelines; households with income between 130 and 185 percent of the Federal poverty guidelines are eligible for reduced-price school meals.

[36] A 1979 study by the U.S. General Accounting Office (1979) concluded that nearly all WIC participants were given the maximum allowable quantities of WIC foods without any attempts to tailor the kinds and amounts of food to meet the nutritional needs of individuals.

[37] This is the Federal share of benefits received. States may provide additional benefits.

[38] Federal grants to WIC State agencies are divided into food grants and nutrition services and administration (NSA) grants.

[39] P.L. 104-193 replaced AFDC with the Temporary Assistance for Needy Families program in 1996.

[40] Eligibility rules and practices in some States now enable people with incomes above 185 percent of poverty to enroll in Medicaid and therefore be income eligible for WIC.

[41] Although breastfeeding was always an area of concern in the WIC program, the level of concern rose as the program grew because of the increasing number of women being served and WIC's growing share of the infant formula market (Schwartz et al., 1992).

[42] Dual participation refers to simultaneous participation in the WIC and Commodity Supplemental Food Program as well as to participation in more than one local WIC program at the same time.

[43] Concerned about the variation in criteria used to determine nutritional risk eligibility among WIC State agencies, Congress directed USDA in 1989 (P.L. 101-147) to conduct a review of risk criteria (USDA 1998). In 1993, USDA awarded a grant to the Institute of Medicine (IOM) to conduct a comprehensive independent review of the nutritional risk criteria in use at that time. Following the publication of the IOM report in 1996 (Institute of Medicine, 1996), a joint National Association of WIC Directors (NAWD)/ FNS workgroup called the Risk Iden-tification and Selection Collaborative (RISC) was formed to review each of the criteria addressed by IOM. In 1998, FNS issued the list of the national nutritional risk criteria (several nutritional risk criteria have been added or modified since then).

[44] There may be other reasons for the higher prices in WIC-only stores. For example, smaller WIC-only stores may be less able to take advantage of economies of scale in their purchases.

[45] P.L. 108-447 (which contained the FY 2005 appropriations for WIC) and P.L. 109-97 (which contained the FY 2006 appropriations for WIC) prohibited the authorization of new above-50-percent vendors except for stores needed to ensure participant access to program benefits or stores that had moved short distances. This prohibition was not continued in succeeding years because P.L. 108-265 required FNS certification of a State agency's vendor cost-containment system for a State agency to authorize above-50-percent vendors. These certifications were completed by the end of FY 2006.

[46] An interim final rule has the full force and effect of a final rule, yet allows the Department to obtain feedback on the provisions while implementation goes forward.

[47] For example, the IOM report recommended adding yogurt to the WIC food packages as a milk substitute for children and women and providing fruit and vegetable vouchers with a cash value of $10 per month for women and $8 per month for children. To maintain cost neutrality, however, the interim final rule did not include yogurt and the cash value of the fruit and vegetable vouchers was reduced to $8 for nonbreastfeeding women and $6 for children.

[48] New York and Delaware were the first States to begin implementing the revised food packages in January 2009.

[49] Some States also contribute funds to WIC.

[50] See for example, Devaney et al., (1990) and U.S. General Accounting Office (1992).

[51] Expenditures for WIC in real terms decreased in 1998, 1999, 2000, and 2006.

[52] For example, the number of infants participating in WIC increased by 14 percent from FY 1999 to FY 2007.

[53] The number of infants in WIC who receive infant formula through the program is not available.

[54] Because States are not required to report all nutritional risks and because of possible variations in the methods States use and the number of risks they report, the data reported here may not provide a complete picture of nutritional risks among WIC participants.

[55] Because local WIC staff provide information on other programs at certification, some WIC participants may apply to other programs *after* information on their participation in other programs is recorded (Bartlett et al., 2007). As a result, participation estimates from other programs reported here may underestimate actual participation by WIC participants in those programs.

[56] The monthly income of most households must be 130 percent or less of the Federal poverty guidelines to be eligible for food stamps. Over time, the number of WIC participants with incomes over 130 percent of the poverty level has slightly increased. For example, PC data indicate that about 13 percent of WIC participants reporting income had incomes of 131 percent of poverty or higher in 1992 compared with about 18 percent in 2006. As a result, a smaller percentage of WIC participants have been eligible for food stamps in recent years.

[57] Under Food Stamp Program rules, households may have no more than $2,000 in countable resources, such as a bank account ($3,000 if at least one person in the household is age 60 or older or is disabled). Certain resources are not counted, such as a home and lot. Special rules are used to determine the resource value of vehicles owned by household members (http://www. fns.usda.gov/fsp/applicant_recipients/ eligibility.htm).

[58] WIC regulations define "family" as a group of related or nonrelated individuals living together as one economic unit, but does not include residents of a homeless facility or an institution (7 CFR 246.7).

[59] The legislation (P.L. 101-147) establishing adjunct income eligibility for food stamp, Medicaid, and AFDC participants was intended to simplify the WIC application process since, at the time the legislation was enacted in 1989, the income eligibility criteria for these other programs were lower than those for WIC.

[60] Figures are based on income eligibility levels under Medicaid or State Children's Health Insurance Program (SCHIP) funded Medicaid expansions. The source of the data is the Kaiser Family Foundation website at http:// www.statehealthfacts.org/compare-table.jsp?ind=203&st=3, accessed October 2008.

[61] An average of 16 percent of WIC households included in the eight PC reports published from 1992-2006 did not report income. FNS is currently conducting an income verification study for the WIC program that will provide more information on the income of WIC recipients.

[62] Between 1997 and 2007, WIC caseloads in States with Medicaid limits at or below 185 percent of poverty increased 13 percent compared with a 12-percent increase in WIC caseloads in States with higher Medicaid eligibility limits (Greenstein, 2008).

[63] The nutritional risks reported in the various PC reports were not examined in this report due to differences in the methodology used to collect the information that affect comparisons across years. For example, prior to 1999, the nutritional risk criteria used to determine eligibility varied from State to State. In 1999, FNS implemented nationally uniform standards that were first refl ected in PC2000. Beginning in PC2006, States could report up to 10 nutritional risks for participants, whereas prior to 2006, only 3 nutritional risks could be reported.

[64] Some have referred to the provision of increased WIC benefits to families based on some measure of need as "WIC-Plus."

[65] December 2007 marked the beginning of the current recession (National Bureau of Economic Research, 2008).

[66] Some States, however, use their own funds to supplement the Federal grant.

[67] Besharov argues that WIC has expanded to serve less needy families. For example, in some States, Medicaid participants with income up to 300 percent of the Federal poverty guidelines are adjunctively income eligible for WIC.

[68] Based on information provided by FNS in October 2008.

[69] Federal regulations require that each State establish a maximum reimbursement amount that it will pay WIC-approved vendors for WIC food instruments. The maximum reimbursement amount was typically set high enough to cover the higher costs associated with small stores. Regular stores generally set their prices for WIC food items in a competitive fashion, usually considerably below the maximum allowed in order to attract non-WIC shoppers. Data suggest that food instruments from WIC-only stores tend to be closer to the maximum allowable reimbursement levels (Neuberger and Greenstein, 2004).

[70] P.L. 108-265, enacted in 2004, largely eliminated the giveaway of incentive items at WIC-only stores.

[71] The authors first heard of the term "orphan program" to describe WIC during a discussion in 2006 with Larry Sawyer, former Director of Government Relations at General Mills.

[72] An association of WIC-only stores and three food companies filed suit in December 2005 to stop the Federal legislation, claiming that it would reduce the stores' WIC reimbursements to an unsustainable level (U.S. Government Accountability Office, 2006b). The case was dismissed in February 2006.

[73] The association of WIC-only stores that filed the lawsuit to stop implementation of the 2004 Federal regulations aimed at stopping the growth in the number of WIC-only stores characterized themselves as small businesses (U.S. Government Accountability Office, 2006b).

[74] According to FNS, "salary costs represent by far the most significant contributor to WIC NSA costs" (64 *Federal Register* 56670).

[75] WIC State agencies typically retain about a fourth of the funds for State-level operations and distribute the remaining funds to local WIC agencies (U.S. General Accounting Office, 2001b).

[76]The amount allocated for NSA on a national level is based on the national average of NSA grant expenditures that were made per participant per month in 1987, adjusted for infl ation.

[77] The average NSA grant per person in FY 2008 was $15.71.

[78] Little is known about how much meeting these additional requirements costs the program. Costs have been estimated for only two of these requirements. USDA estimated that strengthening vendor monitoring would cost States and local agencies about $7 million annually. The National Association of WIC Directors (the predecessor of the National WIC Association) estimated that increasing the emphasis on immunization education, documentation, and referrals could cost as much as $37 million annually. Officials from the Centers for Disease Control and Prevention agreed with this cost estimate (U.S. General Accounting Office, 2001b).

[79] Many managed care organizations are not colocated with WIC clinics and lack knowledge of WIC services, thereby increasing the barriers to coordination (Bell et al., 2007).

[80] For example, MIS should be able to automatically assess whether an applicant's income exceeds the maximum income level for eligibility based on data entered into the system (U.S. General Accounting Office, 2001b).

[81] For example, a GAO site visit found staff counting the number of participants manually to generate the monthly participation report required by the State because the agency's MIS was not capable of automatically preparing the report (U.S. General Accounting Office, 2001b).

[82] Other sources of funding—such as special grants or set-asides—have also become more difficult to access. For example, although the 2005 WIC reauthorization legislation established a $30 million annual set-aside for MIS, in FY 2006, the appropriations legislation overrode the reauthorization set-aside and provided $20 million for MIS if contingency funds are not needed to serve eligible applicants (Neuberger and Greenstein, 2006). Unfortunately, the contingency funds have been needed, and, as a result, the funds have been unavailable for MIS.

[83] As of March 2008, only two EBT systems have been implemented statewide (Wyoming and New Mexico) (http://www.fns.usda.gov/wic/EBT/ wicebtstatus.htm). Burger (2008) estimated that the costs of not converting to EBT are quite high. For example, cost studies for EBT pilot studies in Michigan and New Mexico suggest that the paper systems cost $0.05 more per participant per month than EBT. He estimated that it would take less than 8 years to recoup the costs of implementing WIC EBT nationally.

[84] An interim final rule allows FNS to obtain feedback on the major changes while allowing implementation to move forward. The interim final rule comment period ends on February 1, 2010. USDA will issue a final rule after review and analysis of public comments.

[85] Some of the changes to the food packages also have the potential to reduce participant satisfaction. For example, some participants may become dissatisfied with the reduced amounts of some WIC foods (such as milk, eggs, and juice), the reduced amount of cheese that can be substituted for fl uid milk, the elimination of whole milk from the food packages for women and children age 2 and older (unless participants with qualifying conditions provide medical documentation requesting otherwise), and some of the changes in the infants' food packages.

[86] Fruits and vegetables were not added to the food package for infants younger than 6 months.

[87] Note that increased store sales of fresh fruits and vegetables may not necessarily translate to increased total consumption of fruits and vegetables by WIC participants. For example, households may substitute fresh fruits and vegetables for processed fruits and vegetables, and/or other household members may increase their consumption of fruits and vegetables but the WIC participant may not.

[88] WIC State agencies must authorize *fresh* fruits and vegetables in their food packages; canned and frozen fruits and vegetables are options.

[89] WIC State agencies have the option to increase these requirements and to specify whether vendor fruit and vegetable stocking requirements must include fresh forms. WIC State agencies also have the option to establish different minimum requirements for different vendor peer groups, thereby taking into account the difficulty that some small vendors may have in stocking a wide variety of fruits and vegetables, particularly in fresh form. Larger vendors may be required to stock a wider variety of WIC foods.

[90] Most of the initial difficulties were easily addressed. For example, lack of participant familiarity with a produce scale was solved by laminating simple instructions in both English and Spanish near the scales. The biggest issue was explaining to WIC participants that a red-skinned potato was still a "white potato" and was therefore not eligible for the voucher (Klein, 2008).

[91] In the interim final rule, FNS asked the food industry to notify them of whole-wheat and whole-grain products that meet the new WIC food requirements.

[92] The clearest example of how WIC nutritional standards have infl uenced manufacturers' behavior in the past focuses on WIC's requirement that adult cereals be iron fortified and contain no more than 6 grams of sugar per ounce. Manufacturers responded by reformulating some of their cereals. Many of the cereals currently available to U.S. consumers meet these requirements, including popular brands, such as Cheerios, Corn Flakes, Kix, Life, Honey Bunches of Oats, Grape Nuts, Special K, Total, Wheaties, and Cream of Wheat.

[93] Several manufacturers informed FNS that they are making new WIC foods available to meet the requirements of the interim final rule (based on communication with FNS on October 3, 2008).

[94] WIC has previously been shown to increase the price of food to non-WIC consumers. An ERS study by Oliveira et al. (2004) determined that WIC and its infant formula rebate program resulted in modest increases in the supermarket prices of infant formula, especially in States with a high percentage of WIC formula-fed infants. Infant formula, however, is unique among WIC-authorized foods since WIC accounts for over half of all infant formula sold in this country. WIC is not expected to account for nearly as much of the market share for the new foods included in the revised food packages.

[95] The take-up rate of tofu is based on market consumption data, indicating that about 3 percent of all U.S. households with WIC-eligible incomes purchased tofu (72 *Federal Register* 68965-69032), and the fruit and vegetable redemption rate is based on a 2004 evaluation of a WIC fruit and vegetable intervention in Los Angeles (Herman, 2004).

[96] The maximum value of the vouchers is adjusted annually in whole-dollar increments using the Consumer Price Index (CPI) for fresh fruits and vegetables (7 CFR 246.16). That is, the maximum value of the vouchers will not change until the cumulative increase in the CPI is sufficient to raise the voucher's value by a dollar.

[97] Although the fruit and vegetable vouchers may be adjusted annually for infl ation, the adjustment would be made at the national, and not the State, level (7 CFR 246.16).

[98] Pre-rebate costs refl ect the estimated retail cost of infant formula at the time of the purchase, while post-rebate costs refl ect actual reported costs and take into account savings from infant formula rebates (USDA, 2007b).

[99] While the use of infant formula rebates has lowered program costs and enabled more people to participate in WIC, not everyone encourages the practice. For example, Burstein (2001) argued that "it is hard to defend the government's using its monopsony power to extract an involuntary program subsidy from an industry."

[100] States can either hold an individual contract for infant formula or be part of a multistate group contract or alliance whereby WIC State agencies join in a single rebate agreement to obtain infant formula. In this way, WIC State agencies with fewer clients can pool their buying power to leverage higher rebates. In 2004, however, Congress limited the use of this cost-saving practice. P.L. 108-265 prohibits the formation of multistate alliances for the purchase of infant formula if the total number of infants served by the States exceeds 100,000 (except alliances that had 100,000 infants as of October 2003). Any alliance in existence as of October 2003 may expand to serve more than 100,000 infants, but may not expand to include any additional WIC State agencies (an exception is made if the WIC State agency to be added served fewer than 5,000 infants as of October 2003). The belief is that this regulation—which grew out of concern that not all infant formula manufacturers would be able to compete for the larger multistate contacts due to production capacity—will help maintain competition among the infant formula manufacturers by helping to ensure that all manufacturers can compete for the rebate contracts (73 *Federal Register* 11308).

[101] Rebate contracts contain infl ation-ary provisions. In the event of an increase in the wholesale price after the date of the bid opening, there is a cent-for-cent increase in the rebate amounts so the net price remains the same.

[102] Infant formula manufacturers sell their product at the wholesale price to retailers who are reimbursed by WIC for the formula purchased via WIC vouchers and coupons. The manufacturers then give a portion of the wholesale price to WIC in the form of rebates. As a result, the net wholesale price can be thought of as what WIC ultimately pays manufacturers for the formula.

[103] All States, except Mississippi and Vermont (along with parts of Chicago, IL), use the retail food delivery system to provide infant formula to WIC infants.

[104] Although retailers are reimbursed by WIC for the full retail price of infant formula, they purchase the infant formula from infant formula manufacturers at the wholesale price. Retailers add a retail markup to the wholesale price and sell the formula to consumers, including WIC. So, the retail markup can be thought of as what WIC ultimately pays retailers for the formula purchased through the program.

[105] Retail markup can vary widely depending on a store's pricing strategy. For example, at one extreme, some retailers may use infant formula as a loss leader, whereby they price the product below cost to attract people into their store to purchase other items at full markup.

[106] Although this claim is often used to highlight WIC's effectiveness, in general, it should be noted that these studies were limited to examining the effects solely from *prenatal* participation in WIC.

[107] Others have reviewed WIC evaluation studies with similar conclusions (see, Abrams, 1993; Ku et al., 1994; Owen and Owen, 1997; and Rossi, 1998).

[108] The authors theorize that the finding regarding Black twins was "confounded by the waning of the crack-cocaine epidemic."

[109] WIC does not systematically collect data on the number and characteristics of participants receiving nutrition education, the types of nutrition education provided, the length and frequency of nutrition education, or the outcomes of nutrition education (U.S. General Accounting Office, 2004).

[110] Research published prior to 1995 was eliminated from the study to better examine the program as it currently operates.

[111] FNS also funded a nutrition education demonstration study aimed at WIC's child participants. The study consisted of a preschool lesson that focused on the Food Guide Pyramid, variety in the diet, and making healthy food choices for 3- and 4-year-old children (Randall et al., 2001a). Results of the study found that children who received the preschool lesson scored significantly higher on the nutrition knowledge test than children not exposed to the preschool lesson. Although the study's findings appear to indicate that nutrition education for young children in WIC settings has limitations, the researchers concluded that providing nutrition education directly to 3- and 4-year old WIC participants is feasible and can increase nutrition knowledge.

[112] For example, the percentage of women in each site who received two contacts during the prenatal period ranged from a low of 24 percent to a high of 92 percent. Among postpartum women, the maximum percentage for receipt of two nutrition education contacts ranged from 5 to 59 percent.

[113] An FNS-funded study estimated that nutrition education seminars in 1988 averaged 15 minutes (Williams et al., 1990).

[114] Possible program enhancements cited by Besharov and Germanis include additional or enhanced nutrition education services to families with obese children or parents with a drug- or alcohol-abuse problem and supplementing nutrition education classes with individual counseling sessions.

[115] Children with body mass index (BMI) values at or above the 95th percentile of the sex-specific BMI growth charts were categorized as overweight.

[116] For example, see Besharov (2002).

[117] A child with weight-for-height at or above the 85th percentile and less than the 95th percentile was classified as at risk of being overweight, and a child with weight-for-height at or above the 95th percentile was classified as overweight.

[118] In 2001, FNS added a new nutritional risk criteria for infants and children—at risk of becoming overweight—to the allowable criteria that may be used to establish WIC program eligibility (USDA, 2001). The new criteria, based on expert recommendations, classify children 24 months old and over with weight-for-height at or above the 85th percentile as being at risk for becoming overweight. The new criteria also include the existence of one or both obese parents as an allowable contributing factor to the overall risk of a child becoming overweight or obese in later years. This factor was based on scientific evidence suggesting that the presence of obesity in a parent greatly increases the risk of overweight in preschoolers (Whitaker, 2004).

[119] An ERS study estimated that a minimum of $3.6 billion would be saved if breastfeeding rates increased from 1996 levels (64 percent in-hospital, 29 percent at 6 months) to those recommended by the U.S. Surgeon General in 2000 (75 and 50 percent, respectively) (Weimer, 2001). Riordan (1997) estimated that not breastfeeding was associated with over $1 billion of extra health care costs each year associated with three health conditions—otitis media, infant diarrhea, and respiratory syncytial virus. Ball and Wright (1999) estimated that these three conditions cost the managed care health system between $331 and $475 per never-breastfed infant during the first year of life.

[120] While breastfeeding rates, both in-hospital and at 6 months, have generally increased since 1990, they remain below the breastfeeding goals set in *Healthy People 2010*, the U.S. Government's statement of national health objectives designed to identify the most significant preventable threats to health and to establish national goals to reduce these threats (U.S. Department of Health and Human Services, 2000). *Healthy People 2010's* breastfeeding goals are 75 percent in the early postpartum period, 50 percent at 6 months, and 25 percent at 1 year.

[121] "Breastfeeding initiation" is not necessarily synonymous with "exclusively breastfeeding," even in the first days of an infant's life. For example, a study of breastfeeding in California hospitals found large differences in the intensity of breastfeeding even in the hospital. In some hospitals, large proportions of mothers reporting "any breastfeeding" were accompanied by very small proportions reporting "exclusive breastfeeding" (California WIC Association and UC Davis Human Lactation Center, 2007).

[122] For, example, Chatterji and Brooks-Gunn (2004) found that WIC participation was associated with small increases in the probability of initiating breastfeeding, while Bitler and Currie (2005) found that WIC participation was associated with decreased likelihood of breastfeeding. Jacknowitz et al. (2007) found that WIC participation was associated with decreased likelihood of exclusive breastfeeding.

[123] Because a fully breastfed infant receives no WIC foods during its first few months, it is important to look at the infant/mother pair.

[124] The IOM-proposed food packages differ only very slightly from the revised food packages; mostly the proposed food package allowed yogurt in the women's food packages and did not allow for any infant formula for partially breastfed infants during the first month of life. All cost estimates are based on breastfeeding for 12 months.

[125] As already mentioned, there are very few differences between the proposed and revised food packages, and they are not likely to affect these estimates by much.

[126] In 2003, 21 percent of WIC women and 43 percent on non-WIC women breastfed at 6 months (Figure 21).

In: Child Nutrition and the WIC Program
Editor: Dominic J. Lombardi

ISBN: 978-1-61209-142-6

Chapter 3

CHILD NUTRITION AND WIC REAUTHORIZATION: ISSUES AND LEGISLATION IN THE 111TH CONGRESS

Joe Richardson

SUMMARY

A comprehensive congressional review ("reauthorization") of the primary laws governing child nutrition and WIC programs (the Richard B. Russell National School Lunch Act and the Child Nutrition Act) was scheduled for 2009 (the last reauthorization was in 2004). Congress did not meet the September 30, 2009, deadline for comprehensive reauthorization. Instead, a one-year extension (through September 30, 2010) was included in the FY2010 Agriculture Department appropriations measure to give Congress time to consider a full reauthorization bill. The delay in child nutrition/WIC reauthorization was primarily due to a lack of agreement on how to fund any new child nutrition initiatives subject to congressional "pay-go" rules. The Administration had proposed spending $10 billion over the next 10 years on expanding child nutrition efforts to "end childhood hunger by 2015," but did not offer specific policy changes or spending/revenue offsets. In 2010, Congress has moved to begin the process of enacting the most sweeping changes in child nutrition and WIC programs since the 1970s.

In May, the Senate Agriculture, Nutrition, and Forestry Committee reported the Healthy, Hunger- Free Kids Act of 2010 (S. 3307; S.Rept. 111-178). It makes substantial changes in child nutrition and WIC programs (most importantly, increasing federal financing for school lunches) that are estimated to cost just under $5 billion over the next 10 years. It also included spending reductions in other programs that offset this cost—most significantly, reduced payments under the Agriculture Department's Environmental Quality Incentive Program (EQIP) and a long-term cut in spending for the nutrition education component of the Supplemental Nutrition Assistance Program (SNAP, formerly the Food Stamp program). On August 5, 2010, the Senate approved an amended version of S. 3307. It differs from the Committee-reported version of the bill in that it replaces savings from the EQIP offset with spending reductions achieved by reducing future benefits under the Supplemental Nutrition Assistance Program (SNAP, formerly the Food Stamp program).

In July 2010, the House Education and Labor Committee approved the Improving Nutrition for America's Children Act (H.R. 5504, as amended in committee). This bill includes provisions that are much the same as the Senate initiative, but the anticipated cost is larger because it includes some provisions expanding child nutrition efforts beyond those in the Senate's bill and there are only relatively minimal offsets.

Although the Senate and House bills have now placed an extensive menu of policy changes on the table, how to pay for them is still the overriding issue. Little time is left on the congressional calendar for enactment of a comprehensive child nutrition/WIC reauthorization measure. If there is no reauthorization bill enacted before September 30, 2010, another extension (as was done in 2009) is most likely.

RECENT DEVELOPMENTS

On August 5, 2010, the Senate approved an amended version of its child nutrition/WIC reauthorization bill (S. 3307). As passed by the Senate, the bill differs from the bill as reported by the Senate Agriculture, Nutrition, and Forestry Committee in one major aspect. The committee's bill included a spending reduction offset for its costs that lowered payments under the Agriculture Department's Environmental Quality Incentives Program (EQIP); the Senate-passed bill replaces this offset with an amendment that effectively reduces benefits under the Supplemental Nutrition Assistance Program (SNAP, formerly the Food Stamp program) as of October 31, 2013—saving some $2.5 billion. This reduction would be accomplished by terminating an across-the-board SNAP/food stamp benefit increase (above and beyond that dictated by food price inflation) stipulated in the 2009 American Recovery and Reinvestment Act (ARRA; P.L. 111-5), thereby returning SNAP/food stamp benefits to levels they would have been under pre-ARRA law (i.e., based on food price inflation) and reducing benefits by an estimated $10-$ 15 per person per month.

BACKGROUND

Child nutrition programs (like school meal programs, after-school meal/snack programs, and those serving children in child care settings) and the Special Supplemental Nutrition Program for Women, Infants, and Children (the WIC program) were scheduled for a comprehensive review ("reauthorization") in 2009. However, because of concerns over the *cost* of any renewal of expiring child nutrition and WIC program authorities and of new proposals that went beyond current law (and how to pay for these new initiatives), Congress delayed action on a comprehensive bill and enacted a one-year extension (through September 30, 2010) of expiring authorities as part of the FY20 10 appropriations law for the Agriculture Department.[1]

The Administration has proposed spending $10 billion over the next 10 years in an effort to "end childhood hunger by 2015," but it has not advanced specific program changes or ways to offset any new costs. While they include the most extensive changes in child nutrition/WIC programs since the 1 970s, the pending House and Senate child nutrition/WIC reauthorization bills (H.R. 5504 and S. 3307) would require less new spending than the Administration has called for and, as noted below, substantial issues remain about how to pay for any new initiatives.

Child nutrition and WIC programs were last amended in a substantial way by the Child Nutrition and WIC Reauthorization Act of 2004 (P.L. 108-265); these revisions are covered in CRS Report RL33299, *Child Nutrition and WIC Legislation in the 108th and 109th Congresses*, by Joe Richardson. How child nutrition and WIC programs work is addressed in CRS Report R40397, *Child Nutrition and WIC Programs: A Brief Overview*, by Joe Richardson.

THEMES IN CHILD NUTRITION AND WIC REAUTHORIZATION LEGISLATION

The Senate (S. 3307) and House (H.R. 5504) committees of jurisdiction (the Senate Agriculture, Nutrition, and Forestry Committee and the House Education and Labor Committee) have now approved child nutrition/WIC reauthorization measures. They both represent the most far-reaching (and costly) changes to child nutrition and WIC programs since the 1970s and would add significant new funding (above inflation-indexed payments).

Basically, the Senate and House proposals have the same themes, although the House bill is somewhat more expansive and is anticipated to be significantly more expensive. Each proposes to

- increase funding for school lunches and link this new money to schools meeting updated nutrition standards;
- provide for gradually increasing prices for school lunches served to paying (non-poor) students;
- increase access to free school meals by (1) expanding automatic (direct) certification of those receiving public assistance benefits, and (2) giving schools new options to offer free meals to all students;
- require updated school meal nutrition standards and professional standards for school meal providers;
- broaden coverage of and support for local school “wellness policies”;
- establish nutrition standards for foods sold in competition with school meals (e.g., a la carte foods and those sold from vending machines);
- encourage “farm-to-school” and other initiatives to combat childhood obesity;
- expand support for food service through summer programs and after-school and outside-of-school programs;
- add to food safety requirements for foods served on school campuses and foods provided by the Agriculture Department;
- improve food procurement practices used by schools;
- increase WIC program support for breastfeeding;
- establish a time frame for introducing electronic benefit transfer systems to the WIC program;

- provide for rules governing added ingredients in WIC foods that purport to increase their nutritional value;
- improve schools' accountability for proper program operations;
- introduce new rules for nutrition standards and heightened physical activity in child care settings; and
- support and finance state and local initiatives to end childhood hunger.

MAJOR ISSUES

With a few exceptions (noted below), there is little controversy over the Senate and House policy provisions carrying out the themes listed above. The single, overwhelming issue in the child nutrition/WIC reauthorization debate is the costs associated with the proposed revisions (and how to offset them).

The bill reported by the Senate Agriculture, Nutrition, and Forestry Committee (with costs of just under \$5 billion over 10 years) included four offsets. There has been no opposition to the two smallest offsets—changes in how to count "bonus" commodities in meeting minimum requirements for commodity aid to schools and additional independent review of eligibility for free and reduced-price school meals. Together, they account for about one-fifth of the new spending in the Senate's measure. However, the two larger offsets have been controversial. One would substantially reduce payments for the Agriculture Department's Environmental Quality Incentive Program (EQIP) and the other would effectively cut spending for the nutrition education component of the Supplemental Nutrition Assistance Program (SNAP, formerly the Food Stamp program). Critics have argued that these two efforts deserve the support they get under current law; supporters see few other offsets to use under House/Senate "pay-go" rules.

Largely in response to criticism of the EQIP offset from the agricultural community and others, the child nutrition/WIC reauthorization bill passed by the Senate on August 5, 2010, replaces it with a provision that reduces future SNAP/food stamp benefits by terminating an across-the- board benefit increase legislated in the 2009 American Recovery and Reinvestment Act (ARRA; P.L. 111-5) in November 2013. This offset has, in turn, become controversial among advocates for food assistance programs, who see it as simply transferring SNAP/food stamp funding meant for low-income households to pay for other nutrition programs primarily affecting the same households—not new spending on food assistance.

The House bill is anticipated to have costs above the Senate's and includes only the two smallest (and non-controversial) offsets.

As a result, further progress on child nutrition/WIC reauthorization legislation largely hinges on how the cost issue is dealt with.

Beyond cost/offset issues, three major policy questions remain:

- To what degree should the federal government step in with rules governing the types of "competitive foods" served outside the school meal programs (e.g., a la carte items and foods sold from vending machines)? While both the Senate and House bills would require the establishment of federal rules for these foods, there are those who argue that the decision is better left to states and schools.

- Should there be federal rules effectively requiring minimum prices for school lunches served to non-poor children? Both the Senate and House bills envision a gradual increase in these prices (although they would achieve this in different ways). This is based on studies indicating that federal school meal payments effectively "cross-subsidize" the price of food served to non-poor children and items offered outside the school meal programs (for example, "paid" meals served to non-poor children often are priced below the full federal subsidy for a free meal). In effect, supporters are concerned that federal dollars intended for
- services to poor children are being "diverted" to aid in paying for meals for those who could afford to pay more. On the other hand, opponents contend that the current system brings higher participation among non-poor children (and bigger revenues for school food service authorities) that allows authorities to serve
- better meals, and they are concerned that higher prices would be charged to "non-poor" children whose family income is just above the cutoff for free and reduced price meals (i.e., the near poor).
- Should there be rules governing when the WIC program will pay for foods (like infant formula) where new ingredients have been added that purport to increase their nutritional value? The Senate's bill would give the Agriculture Department authority to bar foods where increased costs outweighed any increased nutritional value; the House bill takes a longer-range approach and calls for a review of the benefits of any new or emerging ingredients.

ENACTED LEGISLATION

Two items of legislation affecting child nutrition programs and the WIC program have been enacted thus far in the 111th Congress: (1) the 2009 American Recovery and Reinvestment Act (the ARRA; P.L. 111-5), and (2) the FY20 10 Agriculture Department appropriations measure (P.L. 111-80).[2]

The ARRA provided a one-time appropriation of $100 million for grants to states and schools to improve school food service infrastructure ("equipment grants"). It also appropriated an extra $500 million for the WIC program. Some $100 million of this funding is being used for various projects supporting improved WIC management information systems and the expanded use of electronic benefit transfer systems to deliver WIC benefits; the remaining $400 million has been placed in a contingency reserve to cover unanticipated WIC costs due to economic conditions.

In addition to regular annual appropriations for child nutrition and WIC programs, the FY20 10 Agriculture Department appropriations law made changes in the operations of child nutrition programs and extended expiring child nutrition legislative/funding authorities through September 30, 2010.

The FY2010 appropriations act revised the current rules governing child nutrition and WIC programs by

- adding three states and the District of Columbia to the 10 states authorized to receive federal subsidies for suppers served in after-school programs,

- requiring that military combat pay be disregarded for judging eligibility for free or reduced-price meals in child nutrition programs and the WIC program, and
- allowing state WIC agencies to exceed regulatory maximums on the amount of reconstituted liquid concentrate infant formula given to WIC recipients.

The appropriations law also provided funding for a number of new child nutrition initiatives, including money for (1) projects testing new methods of providing access to food for children during summer months, (2) support to states wishing to improve "direct certification" of SNAP (food stamps) recipients for free school meals, (3) grants for the purchase of food-service-related equipment, (4) grants to improve the health and nutrition status of children in child care settings served by the CACFP, (5) bonus payments to state WIC agencies demonstrating high proportions of breastfed infants, and (6) school garden projects.

CRS Report R40721, *Agriculture and Related Agencies: FY2010 Appropriations*, coordinated by Jim Monke, provides further and more-detailed information on child nutrition provisions in the FY2010 appropriations act.

The Senate Child Nutrition and WIC Program Reauthorization Bill (S. 3307)

On May 5, 2010, the Senate Agriculture, Nutrition, and Forestry Committee reported the Healthy, Hunger-Free Kids Act of 2010 (S. 3307; S.Rept. 111-178). This bill would reauthorize all expiring child nutrition and WIC authorities/programs (now scheduled to terminate September 30, 2010) through FY2015 and make numerous and wide-ranging changes in the operations of these programs (summarized below).

The Congressional Budget Office (CBO) estimates that the proposed revisions would cost some $4.65 billion/$4.56 billion (mandatory budget authority/outlays) over the next 10 years (FY2011–FY2020) and $1.67 billion/$1.59 billion (mandatory budget authority/outlays) over the next five years (FY2011–FY2015).

These costs were offset by savings expected from four provisions in the bill (discussed below) that were anticipated to generate total savings that effectively meet or exceed costs. In committee consideration, the makeup of the package of savings, particularly the change proposed for the Agriculture Department's Environmental Quality Incentives Program (EQIP), was the major point of contention.

On August 5, 2010, the Senate approved an amended version of S. 3307. Differing from the committee-reported bill, the Senate-passed bill drops reductions in EQIP payments and replaces them with an offset accomplished by reducing future benefits under the Supplemental Nutrition Assistance Program (SNAP, formerly the Food Stamp program). This reduction, scheduled for November 2013, would terminate an across-the-board increase in SNAP/food stamp benefits enacted as part of the 2009 American Recovery and Reinvestment Act (ARRA; P.L. 111-5) and is expected to result in monthly benefit reductions averaging some $10-$ 15 per person.

The largest savings in the Senate committee bill would have come from an amendment to ***EQIP*** law; the EQIP provides financial assistance to agricultural producers to implement conservation practices. Section 442 would substantially reduce annual mandatory funding for the EQIP for total savings of $2.87 billion/$2.2 billion (budget authority/outlays) over 10 years and $1.35 billion/$0.75 billion (budget authority/outlays) over five years.[3]

A second revision to the law governing the ***nutrition education*** component of the Supplemental Nutrition Assistance Program (SNAP, formerly the Food Stamp program) is expected to cut mandatory spending by $1.3 billion (budget authority and outlays) over 10 years and $250 million (budget authority and outlays) over five years. Section 241 would establish a new grant program for nutrition education and obesity prevention, replacing the current program under which state spending (both cash and in-kind) on nutrition education for SNAP recipients is matched by the federal government as part of their SNAP administrative costs (the federal share is 50%). The bill would instead provide $375 million for grants in FY20 11 (approximately the value of the current federal share), and adjust that amount for inflation in future years. These funds would be distributed by formula to the states and there would no longer be a requirement for state matching funds.[4] States could use the money to provide nutrition education and operate obesity prevention programs for SNAP recipients and other low-income individuals.

Extension of the Agriculture Department's authority to count certain ***"bonus" (surplus) commodities*** toward meeting a minimum threshold for commodity support of child nutrition programs (in Section 401 of the bill) is estimated to produce savings of $1 billion (budget authority and outlays) over 10 years and $500 million (budget authority and outlays) over five years. This authority was most recently extended (through September 30, 2010) in the FY20 10 Agriculture Department appropriations measure. A detailed discussion of this authority is found in CRS Report R40721, *Agriculture and Related Agencies: FY2010 Appropriations*, coordinated by Jim Monke.

Finally, Section 304 of the bill would require local educational agencies (LEAs) that demonstrate high levels of administrative error to have an additional person ***independently review eligibility determinations*** for free and reduced-price school meals. This change in program operations is estimated to save $63 million/$62 million (budget authority/outlays) over 10 years and $26 million/$25 million (budget authority/outlays) over five years.

Summary of Provisions

In addition to reauthorization of all expiring authorities/programs in the Richard B. Russell National School Lunch Act and the Child Nutrition Act and the four cost-saving proposals noted above, the Senate committee's initiative includes major changes in the way child nutrition programs operate and provides substantial new funding.

Federal Funding for and Pricing of School Lunches

Section 201 ***increases funding for school lunches*** served in participating schools by raising all per-lunch federal subsidies by 6 cents (indexed for inflation) for schools that meet updated meal pattern and nutrition standards required by the bill. This "performance-based" increase in federal school lunch subsidies represents the largest cost item in the Senate bill—about 70%–75% of total costs.

Section 205 requires participating schools to ***gradually increase the price charged for "paid" school lunches*** (i.e., those not served free or at a reduced price) so that prices charged to "paying" students eventually match at least the difference between the federal subsidy for free and paid lunches—unless non-federal funds are used to compensate.

Expanded Access to Free School Meals

Sections 101 and 103 change rules governing the ***"direct certification"*** method of determining eligibility for free school meals. Under current direct certification rules, schools may enter into agreements with SNAP/food stamp agencies to certify children in SNAP/food stamp households eligible for free school meals without requiring a separate application from the family; direct certification effectively allows schools to "piggyback" on the more in-depth eligibility certification done for SNAP/food stamps and reduces errors that may occur in school lunch application eligibility procedures that are otherwise used. Section 101 provides funding ($4 million a year) for "performance awards" for states demonstrating outstanding or substantially improved performance in direct certification activities. It also requires "continuous improvement plans" for states failing to meet goals set for increasing direct certification. Section 103 aims to extend direct certification by establishing a demonstration project to directly certify most children in ***Medicaid*** households as eligible for free school meals.

Section 102 places into law a provision (similar to current regulations) making ***foster children*** categorically (automatically) eligible for free school meals.

Section 104 would give LEAs ***two new options to offer free meals to all schoolchildren***. Under current law, schools with high proportions of low-income children can choose to offer free meals to all children; these provisions of law are generally called "Provision 2 and Provision 3." Schools taking these options must, however, take applications in a "base" year and use the results of those approved applications to determine the proportion of meals/students that would otherwise be served free or at a reduced price, thereby establishing the amount of their federal school meal subsidies for the next four years. In effect, schools taking advantage of these provisions save the administrative cost of determining eligibility for free and reduced-price meals and counting them separately and must cover the extra costs associated with losing charges received from paying students. The Senate committee bill would add two more choices for schools wishing to serve free meals to all students; in both cases, taking of applications would not be necessary and schools would (as under current law) be required to find funding for any costs above those covered by federal subsidies. Under a ***"direct certification" option***, schools with relatively high proportions of students directly certified as eligible for free school meals because they are public assistance (e.g., SNAP-food stamp/Medicaid) recipients could choose to receive federal school meal subsidies derived from the proportion of students directly certified. Under a ***"survey" option***, the Agriculture Department would be permitted to use Census and other socioeconomic surveys and data sources to approximate the makeup of students and replace the collection of household applications to determine the proportion of children eligible for free and reduced-price meals.

Nutrition, Nutrition Education, Wellness, and Farm-to-School Policies

Section 201 establishes a time frame for the Agriculture Department to promulgate regulations ***updating meal patterns and nutrition standards for school meal programs*** based on recommendations from the National Academy of Sciences. Schools meeting the new requirements would be eligible for the increased federal subsidies (6 cents a lunch) noted above. It also provides funding for technical assistance to help implement new meal patterns and nutrition standards.

Section 202 changes rules governing ***milk*** served in school meal programs to effectively bar federal subsidies for whole milk (i.e., milk must be "consistent with the Dietary Guidelines for Americans").

Section 203 requires that schools participating in school meal programs offer free, potable ***water*** in meal service areas.

Section 204 replaces existing requirements that LEAs establish ***"wellness policies"*** with a similar (but expanded) requirement that all LEAs participating in school meal programs have wellness policies (designed locally) that include goals for nutrition education, increased physical activity, and other policies that promote student wellness—including guidelines for *all* foods available on the school campus during the school day and periodic reassessments of policies. The Agriculture Department (in conjunction with the Education Department and the Centers for Disease Control and Prevention) also is required to provide technical assistance to LEAs in carrying out the wellness policy directive.

Current federal child nutrition law does not give the federal government any significant say over foods served/offered in schools outside of meals that are federally subsidized (e.g., a la carte food items and those served from vending machines). Section 208 requires the Agriculture Department to establish "science-based" nutrition standards for *all* foods offered in participating schools— throughout the school campus and until the end of the school day. This is intended to establish minimum national standards for so-called ***"competitive foods"*** in schools participating in meal programs.

Section 209 requires LEAs to periodically ***report information on the "school nutrition environment"*** of schools under their jurisdiction to the Agriculture Department and the public and authorizes the department to provide technical assistance to support assessment of and reporting on schools' nutrition environments. Information called for under this amendment would cover food safety, local wellness policies, program participation, and the nutritional quality of meals.

Section 210 authorizes a pilot project of competitive grants aimed at increasing the quantity of ***organic foods*** provided through the School Lunch program.

Section 243 provides mandatory funding ($5 million a year) for competitive grants (with a 75% federal match) to assist schools and nonprofit entities in establishing ***"farm-to-school" programs*** that improve schools' access to locally produced foods.

Section 244 authorizes the Agriculture Department (in consultation with the Health and Human Services Department) to establish a research, demonstration, and technical assistance program to ***promote healthy eating and reduce the prevalence of obesity***, especially among children.

After-School and Outside-of-School Initiatives

Section 122 makes all states eligible to receive federal subsidies for ***suppers served in after- school care programs*** (in addition to the District of Columbia and the 13 states covered by current law). Section 337 requires the Agriculture Department to study ways of bringing in more sponsors for after-school supper programs.

Child and Adult Care Food Program (CACFP)

Section 121 makes it easier for ***family day care homes*** to qualify as "Tier I" homes and thereby receive higher federal subsidies.

Section 221 requires the establishment of ***new nutrition requirements for meals served under the CACFP*** and generally conforms these requirements to those used for school meal programs. Mandatory funding of $10 million is provided to support ***promotion of physical activity and limited electronic media use*** in child care venues.

Section 222 requires that the Agriculture Department and Health and Human Services Department coordinate efforts to encourage state child care agencies to include nutrition and child wellness standards in ***state child care licensing rules***.

Section 223 requires the Agriculture Department (in consultation with the Health and Human Service Department) to conduct a national study of child care centers and family day care homes to ***assess the nutritional quality of foods served and opportunities for physical activity***. Mandatory funding of $5 million is provided for the study.

Sections 331–333 include provisions ***easing administrative rules*** applied to day care providers, making clear that aggrieved providers' have access to hearings and payment for valid claims, and allowing family day care home providers to help families in preparing and transmitting application forms that are used in determining homes' eligibility for higher CACFP benefits.

Section 334 ***standardizes (and generally increases) federal administrative payments to family day care home sponsors*** and allows sponsors to carry over a portion of these funds (if unspent) into the next fiscal year.

Section 335 increases funding for ***audits*** of entities participating in the CACFP.

Section 336 requires the Agriculture Department to continue efforts to ***reduce paperwork*** required of providers and sponsors under the CACFP.

Summer Food Service

Section 111 eliminates current rules limiting the number of sites ***nonprofit summer program sponsors*** can operate, aligning eligibility rules between public and nonprofit sponsors.

Section 112 requires schools to conduct ***outreach efforts*** to inform families of the availability and location of summer program meal sites (and the availability of school breakfasts).

Section 113 authorizes appropriations ($20 million a year) for ***competitive grants to support improvement and expansion*** of summer food service programs.

Sections 321-322 ***ease administrative rules*** for summer program sponsors, establish procedures for termination of sponsors, and require the maintenance of a list of disqualified sponsors.

Safety and Procurement Practices

Section 242 requires the Agriculture Department to develop ***model product specifications and practices for procurement*** of food used in child nutrition programs (including how to follow "Buy American" rules).

Section 302 mandates that ***food safety rules*** established for school meals apply to any facility or part of a facility in which foods are stored, prepared, or served under any school nutrition program.

Section 308 requires the Agriculture Department to improve ***procedures for dealing with suspect food items*** purchased by the department for use in school meal programs (e.g., product recall rules).

Special Supplemental Nutrition Program for Women, Infants, and Children (the WIC Program)

Section 131 allows states to ***certify children eligible for WIC benefits for up to one year*** at a time (as opposed to the current six months) if the child receives regular health and nutrition assessments.

Section 231 expands the Agriculture Department's mandate to promote ***breastfeeding*** through the WIC program and recognize exemplary breastfeeding practices by local WIC agencies.

Section 232 specifies that the Agriculture Department conduct a ***review of food items provided under the WIC program*** at least every 10 years.

Section 351 provides for ***sharing information on WIC nutrition education and breastfeeding promotion practices*** with projects operating the Commodity Supplemental Food Program or the CACFP.

Section 352 makes several changes affecting ***WIC program operations***. It increases funding for WIC program evaluation efforts, makes changes to administrative rules governing competitive bids for supplying WIC food items, mandates the use of electronic benefit transfer (EBT) systems in providing WIC benefits by October 2020, and allows states (under limited conditions) to use rebates received from infant formula manufacturers to pay for food costs incurred in the previous fiscal year.

Section 353 provides the Agriculture Department with ***authority to disallow food products for use in the WIC program*** based on a determination as to whether the ingredients in the product yield a benefit relative to its cost.

Miscellaneous and Administrative Proposals

Section 141 provides $10 million for research on the causes and consequences of ***childhood hunger*** and $40 million for demonstration projects that test innovative strategies to end childhood hunger.

Section 142 authorizes the Agriculture Department to award ***State Childhood Hunger Challenge Grants*** to governors to carry out comprehensive strategies to end childhood hunger.

Section 143 requires the department (in conjunction with states and LEAs) to examine current practices regarding ***extending credit to children to pay for school meals and providing "alternate" meals to children without cash on hand.*** The department must report on the review and may implement national standards for meal charges and the provision of alternate meals.

Section 206 requires that ***revenue from the sale of "non-program foods"*** (food items other than federally subsidized school meals sold in competition with school meals) that are purchased with funds from a school's food service account must effectively equal or exceed the costs associated with obtaining the food.

Section 207 places into law provisions for an ***expanded audit and compliance review system*** for participating schools that covers both financial and nutritional requirements; it also directs that review results be made publicly available.

As a privacy protection measure, Section 301 changes rules governing the provision of ***Social Security account numbers*** to require that only the last four digits of the account number of the primary wage earner be provided when applying for free or reduced-price school meals.

Section 303 provides the department with authority to ***levy fines*** on schools and state agencies with serious violations of child nutrition program rules.

Section 305 requires states and child nutrition program providers to cooperate with the department in the conduct of ***program evaluations and studies***.

Section 306 requires the department to establish ***professional standards*** for certification of state and local school food service directors and provide necessary training to those affected. Mandatory funding ($5 million in the first year and $1 million a year in later years) is provided for management of training and certification activities—which may be carried out through professional food service management organizations.

Section 307 requires the department to issue a guidance to schools as to ***charging school food service budgets for indirect costs*** (those not directly associated with food service like trash collection and phone and computer services). It also provides for a study of the extent to which these charges are made, and (after the study) further guidance and regulations on the types of indirect costs that are reasonable and necessary to provide school meals. Mandatory funding ($2 million) is made available to carry out these activities.

Section 361 requires that agreements between the department and state agencies administering child nutrition and WIC programs include provisions that support full use of federal funds for administration of these programs and ***exclude federally funded activities from state budget limitations*** (such as hiring freezes, work furloughs, and travel restrictions).

Section 362 ***bars eligibility for child nutrition providers*** (for *any* child nutrition program) if they have been terminated from a child nutrition program and are on a disqualification list for the Summer Food Service program or the CACFP.

Section 406 increases mandatory ***funding for the Food Service Management Institute (FSMI)*** from $4 million to $5 million a year.

Section 407 provides mandatory ***funding for federal administrative support*** of child nutrition program operations (e.g., training and technical assistance related to improving program integrity, reviewing administrative practices of local agencies) of $4 million a year.

THE HOUSE CHILD NUTRITION AND WIC PROGRAM REAUTHORIZATION BILL (H.R. 5504)

On July 15, 2010, the House Education and Labor Committee approved an amended version of H.R. 5504, the Improving Nutrition for America's Children Act—reauthorizing expiring authorities through FY20 15 (as in the Senate bill) and making substantial changes to child nutrition and WIC programs. No fully compiled version of the amended bill is yet available and a report to accompany the bill has not been filed.

While no official Congressional Budget Office (CBO) cost estimate has been completed, it appears that it will cost substantially more than the Senate committee's measure because it includes amendments not included by the Senate. Unlike the Senate bill, only two relatively small offsetting savings are provided (both are also included in the Senate bill). The House offsets are in Section 401 (the same as the ***"bonus" commodity offset*** in the Senate, which the CBO estimates will save $500 million over five years and $1 billion over 10 years) and Section 310 (the same as the ***independent review of eligibility applications*** in the Senate, which the CBO estimates would save some $25 million/$26 million (budget authority/outlays) over five years and $62 million/$63 million (budget authority/outlays) over 10 years.

Summary of Provisions

In addition to reauthorization of all expiring authorities/programs in the Richard B. Russell National School Lunch Act and the Child Nutrition Act (as in the Senate's bill), the House committee's initiative includes extensive changes in the way child nutrition and WIC programs operate and major new funding. Many are the same as or very similar to those in the Senate bill and the reader should refer to the earlier summary of the Senate bill's provisions when they are noted for additional detail.

Federal Funding for and Pricing of School Lunches

As in the Senate bill, Section 201 ***increases funding for school lunches*** by raising federal per- lunch subsidies by 6 cents (indexed for inflation) for schools that meet updated meal pattern and nutrition standards.

Section 409 requires that participating schools ***gradually increase their revenues from nonfederal sources*** (including prices charged to paying students) so as to ensure that the average per-lunch revenue from federal and non-federal sources matches at least the federal subsidy for a free lunch.

Expanded Access to Free School Meals

As in the Senate bill, Section 101 places into law a provision making ***foster children*** categorically eligible for free school meals. In addition, it makes clear that Indian children placed in foster care are covered.

As in the Senate bill, Section 102 changes rules governing the ***"direct certification"*** method of determining eligibility for free school meals (i.e., provides for performance bonuses and requires "continuous improvement plans" for non-performing states). Similar to the Senate bill, Section 103 allows an increasing number of states to directly certify most children in ***Medicaid*** households as eligible for free school meals.

With few differences from the Senate bill, Section 104 offers LEAs ***two new options to offer free meals to all schoolchildren***—one based on the proportion of children "directly certified" for free meals based on public assistance participation and the other based on Census or other socioeconomic survey information.

Section 107 permits LEAs to automatically certify as eligible for free school meals any child in a ***military household*** receiving a Defense Department "supplemental subsistence allowance for low-income families." Section 146 requires the Agriculture Department (in consultation with the Defense Department) to examine the access children in military households have to free and reduced-price school meals and recommend strategies that could better meet their needs.

Nutrition, Nutrition Education, Wellness, and Farm-to-School Policies

Like the Senate bill, Section 201 establishes a time frame for the Agriculture Department to ***update meal patterns and nutrition standards for school meal programs*** and provides funding for technical assistance to help implement the new meal patterns and nutrition standards.

As with the Senate bill, Section 202 changes rules governing ***milk*** served in school meal programs to effectively bar federal subsidies for whole milk. It also clarifies rules governing the substitution of non-milk products for milk.

Like the Senate bill, Section 203 requires schools to offer ***water*** in meal service areas.

Similar to the Senate bill, Section 204 requires minimum standards for ***"competitive foods"*** (e.g., a la carte food items and those sold from vending machines), but the standards would apply somewhat more broadly (i.e., throughout the "extended school day").

Similar to the Senate bill, Section 205 includes expanded requirements for local ***"wellness policies"*** and provides for technical assistance in establishing these policies.

Similar to the Senate bill, Section 206 requires LEAs to report information on the ***"wellness environment"*** in their schools.

Section 207 establishes and funds a new ***Nutrition and Wellness Promotion program*** to support nutrition education and other promotion and compliance activities. Each state would receive an annual amount equal to a 1/2 cent for each lunch subsidized under the School Lunch program (totaling approximately $25 million–$30 million).

Similar to the Senate bill, Section 208 provides mandatory funding ($10 million a year) for competitive grants to assist schools and nonprofit entities in establishing ***"farm-to-school"*** programs that improve schools' access to locally produced foods.

Similar to the Senate bill, Section 243 authorizes the establishment of a research, demonstration, and technical assistance program to ***promote healthy eating and reduce the prevalence of obesity***.

Section 244 authorizes the Agriculture Department (in consultation with the Education and Health and Human Services Departments) to conduct a study on the extent and types of ***marketing of foods and beverages in schools*** (including, for example, assessment of the nutritional quality of the items marketed).

Section 247 authorizes the department to award competitive matching ***"partnership for wellness" grants*** for projects that leverage community resources and support student access to physical activity, nutrition education, and nutritious foods during the regular school year.

Similar to the Senate bill, an as yet unnumbered section authorizes a pilot program of competitive grants to schools to increase the quantity of ***organic foods*** served in school lunches.

An as yet unnumbered section establishes a pilot project under which the department would deliver ***plant-based alternate protein products*** to schools for the meal programs—in addition to other commodities provided to schools.

Section 249 requires the department to ensure that schools and other child nutrition providers have information as to the levels of ***mercury*** in the food they serve and calls for guidance and technical materials to help ensure that foods and meals are safe with respect to mercury levels.

Section 250 authorizes a pilot program of grants to schools to encourage the consumption of ***milk*** outside of school meal programs.

Section 363 authorizes the establishment of a ***Nutrition Corps*** under the Corporation for National and Community Service. It would support programs to increase access to and participation in nutrition programs, improve the quality of these programs, and support local agriculture and farm-to-school initiatives.

After-School and Outside-of-School Initiatives

Section 105 establishes a project of competitive grants to five states to provide meals and snacks (***"out-of-school meal service"***) to children participating in outside-of-school educational or other programs.

Similar to the Senate bill, Section 123 makes all states eligible to receive federal subsidies for ***suppers served in after-school care programs***.

Section 144 requires a ***study of after-school meal service programs***, including "best practices" for soliciting sponsors for the programs and any requirements that may be a barrier to sponsor participation.

Section 145 establishes and funds (at $10 million a year) a pilot program under which the department would provide food commodities to entities like schools and food banks to be used to provide ***food to at-risk school children on weekends and during extended school holidays.***

Commodities

Section 242 requires the Agriculture Department to develop ***model product specifications and procurement practices for procurement*** of food used in child nutrition programs.

Section 306 requires the department to develop new guidelines to determine the circumstances under which it is appropriate to place a "hold" on ***suspect foods supplied by the department*** and to establish rules for improving department hold and recall procedures.

Section 307 requires the department to make available to states and schools ***information on vendors supplying commodity foods*** to the department.

Section 312 allows the department to ***retain title to commodities provided by the department*** and delivered to a processor on behalf of a state recipient agency until the finished, processed commodity is delivered to the state agency. It also requires the department to issue regulations to ensure ***accountability for commodities provided to processors***, especially in the event of a food safety issue.

Section 441 allows ***dried fruit and frozen fruit*** to be included in offerings under the Fresh Fruit and Vegetable program.

An as yet unnumbered amendment requires the department to purchase ***low-fat cheeses*** (valued at up to $1 million a year) for use in school meal programs, in addition to other commodities the department supplies to schools.

Child and Adult Care Food Program (CACFP)

As in the Senate bill, Section 121 makes it easier for ***family day care homes*** to qualify as "Tier I" homes and thereby receive higher federal subsidies.

Section 122 provides for federal subsidies for additional meal/snacks served to ***children in child care for more than eight hours a day***—in no more than five states.

Like the Senate bill, Section 221 requires the establishment of ***new nutrition requirements for meals served under the CACFP,*** generally conforms these requirements to those used for school meal programs, and provides mandatory funding of $10 million to support ***promotion of physical activity and limited electronic media use*** in child care venues. It also provides mandatory funding of $25 million for competitive grants to promote health and nutrition in child care settings.

As in the Senate bill, Section 222 provides funding for a study of child care centers and day care homes to ***assess the nutritional quality of food served and the opportunities for physical activity***.

Like the Senate bill, Sections 331–336 ***ease administrative rules*** applied to day care providers (including making clear that aggrieved providers' have access to hearings and payment for valid claims and allowing day care home providers to help with application forms), ***standardize and increase administrative payments*** to day care home sponsors, increase funding for ***audits***, and mandate continued efforts to reduce CACFP ***paperwork requirements***. In addition, Section 337 allows for ***advance payments for administrative costs*** to family day care home sponsors.

Summer Food Service

As in the Senate bill, Section 111 aligns eligibility rules between public and ***nonprofit summer program sponsors.***

Like the Senate bill, Section 112 requires summer program ***outreach efforts***.

Section 113 authorizes and funds a competitive grant program to provide up to 10 states with federal subsidies for meals and snacks served by non-public entities wishing to implement ***"year-round" food service programs*** that effectively operate like summer food service programs (e.g., they operate at sites during the regular school year that serve meals/snacks outside of school hours, on weekends, or during school holidays/vacations; are located in low-income areas; and receive federal subsidies based on summer program rather than school meal program rules).

Section 114 authorizes competitive grants to assist summer program sponsors with technical assistance, site improvement and transportation costs, and other activities ***supporting sponsor retention.***

Section 115 lowers the threshold for qualifying as a low-income area in the summer program for rural areas—potentially making more ***rural sponsors of summer programs*** eligible.

As in the Senate bill, Sections 321-322 ***ease administrative rules*** for summer program sponsors.

Section 323 increases funding for ***health inspections*** of summer food projects.

Section 441 loosens ***"low-income area eligibility" rules***, potentially making more sponsoring organizations eligible to operate summer programs.

School Breakfasts

Section 106 establishes a competitive grant program for schools (with mandatory funding of $10 million) to help them ***expand the School Breakfast program***.

Safety and Procurement Practices

Section 242 requires the Agriculture Department to provide ***technical assistance, guidance, and training*** to state and local child nutrition agencies on how to procure foods for meal programs (including how to follow "Buy American" rules) and mandates that the department develop ***model product specifications and practices for procurement*** of food used in child nutrition programs. It also provides mandatory funding of $4 million to carry out these activities.

Like the Senate bill, Sections 305 and 306 mandate that ***food safety rules*** apply throughout the school campus and require the department to improve ***procedures for dealing with suspect foods*** (e.g., product recall rules) it may purchase.

Special Supplemental Nutrition Program for Women, Infants, and Children (the WIC Program)

As in the Senate bill, Section 131 allows states to ***certify children eligible for WIC benefits for up to one year*** at a time.

As in the Senate bill, Sections 231 and 232 expand the Agriculture Department's mandate to promote ***breastfeeding*** and specify that a ***review of WIC food items*** be conducted at least every 10 years.

Like the Senate bill, Sections 351 and 352 require ***sharing information on WIC nutrition education and breastfeeding practices*** and change rules governing ***WIC program operations*** (especially requiring the use of electronic benefit transfer systems to deliver benefits by October 2020).

Section 425 mandates that the department (as part of the periodic review of WIC food items noted above) contract for an independent ***review of the benefits of any new or emerging ingredients of potential public health significance that are added or may be added to WIC foods***.

Miscellaneous and Administrative Proposals

As in the Senate bill, Section 141 provides money for research on the causes and consequences of ***childhood hunger***.

Similar to the Senate bill, Section 142 establishes and provides funding for ***State Childhood Hunger Challenge Grants***.

Section 143 requires schools to notify parents about policies with respect to providing school ***meals to children without sufficient funds to buy their meals or who have outstanding debts owed for meals.*** It also requires that unpaid meal fees not affect children's access to regular school meals and establishes rules for dealing with households in arrears on their meal payments. Similar to the Senate bill, it calls for a study of current practices on dealing with children in these circumstances and authorizes national standards.

Section 146 provides specific authority for schools to ***donate unused foods*** to food banks and other charitable organizations.

Section 245 authorizes grants to schools for the purchase of ***food service equipment.*** In addition, an as yet unnumbered section calls for a study of the adequacy of cafeteria equipment commonly used in school meal programs.

Section 246 authorizes the Agriculture Department (in consultation with the Environmental Protection Agency) to establish a ***"green cafeterias"*** pilot program of competitive grants to schools making environmentally suitable changes in their meal programs (e.g., recycling activities and changes to their procurement practices).

As in the Senate bill, Section 301 provides for a guidance, a study, and regulations with regard to ***charging school food service budgets for indirect costs.***

Like the Senate bill, Section 302 requires that ***revenue from the sale of "non-program foods"*** equals or exceeds the costs associated with obtaining them.

As in the Senate bill, Section 303 includes provisions for an ***expanded audit and compliance review system*** and the public reporting of review results. In addition, Section 304 funds a study of effectiveness and efficiency of compliance/accountability reviews of schools.

Similar to the Senate bill, Section 306 calls for establishment of ***professional standards*** for school food service directors. Like the Senate bill, Section 308 changes rules covering the provision of ***Social Security account numbers*** to require that only the last four digits of the number be provided.

As in the Senate bill, Section 309 provides authority to ***levy fines*** on schools and state agencies with serious violations of program rules.

Like the Senate bill, Section 311 requires states and child nutrition providers to cooperate with the department in the conduct of ***program evaluations and studies.***

Section 313 authorizes an examination of states' policies and practices with respect to participation of ***charter schools*** in school meal programs.

As with the Senate bill, Section 361 includes provisions to ensure that ***federally funded activities are excluded from state budget limitations.***

Like the Senate bill, Section 362 bars eligibility for ***providers that have been terminated*** from another child nutrition program.

As in the Senate bill, Section 406 increases funding for ***federal administrative support activities.*** In addition, Section 408 increases funding for the nutrition program ***information clearinghouse*** to $1 million a year.

End Notes

[1] See CRS Report R40721, *Agriculture and Related Agencies: FY2010 Appropriations*, coordinated by Jim Monke, for more detail.

[2] In addition, two resolutions (S.Res. 67 and H.Res. 210) recognizing National School Breakfast Week and the achievements and need for breakfast programs were approved in March 2009 and one resolution (H.Res. 362) supporting the goals of the National School Lunch program was approved in April 2009.

[3] Additional detailed information on the EQIP and the proposal to use funding from EQIP can be found in CRS Report R40197, *Environmental Quality Incentives Program (EQIP): Status and Issues*, by Megan Stubbs.

[4] The formula used to distribute money to the states would be based on the number of participants in the SNAP. However, "hold-harmless" provisions phasing in the use of the formula would limit reductions in individual state amounts.

In: Child Nutrition and the WIC Program
Editor: Dominic J. Lombardi

ISBN: 978-1-61209-142-6

Chapter 4

RISING INFANT FORMULA COSTS TO THE WIC PROGRAM: RECENT TRENDS IN REBATES AND WHOLESALE PRICES

Victor Oliveira, Elizabeth Frazao and David Smallwood

ABSTRACT

The Special Supplemental Nutrition Program for Women, Infants, and Children (WIC) provides participating infants with free infant formula. This study estimated that between 57 and 68 percent of all infant formula sold in the United States was purchased through WIC, based on 2004-06 data, and that formula costs to the WIC program have increased. Typically, WIC State agencies receive substantial rebates from manufacturers for each can of formula provided through the program. Each WIC State agency, or group of agencies, awards a contract to the manufacturer offering the lowest net wholesale price, defined as the difference between the manufacturer's wholesale price and the State agency's rebate. After adjusting for inflation, net wholesale prices increased by an average 73 percent for 26 fluid ounces of reconstituted formula between States' contracts in effect in December 2008 and the States' previous contracts. Most (72 percent) of the increase in real net wholesale prices was due to higher wholesale prices, the rest (28 percent) was due to lower rebates. As a result of the increase in real net wholesale prices, WIC paid about $127 million more for infant formula over the course of a year.

Keywords: Infant formula; Special Supplemental Nutrition Program for Women, Infants, and Children; WIC; infant formula maximum daily allowance; ERS; Economic Research Service; U.S. Department of Agriculture; USDA

ACKNOWLEDGMENTS

The authors thank Ruowei (Rosie) Li and Jian Chen of the Centers for Disease Control and Prevention for providing us with data from the National Immunization Survey (NIS), as well as Priscilla Smith and Wynnice Pointer-Napper for editorial and design support.

SUMMARY

USDA's Special Supplemental Nutrition Program for Women, Infants, and Children (WIC) provides participating infants with free infant formula. Federal law requires that WIC State agencies enter into cost-containment contracts with infant formula manufacturers, with agencies typically receiving substantial discounts (rebates) from manufacturers for each can of formula purchased through the program. Each WIC State agency or group of agencies awards a contract to the manufacturer offering the lowest net wholesale price, defined as the difference between the manufacturer's wholesale price and the rebate. In exchange for the rebate, a manufacturer is given an exclusive right to provide its infant formula to WIC participants in the State. In fiscal 2008, infant formula rebates totaled $2.0 billion, compared with total WIC expenditures (after rebates) of $6.2 billion.

What is the Issue?

Because of the large volume of infant formula purchased through WIC, even small increases in net wholesale price can result in large increases in total costs to the program. WIC is a discretionary grant program funded annually by appropriations law. The number of participants who can be served within a fixed budget depends heavily on the program's food package costs, which in turn are significantly affected by rebates and the cost of infant formula.

What Did the Study Find?

This study found that between 57 and 68 percent of all infant formula sold in the United States in 2004-06 was purchased through WIC. Nearly all WIC State agencies paid more for milk-based powdered formula (the primary type of infant formula) in their rebate contracts that were in effect in December 2008 than in their previous contracts, even after adjusting for infla-tion. Excluding Mississippi and Vermont, which do not distribute WIC foods through retail foodstores, 45 of 48 States, the District of Columbia, and 5 U.S. territories saw an increase in their real net wholesale price (December 2008 dollars). Across WIC State agencies, real net wholesale prices increased by an average 21 cents for 26 fluid ounces of reconstituted formula (WIC's maximum daily allowance during the study period) between States' previous and current rebate contracts (i.e., those in effect in December 2008). As a result of the increase in real net wholesale prices, WIC State agencies paid about $127 million more for infant formula over the course of a year. This was equivalent to the cost of supporting 134,200 persons in WIC for a year or about 2 percent of all women, infants, and children participating in WIC in fiscal 2008.

Seventy-two percent of the increase in real net wholesale price was due to an increase in the real wholesale price of infant formula. All rebate contracts in effect in December 2008 were based on formulas supplemented with the fatty acids docosahexaenoic acid (DHA) and arachidonic acid (ARA), whereas most of the previous contracts were based on unsupplemented formulas. Because wholesale prices of DHA/ARA-supplemented formulas are higher than wholesale prices of unsupplemented formulas, wholesale prices of infant formula increased more in States that switched to the more expensive DHA/ARA-supplemented formula in their contracts that were in effect in December 2008.

The remaining 28 percent of the increase in real net wholesale price was due to a decrease in real rebates. The average percentage discount (i.e., the rebate as a percentage of the wholesale price) in the previous contracts was 91 percent. In other words, WIC on average paid only 9 percent of the wholesale price for formula (plus the retailer's markup). The average percentage discount in the contracts in effect in December 2008 fell to 85 percent, indicating that WIC State agencies were paying a greater percentage of the wholesale price than previously.

Several recent developments, such as the country's economic condition and revisions to the WIC food packages, have the potential to affect the net wholesale price to WIC in the future.

How Was the Study Conducted?

In order to examine trends or changes in net wholesale price over time, this report compared the real net wholesale price in a State's contract that was in effect in December 2008 to that of its previous contract. The analysis was based primarily on data on infant formula rebate contracts provided by USDA's Food and Nutrition Service and infant formula wholesale prices as reported in the formula manufacturers' price list catalogs. Proprietary data on infant formula sales obtained from the Nielsen Company were used to examine the characteristics of the infant formula market.

DEFINITIONS

Contract brand—all the infant formula, other than exempt infant formulas, that is produced by the manufacturer awarded the WIC contract. All contract brand formulas are covered by rebate contracts.

Current contract—the contract term (i.e., the period during which the infant formula rebate contract is in effect) varies across WIC State agencies (or multistate alliances). In this report, "current contract" refers to an infant formula rebate contract that was in effect in December 2008.

Exempt infant formula—defined in the Federal Food, Drug, and Cosmetic Act as any infant formula that is represented and labeled for use by an infant who has an inborn error of metabolism or a low birth weight, or who otherwise has an unusual medical or dietary problem (21 U.S. Code 350a). Exempt infant formulas require prescriptions for use in the WIC program and are not covered by rebate contracts.

Infant formula—defined in the Federal Food, Drug, and Cosmetic Act as a food that purports to be or is represented for special dietary use solely as a food for infants by reason of its simulation of human milk or its suitability as a complete or partial substitute for human milk (21 U.S. Code 321 (z)).

Multistate alliance—two or more WIC State agencies that join together for the purpose of procuring infant formula by soliciting competitive bids for infant formula.

Net wholesale price—the difference between an infant formula manufacturer's lowest national wholesale price per unit for a full truckload of infant formula and the rebate level or the discount offered or provided by the manufacturer under an infant formula cost containment contract with a WIC State agency.

New WIC food package—the WIC food package in effect upon implementation of the changes described in the interim rule published December 6, 2007 (*72 Federal Register 68966-69032*). WIC State agencies were required to implement the new provisions by October 1, 2009. The new food package for infants provides different maximum allowances for infant formula, depending on infant's age and breastfeeding status (fully formula-fed, partially breastfed, or fully breastfed).

Old WIC food package—the WIC food package in effect prior to implementation of the new regulations described in the interim rule published December 6, 2007 (*72 Federal Register 68966-69032*). Under the old WIC food package, the maximum allowance of formula was the same for all infants, although amounts could be tailored to meet infants' needs.

Percentage discount—the rebate as a percentage of the manufacturer's lowest national wholesale price per unit, as of the date of the bid opening, for a full truckload of the infant formula.

Previous contract—an infant formula rebate contract that was in effect immediately prior to the current contract.

Primary contract infant formula—the specific infant formula for which a manufacturer submits a bid to a WIC State agency in response to a rebate solicitation and for which a contract is awarded by the WIC State agency as a result of that bid.

Rebate—the amount of money refunded under cost-containment procedures to any WIC State agency from the manufacturer of the particular food product as the result of the purchase of the supplemental food with a voucher or other purchase instrument by a participant in each State agency's program. Such rebates shall be payments made subsequent to the exchange of a food instrument for food.

Retail markup—the difference between the retail price and the wholesale price.

Wholesale price—all wholesale prices cited in this report represent the infant formula manufacturers' lowest national wholesale price per unit for a full truckload of infant formula as reported in each manufacturer's price list catalog.

INTRODUCTION

USDA's Special Supplemental Nutrition Program for Women, Infants, and Children (WIC) provides participating infants with free infant formula. This study estimates that between 57 and 68 percent of all infant formula sold in the United States in 2004-06 was purchased through WIC (see appendix A for information on how WIC's share of the infant formula market was estimated). As a result, infant formula accounts for a large share of WIC's program costs.

WIC is a discretionary grant program funded annually by appropriations law.[1] The number of participants who can be served within a fixed budget depends heavily on the program's food package costs, which in turn are significantly affected by the cost of infant formula. To reduce the cost of infant formula to WIC, Federal law requires that WIC State agencies enter into cost-containment contracts with the manufacturers of infant formula. In these contracts, WIC State agencies receive discounts in the form of rebates from the manufacturers for each can of formula purchased through WIC, and the manufacturer is given the exclusive right to provide its infant formula to WIC participants in that State. The rebates have been a major source of funds for WIC. In fiscal year 2008, infant formula rebates totaled $2.0 billion compared to total program expenditures (after rebates) of $6.2 billion. The savings generated by rebates are used to provide benefits to more participants within the same total budget. Since the mid-1990s, rebates have supported about one-quarter of all WIC participants (figure 1).

WIC infant formula rebate contracts are awarded to the manufacturer offering the WIC State agency the lowest net wholesale price (the difference between the manufacturer's wholesale price and the rebate).[2] Because wholesale prices differ across manufacturers and manufacturers offer different rebates to different States, net wholesale prices vary widely across States (figure 2).

Net wholesale price is only one of the costs that WIC pays for infant formula. Most WIC participants purchase infant formula from authorized retail vendors using a WIC voucher or coupon. The WIC State agency then reimburses the vendor for the full retail price (equivalent to the wholesale price plus the retail markup) for the formula purchased by WIC participants. The manufacturer then issues a rebate to the State agency. Thus, the cost to WIC for each can of infant formula sold through the program can be expressed as:

Cost to WIC = Net Wholesale Price + Retail Markup,

where

Net Wholesale Price = Wholesale Price – Rebate

and

Retail Markup = Retail Price – Wholesale Price

The cost of formula to WIC can also be expressed as the retail price minus the manufacturer's rebate. Although this is a simpler way of expressing infant formula's costs to WIC, this report retains the fuller expression in order to emphasize that costs to WIC are established by two different market agents—infant formula manufacturers and foodstore retailers.

Figure 3 illustrates the various cost components of a can of infant formula provided through the WIC program. An earlier Economic Research Service analysis based on 2004 data found that, in most States, the retail markup—not the net wholesale price—was the largest component of infant formula costs to WIC (Oliveira and Davis, 2006). However, the relatively small net wholesale prices are a reflection of the effectiveness of the rebate program. Rebates are generally large—averaging about 85 percent of the wholesale price in recent contracts—and the increase in WIC program costs, if the rebates were to decrease, could potentially dwarf the effect of the retail markup. For example, without the rebates, infant formula would be the single most expensive food item provided by WIC, accounting for 44 percent of all food costs in fiscal 2005, compared to only 17 percent after taking into account the savings from rebates (USDA, 2007).

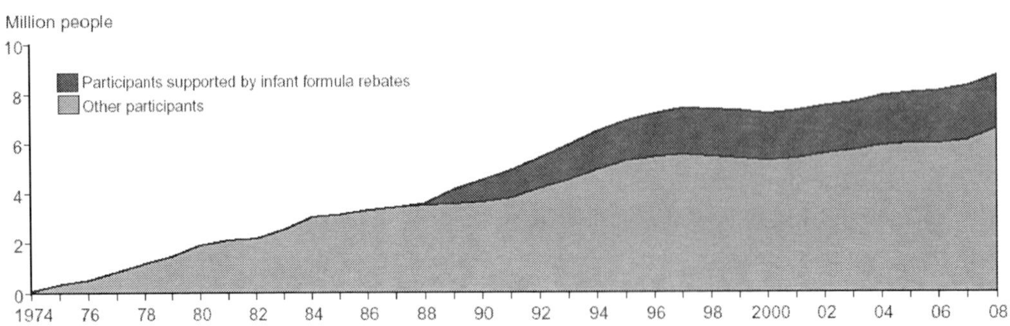

Note: The number of WIC participants supported by infant formula rebates was calculated by multiplying the total number of WIC participants by rebates share of total program expenditures and rebates.

Source: USDA, Economic Research Service calculations based on USDA, Food and Nutrition Service data.

Figure 1. Average monthly number of WIC participants, FY 1974-2008

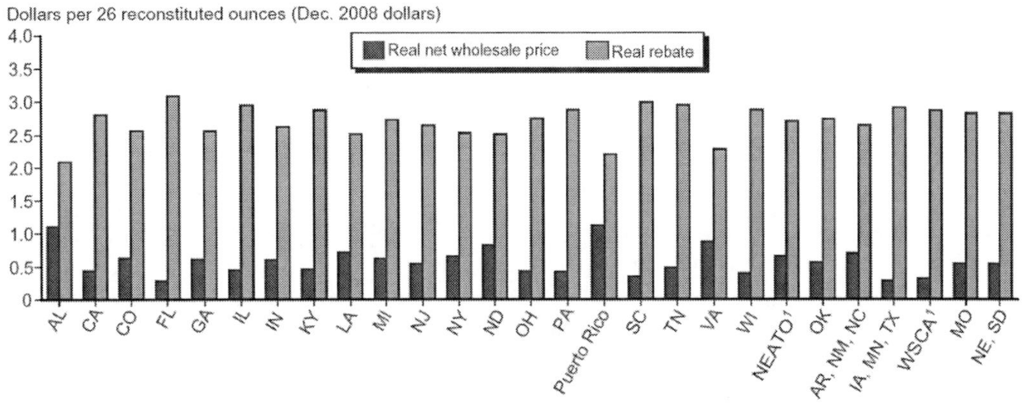

Note: Rebates and net wholesale prices reflect real prices as of the date the State's contract became effective.

[1]NEATO and WSCA are multistate alliances. For a list of members of each alliance, see box, "Multistate Alliances," p.14.

Source: USDA, Economic Research Service calculations based on USDA, Food and Nutrition Service data.

Figure 2. Infant formula rebates and net wholesale prices of milk-based powder by State for contracts in effect in December 2008

This report examines recent trends in infant formula rebates in terms of net wholesale price (ERS is conducting a separate study that examines the retail markup of the infant formula purchased through WIC). Four major questions are addressed:

1. What are the recent trends in the infant formula rebates in terms of net wholesale price?
2. What are the factors behind the trends?
3. What effect do the recent trends have on infant formula costs to WIC?
4. What factors may impact the costs of infant formula to WIC in the future?

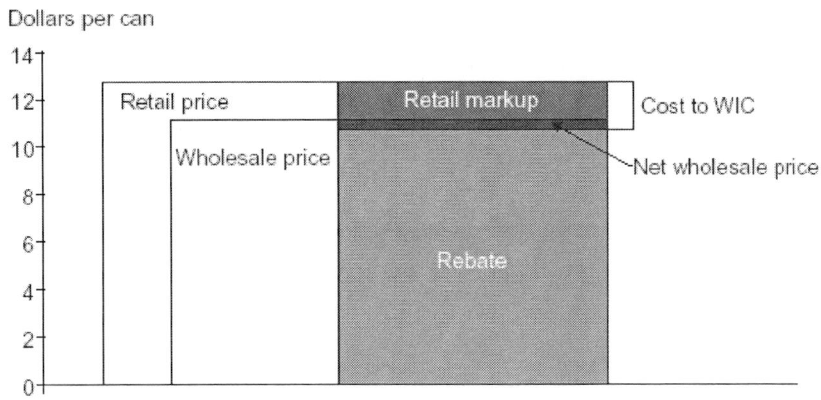

Note: Example based on a 12.9-oz can of Ross Similac with iron (milk-based powder) in the California WIC program during the 2nd quarter of 2004.

Source: Oliveira and Davis, 2006.

Figure 3. Cost components for can of infant formula in WIC

Several different sources of data were utilized in the study. The analysis of changes in net wholesale price was based primarily on data on rebate contracts compiled by USDA's Food and Nutrition Service (FNS), the agency responsible for administering the WIC program, supplemented with data on infant formula rebates compiled by David Davis at South Dakota State University (Davis, 2008). Information from infant formula manufacturers' wholesale price lists was used to examine trends in the wholesale price of infant formula. Information on the characteristics of the infant formula market was based on unpublished scanner-based proprietary data from the Nielsen Company.

The next three chapters provide readers with background information on WIC, the infant formula market, and the infant formula rebate program. Readers familiar with these topics may want to skip those chapters and pick up again in the chapter on "Trends in Infant Formula Rebate Contracts." The remaining chapters discuss how changes in WIC's share of the infant formula market could impact net wholesale price trends and the conclusions.

WIC Program Overview

WIC's mission is to safeguard the health of low-income women, infants, and children ages 1-4 who are at nutritional risk by providing supplemental foods, nutrition education, and referrals to health care and other social services. WIC is based on the premise that early intervention programs during critical times of growth and development can help prevent future medical and developmental problems. Administered by USDA's Food and Nutrition Service, the program provides grants for food benefits, nutrition services, and administration to 90 WIC State agencies, including the 50 States, the District of Columbia, 5 U.S. territories—Guam, the U.S. Virgin Islands, America Samoa, the Commonwealth of Puerto Rico, and the Commonwealth of the Northern Mariana Islands—and 34 Indian Tribal Organizations. Each State agency is responsible for program operations within its jurisdiction, including negotiating rebate contracts with infant formula manufacturers. In fiscal year 2008, an average 8.7 million persons participated in WIC each month, including 2.2 million infants (USDA, 2009a). Over half of all infants born in the United States participate in WIC (figure 4).

To qualify for WIC, a family's income must be at or below 185 percent of the Federal poverty guidelines. For a family of four who lived in the 48 contiguous States as of July 1, 2009, that would be an annual income of $40,793 or lower. Applicants for the WIC program who participate in or who have certain family members who participate in the Supplemental Nutrition Assistance Program (SNAP, formerly the Food Stamp Program), Medicaid, or Temporary Assistance Program for Needy Families (TANF) are deemed to meet the income eligibility criterion automatically. Applicants must also be nutritionally at risk, as determined by a health professional such as a physician, nutritionist, or nurse. A report by the Institute of Medicine (2002) concluded that because nearly all U.S. women and children meet at least one of the nutritional risk criteria established by WIC (e.g., failure to meet the Dietary Guidelines for Americans), the criteria have little effect on restricting program participation.

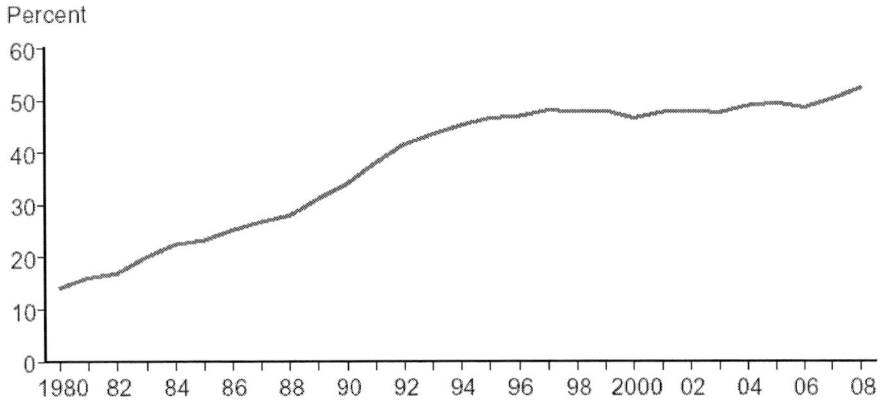

Note: Share was calculated by dividing the average monthly number of infants in WIC (USDA, various years) in a fiscal year by the total number of births in the corresponding calendar year (Hamilton, et al., 2009; and Martin, et al., 2009; and Tejada-Vera and Sutton, 2009). Fiscal years run from October 1 through September 30.

Source: USDA, Economic Research Service calculations.

Figure 4. WIC infants as a share of all U.S. infants, FY 1980-2008

Program participants are prescribed one of seven food packages according to participant category. During the 1998-2008 study period, the WIC food package for infants less than 1 year of age provided up to a monthly maximum allowance of 806 reconstituted fluid ounces of infant formula, equivalent to 26 reconstituted fluid ounces per day.[3] Infant participants are eligible to receive benefits for a 6-month period, but they can be certified up to the infant's first birthday at the WIC State agency's option. According to USDA's Food and Nutrition Service, most States certify infants up to the infant's first birthday.

To provide program participants with supplemental food packages, States may use any one of three types of food delivery systems (or any combination of the three):

- Retail—participants obtain supplemental food free of charge by exchanging a voucher, check, or electronic benefits transfer (EBT) card at authorized retail vendors.
- Home—supplemental foods are delivered to the participant's home.
- Direct distribution—participants pick up supplemental foods from storage facilities operated by the State or local agency.

All States except Vermont and Mississippi distribute WIC foods via the retail food delivery system.[4] Under the retail food delivery system, participants "purchase" the WIC food items from retail food stores using a food instrument (i.e., voucher, check, or electronic benefits transfer (EBT) card) that specifies the types and amounts of foods that can be purchased. In the case of infant formula, the food instrument also specifies the brand of formula to be purchased. Only those vendors (usually supermarkets, grocery stores, or pharmacies) authorized by the WIC State agency may transact and redeem food instruments. At the end of fiscal year 2005 (the latest data available), there were 44,458 authorized WIC vendors nationwide (USDA, 2008).

Generally, vendors submit the food instruments to their bank, which submits them to the WIC State agency's bank. That bank pays the vendors the full retail price (i.e., shelf price) of the WIC food items with funds provided by the WIC State agency in a manner set forth in the State agency's contract with the bank. The WIC State agency bills the infant formula manufacturer for the rebate. The formula manufacturer then issues a rebate to the State.

In the event that WIC does not have the funds to enroll all eligible applicants, WIC has a priority system to ensure that those at the greatest nutritional risk and most likely to benefit from WIC intervention receive program benefits. In general, priority is given to people demonstrating medically based nutritional risks over dietary-based nutritional risks, to infants and pregnant and breastfeeding women over children, and to children over postpartum women. Increases in funding and savings from infant formula rebates during the 1990s allowed a greater number of lower priority applicants, such as children ages 1 to 4, to participate. Anecdotal evidence indicates that funding in recent years has been sufficient to provide benefits to all eligible people seeking to enroll in the program, including those at the lowest priority levels.

The Infant Formula Market

This chapter looks at the characteristics of the U.S. infant formula market and trends in the wholesale prices of infant formula (see box, "Infant Formulas," p. 8).

Characteristics of the Infant Formula Market

Our analyses of retail sales data obtained from the Nielsen Company show that infant formula accounted for about $3.5 billion in sales in 2007 (see section on "Method based on Nielsen market sales data" in appendix A for information on the Nielsen data). This was about the same as the previous year, and up slightly from 2004 and 2005 (figure 5). This small increase in dollar sales was solely the result of price increases as infant formula sales by volume (in reconstituted ounces) actually has declined in recent years (figure 6). For example, between 2004 and 2007, volume sales fell about 5 percent. This is a continuation of a trend found in an earlier ERS analysis of 1994-2000 data (Oliveira, et al., 2004).

The infant formula market is highly concentrated. In 2008, three manufacturers accounted for 98 percent of all dollar sales (figure 7). Abbott (43 percent) and Mead Johnson (40 percent) accounted for the bulk of dollar sales, while Nestlé accounted for another 15 percent. Most of the remaining 2 percent of infant formula sales were accounted for by PBM Nutritionals, producer of the Bright Beginnings line of infant formulas, as well as private-label or store-brand formulas.

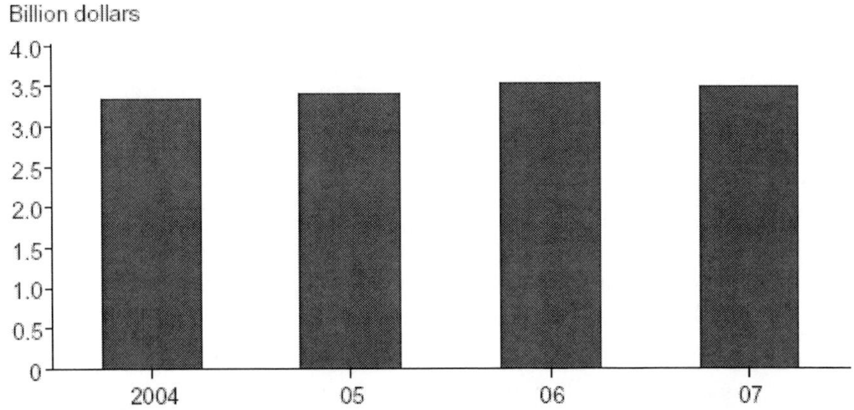

Source: USDA, Economic Research Service calculations based on Nielsen data.

Figure 5. Infant formula dollar sales, 2004-07

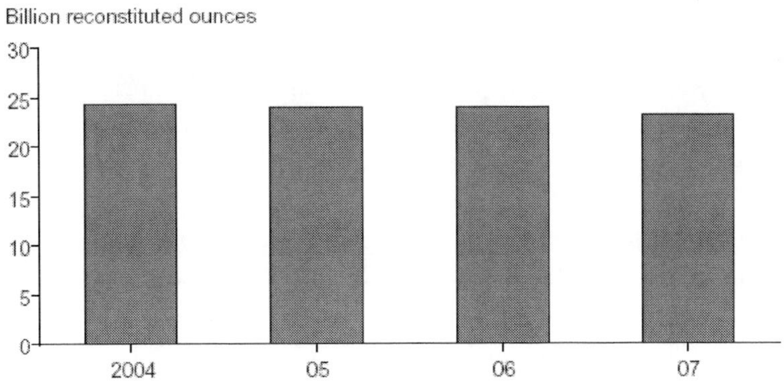

Source: USDA, Economic Research Service calculations based on Nielsen data.

Figure 6. Estimated total infant formula sales by volume, 2004-07

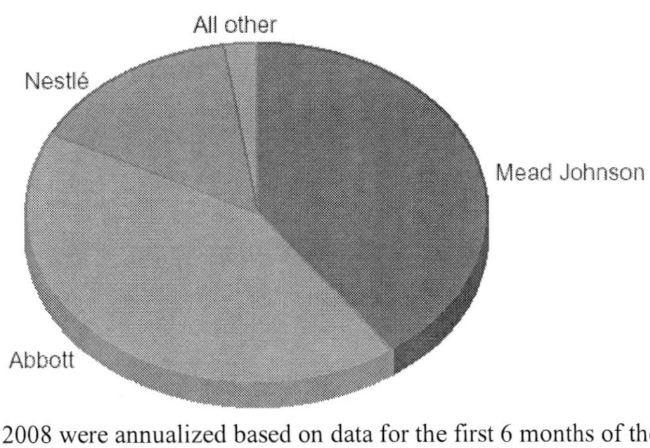

Note: Sales figures for 2008 were annualized based on data for the first 6 months of the year.
Source: USDA, Economic Research Service calculations based on Nielsen data (excludes Walmart).

Figure 7. Share of infant formula dollar sales by manufacturer, 2008

Most of the infant formula sold in this country is in powder form. In a continuation of a long-term trend, the share of infant formula dollar sales in powder form increased from 71 percent in 2004 to 83 percent in 2008 (figure 8). During the same period, sales of liquid concentrate fell from 20 percent to only 10 percent of all formula sales, and ready-to-feed fell from 9 percent to 7 percent.

Powder is about 14 percent less expensive than liquid concentrate on a per-reconstituted-fluid-ounce basis.[5] Unlike liquid concentrate, powdered formula can be mixed in small quantities and the unmixed product keeps without refrigeration. The increased use of powdered formula has been attributed in part to the increase in breastfeeding. Powdered formulas "are commonly used to make up an occasional formula feeding for breastfed infants and many mothers may have continued to use powdered formulas after the cessation of breastfeeding" (Fomon, 2001). The Institute of Medicine (2005) recommends powdered formula for partially breastfed infants in WIC "because the amount of formula prepared can be tailored closely to the amount needed. This may help to reduce waste, food safety concerns, and/or overfeeding of formula to breastfed infants."

A change in the WIC regulations also may have contributed to the increased use of powder. Federal regulations dictate the maximum allowance of infant formula in the WIC food packages. Prior to 2004, the amount that participants could redeem in powder form was determined in part by can size. Since participants cannot purchase partial cans, if the number of dry ounces in a can did not evenly divide into the maximum monthly allowance, participants were not able to redeem the full allotment. The Child Nutrition and WIC Reauthorization Act of 2004 (Public Law (P.L.) 108-265) gave WIC State agencies—for contracts awarded on or after October 1, 2004—the option to round up to the next whole can of infant formula in order to allow all participants to receive the full authorized amount of infant formula, even if this rounding-up option results in participants obtaining more powdered infant formula than the maximum monthly allowance. WIC staff in States utilizing this option may be more likely to prescribe formula in powder than in liquid concentrate form because the powder form yields more reconstituted formula.

Infant Formulas

There are two basic types of infant formula available for routine infant feeding. Milk-based infant formula, containing lactose and cow's milk proteins, is the most widely used formula. Soy-based formula, made with soy protein and free of lactose, provides an alternative protein source for infants with milk-based allergies or with symptoms of lactose intolerance and also is used by parents seeking a vegetarian diet for their infants.

In addition to the standard milk- and soy-based formulas, there are a wide range of infant formulas designed for infants with unique nutritional needs. For example, milk-based, lactose-free formulas are available for infants sensitive to lactose. Hypoallergenic formulas, including protein hydrolysate formulas, are available for infants with food protein allergies. Other types of specialized formula in the marketplace include organic formula, prebiotic formula, formulas marketed to older infants (e.g., age 9 to 24 months), as well as formulas to reduce colic, diarrhea, spit-up, fussiness, and gas. Infant formulas are also available for infants with other special nutritional needs (e.g., low birth weight and premature infants) and medical disorders, such as phenylketonuria (PKU). Most formulas are now supplemented with the fatty acids docosahexaenoic acid (DHA) and arachidonic acid (ARA).

Infant formula comes in three forms: powder (the least expensive form per reconstituted ounce), liquid concentrate, and ready-to-feed (the most expensive form per reconstituted ounce). Formulas are also available in a wide range of package sizes and in two different iron levels: added iron and low iron. The American Academy of Pediatrics (1999) recommends that formula-fed infants receive an iron-fortified formula as a way of reducing the prevalence of iron deficiency anemia. Iron-fortified infant formula is routinely issued in WIC; all low-iron infant formula issued through WIC requires medical documentation.

Most formula is milk-based—80 percent of dollar sales in 2008, up from 76 percent in 2004. Soy-based formula accounted for 14 percent of all dollar sales in 2008 compared to 17 percent in 2004. Other formula bases—primarily protein hydrolysate—accounted for 6 to 7 percent of all 2004-08 sales.[6]

One of the most important developments in the infant formula market in recent years was the introduction of formulas supplemented with the fatty acids doco-sahexaenoic acid (DHA) and arachidonic acid (ARA), which some studies have linked to improved vision and cognitive development in infants.[7] Abbott first introduced these formulas into their U.S. product lines in 2002, with Mead Johnson and Nestlé following in 2003. Sales of DHA/ARA-supplemented formulas increased rapidly, and by 2004 they accounted for 69 percent of all sales. By 2008, DHA/ARA-supplemented formulas accounted for 98 percent of all formula sales (figure 9).

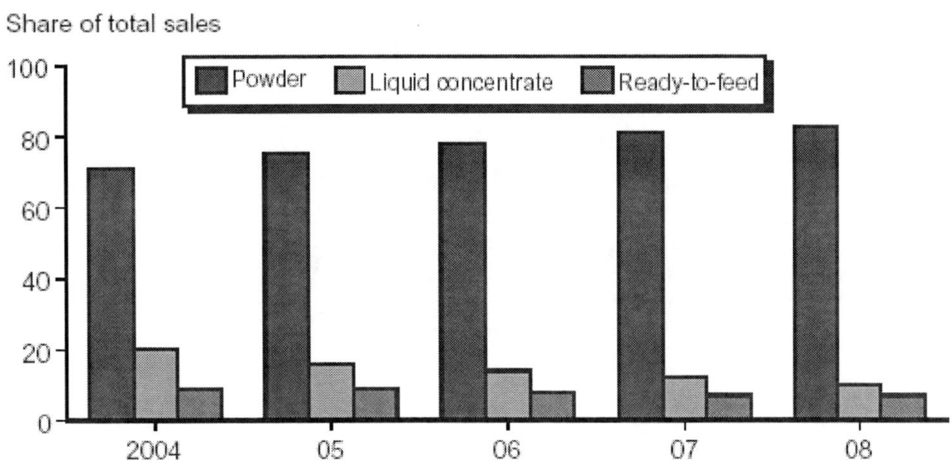

Note: Sales figures for 2008 were annualized based on data for the first 6 months of the year.
Source: USDA, Economic Research Service calculations based on Nielsen data (excludes Walmart).

Figure 8. Share of infant formula dollar sales by form, 2004-08

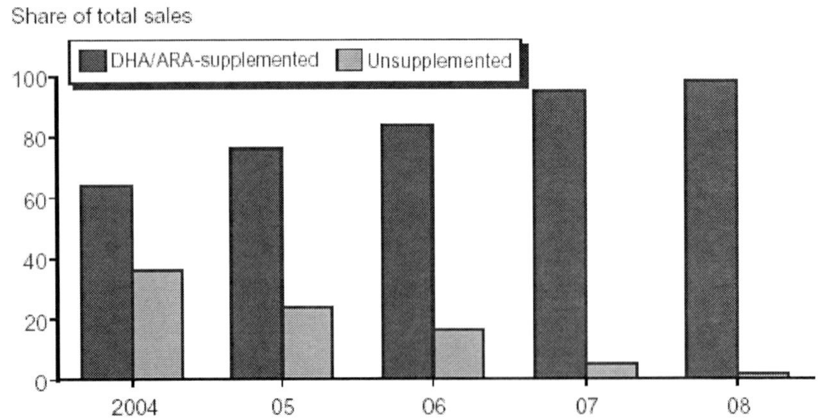

Note: Sales figures for 2008 were annualized based on data for the first 6 months of the year.
Source: USDA, Economic Research Service calculations based on Nielsen data (excludes Walmart).

Figure 9. Share of infant formula dollar sales by supplement status, 2004-08

Wholesale Prices of Infant Formula

Infant formula manufacturers publish a wholesale price list for their products. The listed prices are set at the national level and vary only by volume. Larger volume purchases—up to a truckload of formula—receive a bulk discount. This section examines the national wholesale prices for a full truckload of infant formula produced by the three major manufacturers—Mead Johnson, Abbott, and Nestlé. These three manufacturers currently hold all of the WIC infant formula rebate contracts. Because both the can sizes and reconstitution factors for formula in powder form differ across the three manufacturers (and over time in the case of can size), all wholesale prices cited in this report were converted to a standard unit—26 fluid ounces of reconstituted formula. This volume was chosen because it represents WIC's daily maximum allowance during the study period. This conversion allows for an easy comparison of prices across different package sizes and product forms.

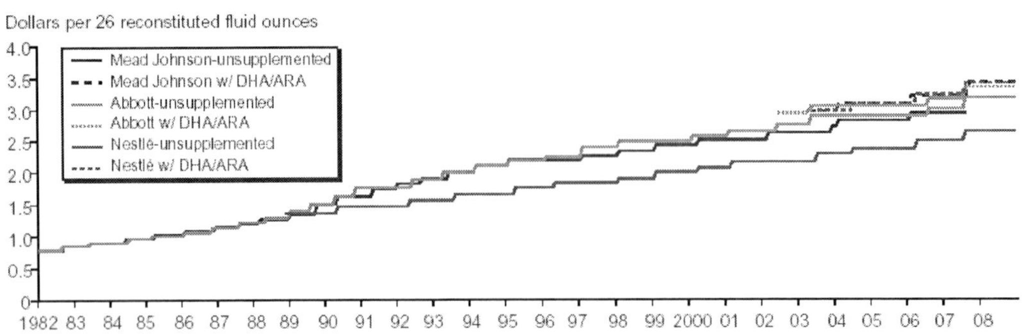

Note: Wholesale prices represent the manufacturers' lowest national wholesale price per unit for a full truckload of infant formula as reported in each manufacturer's price list catalog.
Source: Infant formula manufacturers' product list catalogs.

Figure 10. Nominal wholesale price of infant formula by brand, 1982-2008

Figure 10 shows the wholesale price of the three major infant formula manufacturers' milk-based powder in nominal terms (i.e., not adjusted for inflation) from January 1982 through December 2008 for both the unsupplemented formulas and the DHA/ARA-supplemented formulas (see box, "Infant Formula Products Used in This Analysis," p. 11). In general, wholesale prices for Mead Johnson and Abbott unsupplemented formulas were similar, while Nestlé priced its unsupplemented formula substantially lower. However, the wholesale price of the DHA/ARA-supplemented formulas was comparable among the three companies.

For all three manufacturers, the wholesale price of DHA/ARA-supplemented formulas was substantially higher than the prices of unsup-plemented formulas. For example, in January 2006, the wholesale price of the DHA/ARA-supplemented version of Enfamil was 9.4 percent greater than the wholesale price of the unsupplemented version of Enfamil (figure 11). The difference in wholesale price between the DHA/ARA-supplemented and unsupplemented formula for Similac and Good Start was 5.5 percent and 30.6 percent, respectively.

INFANT FORMULA PRODUCTS USED IN THIS ANALYSIS

From 1998 to 2008, each of the three manufacturers submitted rebate bids based on one of two milk-based infant formulas with iron in their product line, depending on whether or not the formula was supplemented with DHA and ARA (manufacturers began basing their bids on supplemented formulas in 2003). All analyses described in this report are based on these same formulas, shown below:

Unsupplemented formulas:	Powder can size as of January 2007[1]
Mead Johnson—Enfamil	14.3 oz.
Abbott—Similac	12.9 oz.
Nestlé—Good Start Supreme	12.0 oz.
Supplemented formulas:	
Mead Johnson—Enfamil LIPIL	12.9 oz.
Abbott—Similac Advance	12.9 oz.
Nestlé—Good Start Supreme DHA/ARA	12.0 oz.

[1]In March 2002, the can size of Enfamil unsupplemented changed from 16 ounces to 14.3 ounces. In October 2003, the can size of Similac unsupplemented changed from 14.1 ounces to 12.9 ounces. In 2007, Mead Johnson discontinued Enfamil unsupplemented formula.

Each manufacturer has raised the national wholesale price of their unsupplemented and DHA/ARA-supplemented formula numerous times since the early 1980s. Figure 12 shows the wholesale price of infant formula in real terms (adjusted for inflation using the most widely-used measure of general price changes, the Consumer Price Index for All Items (CPI-U)). Note that before each increase in price, the national wholesale price is constant in nominal terms, and the inflation-adjusted real wholesale price declines over time, as inflation erodes the nominal price. Consequently, when manufacturers raise their national wholesale price, the real wholesale price then increases sharply.[8] As indicated by their upward slopes, the real price of the Mead Johnson and Abbot unsupplemented formula rose much faster than the rate of inflation from the early 1980s to the mid-1990s—by over 70 percent—whereas the real wholesale price of Nestlé formula increased only slightly faster than the rate of inflation. (For example, from November 1988—when Nestlé entered the U.S. formula market—to January 1996, the real wholesale price of Nestlé's formula increased by less than 1 percent compared to increases of 35 percent and 32 percent for Mead Johnson's and Abbott's formula). Since about 1998, the real wholesale price of formula for all three brands has remained relatively stable except for the increase associated with the more expensive DHA/ARA-supplemented formulas. That is, the wholesale price of formula has kept pace with inflation in recent years, except when the product changed.

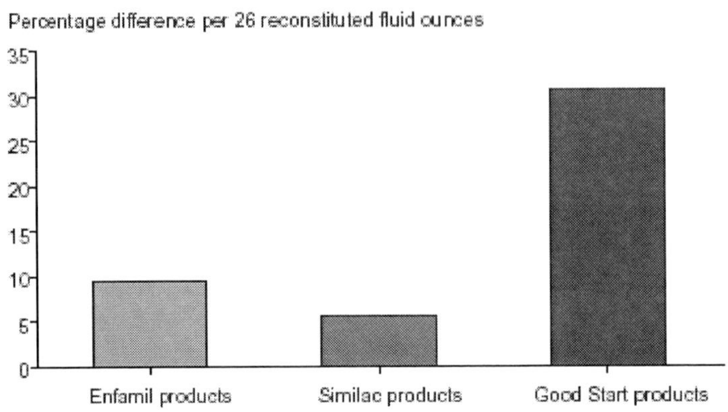

Note: This analysis is based on difference between Enfamil (14.3 oz.) and Enfamil Lipil (12.9 oz.); Similac (12.9 oz.) and Similac Advance (12.9 oz.); and Good Start Supreme (12 oz.) and Good Start Supreme DHA/ARA (12 oz.).

Source: USDA Economic Research Service calculations based on infant formula manufacturers' product list catalogs.

Figure 11. Difference between the wholesale price of supplemented formula and unsupplemented formula by product line, January 2006

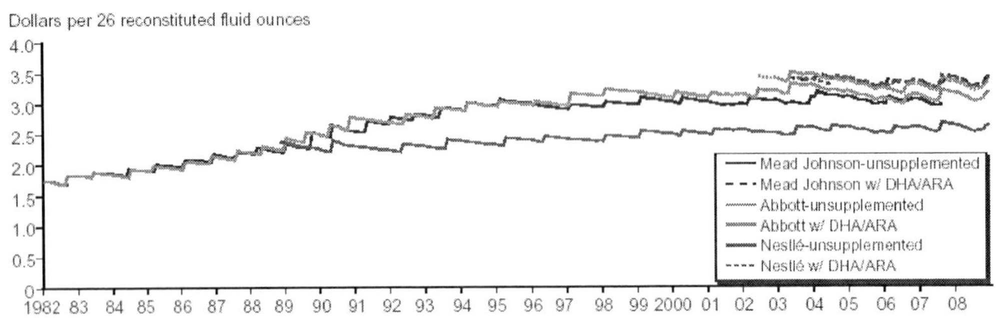

Source: USDA, Economic Research Service calculations of real wholesale prices based on infant formula manufacturers' product list catalogs adjusted by U.S. Department of Labor, Bureau of Labor Statistics' Consumer Price Index for All Urban Consumers for All Items.

Figure 12.Real wholesale price of infant formula by brand, 1982-2008 (December 2008 dollars)

WIC'S INFANT FORMULA REBATE PROGRAM

In the 1980s, infant formula accounted for a large and increasing share of total WIC food costs. In an effort to control costs, Tennessee and Oregon implemented rebate programs with manufacturers of infant formula in 1987 and other States soon followed. As a result of the cost savings realized from these rebate programs, Public Law 101-147 was enacted in 1989 requiring that all WIC State agencies—except those States with home delivery/direct distribution or Indian State agencies with 1,000 or fewer participants—enter into cost-containment contracts for the procurement of infant formula.

How the Contracts Work

Current Federal regulations specify that those WIC State agencies required to operate a cost-containment system for infant formula must use a single supplier (i.e., sole-source) competitive system unless an alternative system provides equal or greater savings (7 CFR 246.16a). Under the sole-source competitive system, a WIC State agency (or a group of WIC State agencies) uses competitive bidding to award a contract to a manufacturer of infant formula in exchange for a rebate for each can of infant formula issued to WIC participants (see box, "Multistate Alliances," p. 14). As a result, the brand of infant formula provided by WIC will vary by State depending on which manufacturer holds the contract for that State.

Solicitation for bids under the sole-source competitive system can take one of two forms—single solicitation or separate solicitations:

- **Under single solicitation**, the winning bidder is required to supply and provide a rebate on all infant formulas it produces that the State agency chooses to issue (except exempt infant formulas). Bidders that do not produce a soy-based infant formula are required to subcontract with another manufacturer to supply a soy-based infant formula. All of these infant formulas are referred to as contract brand infant formulas. The request for bids is for a single iron-fortified, milk-based infant formula that is suitable for routine issuance to most generally healthy, full-term infants. This formula is referred to as the primary contract brand infant formula, and must be offered in all physical forms—liquid concentrate, powder, and ready-to-feed.[9]
- **Under separate solicitations**, bids are issued separately for milk-based and soy-based infant formulas. All relevant infant formulas issued under each contract are considered contract brand infant formulas. The primary contract brand is the milk-based infant formula for which the rebate is being specified (for the milk-based contract) or the soy-based infant formula for which the rebate is being specified (for the soy-based contract).

The sole-source contract is awarded to the bidder offering the lowest total monthly net wholesale price, as determined by the submission of sealed bids, for a specified amount of the primary contract brand infant formula by each of the three forms—powder, liquid concentrate, and ready-to-feed. The amount of the rebate on these contract brand infant formulas is based on the same percentage discount (i.e., the amount of the rebate as a percentage of the wholesale price) for the particular physical form of the primary contract-brand infant formula. For example, if the rebate offered for the primary contract brand of powdered infant formula was 85 percent of the manufacturer's wholesale price, then the rebate for all other powdered forms of the contract-brand infant formula (including soy-based powder under single solicitation) also would be 85 percent of their wholesale price.

MULTISTATE ALLIANCES

States can either hold an individual contract for infant formula or be part of a multistate group contract (alliance) whereby WIC State agencies join in a single rebate agreement to obtain infant formula. In this way, WIC State agencies with fewer clients can pool their buying power to leverage higher rebates. In 2004, Congress limited the use of this cost-saving practice. Public Law 108-265 prohibits the formation of multistate alliances for the purchase of infant formula if the total number of infants served by the States exceeds 100,000 (except alliances that had 100,000 or more infants as of October 2003). Any alliance in existence as of October 2003 may expand to serve more than 100,000 infants, but may not expand to include any additional WIC State agencies (an exception is made if the WIC State agency to be added served fewer than 5,000 infants as of October 2003).

The rationale behind this regulation—which grew out of concern that not all infant formula manufacturers would be able to compete for the larger multistate contacts due to production capacity and/or distribution issues—is that it will help maintain competition among the infant formula manufacturers by helping to ensure that all manufacturers can compete for the rebate contracts (*73 Federal Register* 11308). On the other hand, some view the cap as protecting infant formula manufacturers from extreme rebates. In their 2009 WIC reauthorization legislative agenda, the National WIC Association (2009) recommended that WIC State agencies retain the option to form contracting alliances without limits on the number of participants.

Of the 48 States, the District of Columbia, and the 5 territories operating a competitive sole-source rebate system in conjunction with a retail food delivery system as of December 2008, 34 were part of 1 of 6 multistate alliances:

- The Western States Contracting Alliance (WSCA) is comprised of Alaska, Arizona, Delaware, Hawaii, Idaho, Kansas, Maryland, Montana, Nevada, Oregon, Utah, Washington, the District of Columbia, West Virginia, and Wyoming, as well as American Samoa, Guam, Virgin Islands, the Commonwealth of the Northern Mariana Islands, and three Indian Tribal Organizations (ITOs).
- The New England and Tribal Organization (NEATO) is comprised of Connecticut, Maine, Massachusetts, New Hampshire, Rhode Island, and two ITOs.
- The Mountain Plains Region is comprised of Missouri, Nebraska, and South Dakota.
- The Southwest/Southeast Region is comprised of Arkansas, New Mexico, and North Carolina.
- The Southwest/Mountain Plains/Midwest Regions is comprised of Iowa, Minnesota, Texas, and one ITO.
- The Southwest Region is comprised of Oklahoma and five ITOs.

The remaining 19 States and Puerto Rico held contracts that applied solely to their particular State.

The percentage discount is based on wholesale prices at the time of the bid opening. The contracts contain inflationary provisions. In the event of an increase (decrease) in the wholesale price after the bid opening, there is a cent-for-cent increase (decrease) in the rebate amounts. Thus, the net wholesale price of formula to a WIC State agency remains fixed over the entire span of the contract despite increases (or decreases) in the wholesale price after the contract is initiated. Although the nominal net wholesale price remains constant over time, the real (i.e., inflation-adjusted) net wholesale price will decrease over time due to general price inflation.

Any noncontract brand of formula (including exempt infant formulas and formulas not manufactured by the WIC contract manufacturer) may be issued only with medical documentation (provided by a licensed health care professional authorized to write medical prescriptions under State law) that an infant has a condition that dictates the formula's use. The only exception to this rule is that local WIC agencies may issue noncontract-brand infant formula without medical documentation in order to accommodate religious eating patterns (*65 Federal Register* 51213-51229). In 2004 (the latest data available), noncontract-brand formula was estimated to account for 8 percent of all formula provided to WIC participants (U.S. Government Accountability Office, 2006). The WIC State agency does not receive rebates from noncon-tract-brand infant formula.

Because each WIC State agency operates its own infant formula rebate program, the contract term (i.e., the period during which the infant formula rebate contract is in effect) will vary across States. As a result, the start dates and the expiration dates of each State's contract as well as the length of the contract may vary. Analysis of the most recently completed rebate contracts shows that most were originally for 3-year periods, though some were shorter and some longer. Most contracts were also extended for at least 1 year. As a result, the average infant formula rebate contract, including extensions, lasted 4.3 years (see appendix B).

Recent Legislative Developments

Section 203 of the Child Nutrition and WIC Reauthorization Act of 2004 (P.L. 108-265) made two important changes to the infant formula rebate program.

First, the new law required State agencies or multistate alliances that serve a monthly average of more than 100,000 infants (during the preceding 12-month period) to use separate solicitations in soliciting bids from infant formula manufacturers (except where the Secretary of Agriculture determines that such solicitation procedures are not in the best interest of the program). Among contracts in effect in December 2008, only three States had solicited separate bids for milk-based and soy-based infant formula: California, Florida, and New York. Mead Johnson was awarded both contracts in California, and Nestlé was awarded both contracts in Florida. The only case in which two different manufacturers held infant formula contracts in a single State was in New York, where Mead Johnson was awarded the milk-based contract and Nestlé was awarded the soy-based contract. As a result of the 2004 law, more States or multistate alliances may be soliciting separate bids in the future. For example, three multistate alliances served a monthly average of over 100,000 infants in fiscal 2008: the Southwest/Mountain Plains/ Midwest Region (285,000 infants), the Western States

Contracting Alliance (WSCA) (266,000 infants), and the Southwest/Southeast Region (110,000 infants) (USDA, 2009b).

The rationale behind this new provision was that separate solicitations might increase competition for WIC contracts by allowing new or smaller infant formula manufacturers with a limited product line to bid on contracts (*65 Federal Register* 51213-51229). However, concern has been raised that separate solicitations may increase administrative costs. The National WIC Association argues that since all U.S. infant formula manufacturers now produce both soy-based and milk-based formula products, the separate solicitations requirement is no longer warranted and should be eliminated (National WIC Association, 2009).

Second, the law also requires WIC State agencies to issue the primary contract infant formula—determined by the manufacturer—as the first choice of issuance for all WIC infants, with all other infant formulas issued as an alternative to the primary contract infant formula. This was not an issue in the past when infant formula manufacturers produced only one milk-based infant formula that was suitable for the routine issuance to the majority of generally healthy, full-term infants. Since other options generally were not available, manufacturers submitted bids for this single formula in response to bid solicitations for infant formula rebate contracts, and WIC State agencies issued this formula to infants as the formula of first choice. However, manufacturers now produce a variety of milk-based infant formulas—with varying prices—that are eligible to be bid on in response to a solicitation. A report from the U.S. Senate Committee on Agriculture, Nutrition, and Forestry (2004) stated that "In response to the increased variety of milk-based infant formula, the Committee believes that manufacturers, State agencies, and participants should have a common understanding of the infant formula product that will serve as the primary contract infant formula in each State. To ensure that the competitive bidding process can be effectively carried out, the Committee believes that the infant formula bid in response to a solicitation should be the primary contract infant formula issued to infants."

Prior to the 2004 law, WIC State agencies could select the specific infant formula products in the contract-winning manufacturer's product line to be provided to WIC infants in that State. For example, the WIC State agency could select a less expensive formula product than the primary contract brand and decide not to offer the primary contract brand. However, all contracts resulting from bid solicitations issued on or after October 1, 2004, require that WIC State agencies use the primary contract brand as the first choice of issuance. As a result, it is possible that the primary contract infant formula will not be the least expensive formula produced by the winning manufacturer.[10] (The State agency may continue to issue contract brand and noncontract brand alternatives to the primary contract infant formula, if the alternatives better meet an infant's individual nutritional needs.)

By requiring that States issue the primary contract infant formula—determined by the manufacturer—as the first choice of issuance, the 2004 law may have contributed to the rapid growth of DHA/ARA supplemented formulas and the near-disappearance of unsupplemented formulas from the marketplace (see box, "Did Federal Regulations Expedite the Demise of Unsupplemented Infant Formula?")

Did Federal Legislation Expedite the Demise of Unsupplemented Infant Formula?

The Child Nutrition and WIC Reauthorization Act of 2004 (P.L. 108-265) contained provisions that changed the procedures for determining which infant formulas are provided to WIC participants. The legislation in effect guaranteed large sales volumes for DHA/ARA-supplemented formula products.

Prior to 2004, infant formula manufacturers could submit a bid for the WIC rebate contract based on any product in their product line as long as it was suitable for routine issuance to the majority of generally healthy, full-term infants. WIC State agencies were responsible for identifying the specific infant formula products in the winning manufacturer's product line to be used in the State's WIC program. Consequently, the contract formulas provided to WIC participants in a particular State would not necessarily include the primary contract-brand product specified in the manufacturer's bid. For example, even though some of the winning bids submitted by the formula manufacturers after February 2003 identified the new DHA/ARA-supplemented formulas as the primary contract brand, some States chose not to offer them to their participants.

As a result of P.L. 108-265, for all contracts based on solicitations issued after September 2004, State agencies must now use the primary contract infant formula for which the manufacturer submitted its bid (and for which the contract was awarded) as the first choice of issuance (by physical form), with all other infant formulas issued as an alternative. Therefore, if the winning bid is based on a DHA/ARA-supplemented formula, then the WIC State agency is required to offer that formula to the participants in the State.

After the legislation was enacted, nearly all the bids submitted by the formula manufacturers identified DHA/ARA-supplemented formulas as the primary contract infant formula. As a result, all WIC State Agencies now offer DHA/ ARA-supplemented formulas to their WIC recipients. Since WIC accounts for most of the infant formula sales in the United States, the result of the legislation was to ensure large sales volumes for these newly introduced products while increasing their visibility to non-WIC consumers. In addition, making DHA/ ARA-supplemented formulas the primary WIC brand of formula may have given some non-WIC consumers the impression the new supplemented formulas had the endorsement of the WIC program. While these factors may have helped these more expensive supplemented formulas gain shares in the market, it should be noted that not providing WIC participants with these supplemented formulas would have opened WIC up to criticism that it was providing WIC infants with a cheaper, inferior product.

Trends in Infant Formula Rebate Contracts

This chapter looks at recent trends in net wholesale price for milk-based infant formula in powdered form—the primary type of formula provided through WIC. Because net wholesale price is determined by the wholesale price and the rebate, trends in these two factors also are examined. In addition, the impact of recent changes in net wholesale price on total infant formula costs to the WIC program is estimated. The analyses exclude Mississippi and Vermont, which do not use retail food delivery systems, as well as those Indian Tribal Organizations that are not part of a multistate alliance.

Trends in Net Wholesale Price

In order to examine the changes in net wholesale price over time, we compared the real net wholesale price in a State's current contract—defined as the contract that was in effect in December 2008—to that of its previous contract.[11] Although net wholesale price remains constant over the life of the contract in nominal terms, the real net wholesale price will decrease over time due to inflation. To control for the erosion in the real net wholesale price over the length of a contract, we examined the real net wholesale prices for the two contracts at the time each contract became effective (see appendix B for the date in which each State's contract became effective).

Real net wholesale price increased in 24 of the 27 contracts (figure 13). Some of the contracts in effect in December 2008 are part of multistate alliances and therefore represent more than one State. Excluding Mississippi and Vermont, 45 of 48 States, the District of Columbia, and each of the 5 territories saw an increase in their net wholesale price. *This means that nearly all WIC State agencies are paying more for formula in their current contract than under their previous contract, even after adjusting for inflation.* On average, real net wholesale prices increased by an average 21 cents for 26 fluid ounces of reconstituted formula (WIC's maximum daily allowance during the study period) between States' previous and current rebate contracts.[12] This represented a 73-percent increase in real net wholesale prices.

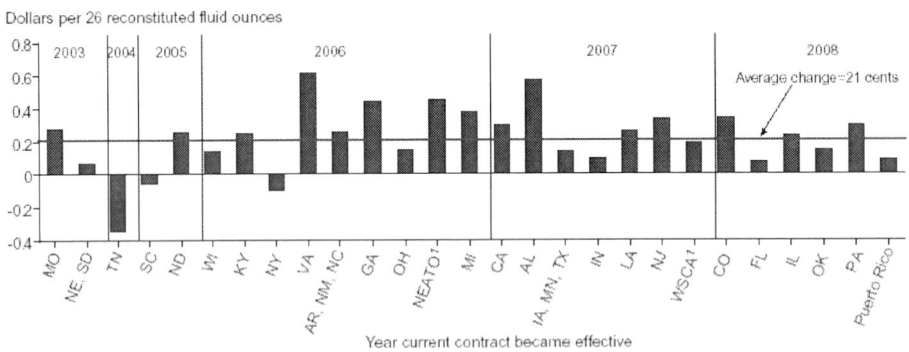

Note: Current contracts refer to contracts that were in effect as of December 2008. Previous contracts refer to contracts that were in effect immediately prior to the current contract. Average change in net price was calculated by weighing the change in real net price for each contract by the number of WIC infants served under the contract.

[1]NEATO and WSCA are multistate alliances. For a list of members of each alliance, see box, "Multistate Alliances," p.14.

Source: USDA, Economic Research Service calculations of changes in real net price based on USDA, Food and Nutrition Service estimates of net prices adjusted by U.S. Department of Labor, Bureau of Labor Statistics' Consumer Price Index for All Urban Consumers for All Items.

Figure 13.Change in real net wholesale price between current and previous contracts, by State (December 2008 dollars)

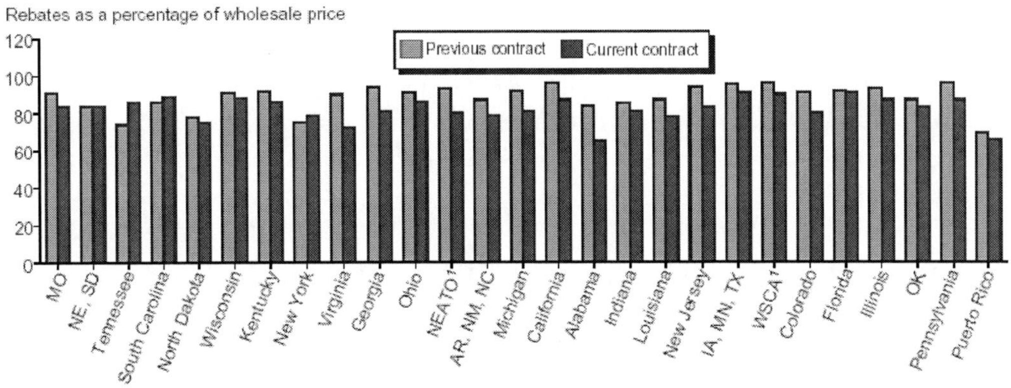

Note: Current contracts refer to contracts that were in effect as of December 2008. Previous contracts refer to contracts that were in effect immediately prior to the current contract.

[1]NEATO and WSCA are multistate alliances. For a list of members of each alliance, see box, "Multistate Alliances," p.14.

Source: Unpublished USDA, Food and Nutrition Service data.

Figure 14. Percentage discount rates for previous and current contracts, by State

Examination of the factors determining real net wholesale price indicates that changes in both real wholesale price and real rebates have contributed to the increase in real net wholesale price. On average, real wholesale prices increased by 5 percent (real wholesale price increased in 18 of the 27 current contracts compared to their previous contracts). This increase in real wholesale prices accounted for almost three-quarters (72 percent) of the overall increase in real net wholesale price between States' previous and current rebate contracts.

At the same time that real wholesale prices increased, the average real rebate (for 26 reconstituted ounces) fell 2 percent (real rebates declined in 15 of the 27 current contracts compared to their previous contracts). This decrease in rebates accounted for 28 percent of the overall increase in real net wholesale price.

The effect of the decline in real rebates is magnified when combined with the increase in real wholesale prices. In order to examine the trends in real rebates in relative terms (i.e., to control for changes in the wholesale price), we examined rebates in terms of the percentage discount, defined as:

Percentage Discount = Rebate as a Percentage of the Wholesale Price

The average percentage discount—calculated as of the date of the bid opening—in the 27 previous contracts was 91 percent. In other words, WIC on average paid only 9 percent of the wholesale price for formula (plus the retail markup). (See box, "How Can Manufacturers Afford To Offer Such High Percentage Discounts to WIC?" p. 21).

The average percentage discount in the 27 current contracts (those in effect in December 2008) fell to 85 percent, indicating that WIC State agencies are now paying a greater percentage of the wholesale price than previously. For 23 contracts (representing 43 States, the District of Columbia, and the 5 territories), the percentage discount fell between the previous and current contract (figure 14). The percentage discount increased in only three contracts (representing three States), each of which became effective in July 2007 or earlier, and in one contract (representing a multistate alliance formed by Nebraska and South Dakota WIC State agencies and enacted in 2003), the percentage discount did not change (however, real net wholesale price increased in the current contract due to an increase in the real wholesale price). Thus, regardless of whether or not the real wholesale price of formula increased, most States experienced a decrease in the percentage discount.

Examination of DHA/ARA Supplementation on Net Wholesale Price

Although all current contracts are based on the DHA/ARA-supplemented formulas, most of the previous contracts were based on the unsupplemented formulas. That is, most of the States switched from unsupplemented formulas in their previous contract to DHA/ARA-supplemented formulas in their current contract. Because the wholesale prices of DHA/ARA-supplemented formulas are greater than wholesale prices of unsupplemented formulas, it might be expected that real net wholesale prices would increase in those States that switched to the more expensive DHA/ARA-supplemented formula holding rebates constant. Therefore, we compared the change in net wholesale prices in those States in which both their previous and current contract was based on DHA/ARA-supplemented formulas (i.e., AL, AR, CA, IN, LA, NC, NJ, NM, NY, OK, PA, and Puerto Rico) to those States that switched to DHA/ARA-supplemented formulas in their current contract.[13] Surprisingly, the results of the analysis indicate that the average change in real net wholesale price for those States in which their last two contracts were based on the DHA/ARA-supplemented formulas (22 cents) was actually slightly greater than that in States that switched to the DHA/ARA-supplemented formulas in their current contract (20 cents).

While the average change in real net wholesale prices was similar between the two types of States, there were substantial differences in each of the two components of net wholesale price. For those States that switched to the DHA/ ARA-supplemented formulas in their current contract, average real wholesale prices increased by 29 cents and average rebates increased by 9 cents (figure 15). However, in those States that already used DHA/ARA-supplemented formula in their previous contracts, the real wholesale price decreased by 6 cents and the real rebate decreased by 28 cents. That is, States in which the real wholesale price decreased still ended up paying higher real net wholesale prices on average due to a large decrease in the amount of the manufacturers' rebate.

How Can Manufacturers Afford to Offer Such High Percentage Discounts to WIC?

Both supply-side and demand-side characteristics of the infant formula market offer possible explanations about how infant formula manufacturers can afford to offer such high percentage discounts. On the supply side, the formula market is highly concentrated—there are only three major manufacturers—a factor which is often associated with higher profit margins (U.S. General Accounting Office, 1998).[1] This, in turn, gives manufacturers a cushion to offer high rebates.

On the demand side, WIC participants purchase over half of all infant formula, ensuring large sales for the contract-winning manufacturer. In addition, manufacturers may realize spillover benefits from winning a WIC contract. For example, retailers generally devote more shelf space and better product placement to the WIC contract brand. This results in greater product visibility, which in turn may spur sales to non-WIC consumers. Sales may also rise if hospitals and/or physicians recommend the WIC contract brand to non-WIC mothers. According to the U.S. Government Accountability Office (2006), "State WIC programs often work with physicians to educate them about the program and the requirement that most WIC participants use the contract brand of infant formula. Physicians may decide to recommend the WIC brand of infant formula to all patients to avoid having to differentiate between those enrolled and not enrolled in WIC. Similarly, some hospitals agree to provide WIC-brand infant formula to new mothers so that they won't have to switch infant formulas after they leave the hospital. It may be easier for hospitals to provide the WIC-brand infant formula to all new mothers."

Other possible spillover effects include: WIC recipients who are satisfied with the WIC contract brand of formula may recommend the brand to non-WIC friends and family members; WIC recipients may stay with the same brand (i.e., demonstrate brand loyalty) during subsequent births even if they leave the WIC program; and, to the degree that the quantity of formula provided by WIC doesn't meet all of their infant's formula needs, mothers of WIC infants may be reluctant to introduce a different brand of formula to their infants and will therefore be likely to supplement the formula provided through WIC by purchasing the same brand of formula out of pocket.

[1]The General Accounting Office (GAO) changed its name in 2004 to the Government Accountability Office.

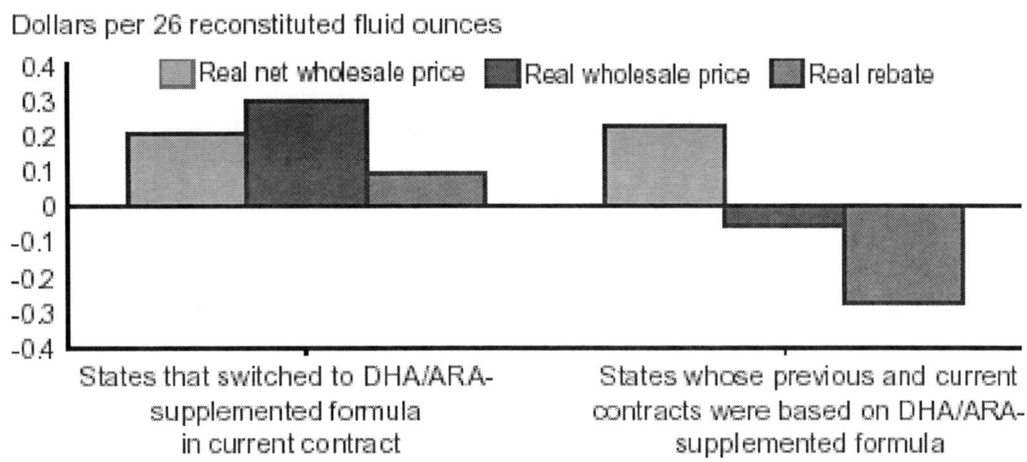

Source: USDA, Economic Research Service calculations based on USDA, Food and Nutrition Service data.

Figure 15. Average change in real net wholesale price, wholesale price and rebate, by State's formula supplementation status

Impact of Higher Net Wholesale Price on Infant Formula Costs

Estimating the impact of the increase in real net wholesale prices on total WIC infant formula costs involved five steps:

1. **Number of WIC infants receiving infant formula**. The number of WIC infants receiving infant formula was estimated on a State-by-State basis. This was done by using data from USDA's Food and Nutrition Service on the average monthly number of infants participating in WIC in 2008 by State (including the five territories and the District of Columbia and excluding Mississippi and Vermont) and multiplying them by .88—the proportion of WIC infants estimated to receive some infant formula through WIC (as reported in table A2 in USDA, 2006). By using the number of infants participating in WIC in only 1 year—2008—we ensure that the estimate of the change in total infant formula costs between previous and current contracts reported here is due solely to increases in net wholesale price and not to increases in the number of infants participating in WIC over time.
2. **Adjustment for use of noncontract formula**. Each of the State estimates of the number of WIC infants receiving formula generated in step 1 were then reduced by 8 percent to account for the estimated 8 percent of infant formula provided to WIC participants that is noncontract (as reported in U.S. Government Accountability Office, 2006) and therefore not eligible for rebate.[14]
3. **Average change in net wholesale price**. The number of infants receiving WIC infant formula subject to rebates by State from step 2 was multiplied by the average change in net wholesale price for 26 reconstituted ounces (the daily maximum allowance of infant formula provided by WIC per infant during the study period) between the previous and current contracts for each State as estimated by ERS.
4. **Adjustment for the amount of formula provided in the WIC packages**. To account for the fact that some WIC infants do not receive the Federal maximum amount of 806 reconstituted ounces of formula per month allowable in WIC (for example, partially breast-fed infants may be prescribed smaller amounts of formula), the State estimates resulting from step 3 were multiplied by .94—the estimated average amount of formula prescribed to WIC infants as a share of the Federal maximum allowed as reported in USDA, 2006. This resulted in an estimate of the impact of the change in net wholesale price per infant per day.
5. **Annualized cost estimate**. The daily State estimates derived in step 4 were multiplied by 365 (the number of days in a year) and summed across States to derive a national annual estimate of the impact of the change in real net wholesale price.

This analysis resulted in an estimated annual cost to WIC attributed to the change in real net wholesale price between the current and previous contracts of $126.7 million. This was equivalent to the cost of supporting 134,200 persons in WIC for a year, or about 2 percent of all women, infants, and children participating in WIC in fiscal 2008.[15] It is important to note that the effect of an increase in net wholesale price between the previous and current contracts lasts for the entire length of the contract (i.e., over 4 years on average based on previous contracts), until the next contract becomes effective. As States implement new contracts, the estimate of the total impact of changes in real net wholesale price to WIC will change due to changes in the mix of current contracts.

While the majority of formula-fed infants in WIC receive milk-based powder, the estimate of the annual increase in infant formula costs reported here assumes that all formula-fed infants in WIC receive milk-based powder formula. However, analysis of changes in the net wholesale prices of milk-based liquid concentrate found similar results: real net wholesale prices increased by an average $.20 for 26 fluid ounces of reconstituted formula (appendix C examines recent trends in net wholesale price for milk-based formula in liquid concentrate form). If all WIC infants received milk-based formula in liquid concentrate form instead of powder, annual costs to WIC would have increased by an estimated $123.3 million (i.e., about the same as if all WIC infants received milk-based formula in power form). Data were not available to estimate the impact of changes in real net wholesale price based on soy-based infant formula.

Changes in WIC's Market Share Could Impact Net Wholesale Price Trends

The results of this analysis indicate that net wholesale prices have increased in recent years, even after adjusting for inflation. Although the exact reasons why manufacturers increased net wholesale price (or stated another way, why rebates decreased relative to wholesale prices) are not known, several hypotheses link the increase in net wholesale price to the increased proportion of infants in the U.S. population who are served by WIC.

It is generally accepted that formula manufacturers are willing to offer such high rebates for the WIC contract in part because the WIC brand of formula has greater market presence (through increased product visibility and better product placement), which results in increased sales to non-WIC customers.[16] However, over time, the share of infants in WIC has increased so that by 2008, over half of all infants born in this country participated in the program (see figure 4). Because WIC mothers are less likely than non-WIC mothers to breastfeed their infants, the share of the formula market attributed to WIC is even greater (Centers for Disease Control and Prevention, 2009).

This study estimated WIC's share of the infant formula market for 2004-06, using two different methods. The first method, utilizing data on breastfeeding and formula-feeding practices, was based on estimates of formula needs of WIC infants relative to the formula needs of all infants. The second method compared the costs of the infant formula purchased through WIC to total infant formula sales. Results of these analyses indicate that between 57 and 68 percent of all infant formula sold in the United States is purchased through WIC (see appendix A for information on how WIC's share of the infant formula market was estimated).

WIC's share of the infant formula market may impact rebate levels directly as well as indirectly. The direct-effect hypothesis holds that as WIC's share of the infant formula market increases, manufacturers have less to gain from the greater market presence resulting from winning the WIC contract because the relative size of the non-WIC segment—that pays full price for their formula—has decreased. As a result, manufacturers are likely to respond by decreasing the amount of the rebate, resulting in higher net wholesale prices for WIC. Besharov and Call (2009) suggest that as the percentage of American infants in WIC increases, "the financial viability of the rebate system declines." Thus, it might be that the high percentage discount received in previous contracts will decline as WIC's share of the formula market increases.

The indirect-effect hypothesis holds that the proportion of infants who are in WIC may affect retail markups, which, in turn, affect rebate levels. Since WIC recipients do not pay for their WIC formula from their personal funds, they are not sensitive to the prices that a store charges for infant formula. An earlier ERS analysis of retail infant formula prices found a positive association between formula identified as the WIC-designated brand and its retail price, especially in areas with a high percentage of WIC infants (Oliveira et al., 2004). That is, as the percentage of infants in WIC increases, so does the retail markup (since there are proportionately more price-insensitive customers), which will result in higher retail prices for the WIC brand of formula.

However, price-sensitive non-WIC consumers, who pay for formula out of pocket, will respond to the higher price of the WIC contract brand by switching to a lower priced brand, resulting in fewer sales of the WIC contract brand in the non-WIC market. There is now less to gain for manufacturers in the non-WIC market by winning the WIC contract, so they will respond by offering lower rebates to WIC State agencies.

In addition, other reasons for the increase in net wholesale prices have been suggested that are not related to WIC's market share. The U.S. Government Accountability Office (2006) suggests that the increase may be related to the increase in the share of formula provided through WIC that is in powdered form. If liquid concentrate formula is more profitable to the manufacturers, the shift to powder could reduce the rebates they offer to the States. Neuberger and Greenstein (2004) suggest that some of the increase in net wholesale price may be related to the growth in the number of WIC-only stores (defined as stores that stock only WIC foods and serve only WIC customers) in the early 2000s. Since shelf space in WIC-only stores does not promote sales to non-WIC customers, as more WIC participants purchase their formula in WIC-only stores, sales of the contract brand of formula to WIC customers in traditional retail food stores decrease. Retail stores likely would respond by stocking less of the WIC contract brand and/or giving it less shelf space. Infant formula manufacturers then may lower their rebate bids as a result of the reduced opportunity to attract non-WIC customers to their products. Since the publication of the Neuberger and Greenstein report, Federal legislation has been enacted to control the growth of WIC-only stores (Oliveira and Frazão, 2009).

Several recent developments have the potential to affect the share of the formula market attributed to WIC infants—either positively or negatively—and, therefore, the net wholesale price to WIC. These factors include the country's economic conditions and recent revisions to the WIC food packages.

Economic Conditions Affect the Number of Infants Eligible for WIC

The number of persons eligible for WIC is largely a function of economic conditions. A weak economy, as indicated by a rising unemployment rate and an increase in the number of persons in poverty, could affect WIC participation in two ways: (1) by increasing the size of the eligible population (i.e., more infants may meet WIC's income eligibility criteria); and (2) by impacting the rate of participation among eligible people. That is, during an economic downturn, families of WIC-eligible infants may be more likely to perceive their economic situation as being serious and long-term and worth the time and effort it takes to apply for WIC benefits.

However, since WIC is a discretionary program, an increase in the demand for WIC services will only translate into an increase in the number of program participants if congressional appropriations are sufficient to cover the costs associated with increased participation. Throughout its history, WIC has received strong congressional support resulting in almost continual annual increases in funding. Even after adjusting for inflation, expenditures for WIC increased each year—except for 1989—up to FY 1997 (Oliveira and Frazao, 2009). As the program reached full funding (whereby every eligible person who applied for WIC was accepted into the program), congressional appropriations flattened out and the increase in real expenditures slowed. In recent years, the program has been able to serve all eligible people who applied for the program.

Poor economic conditions could further increase WIC's share of the formula market by affecting breastfeeding rates among non-WIC population. Since they pay for formula out-of-pocket, more non-WIC mothers may decide to breastfeed their infants instead of paying for formula.

Food Package Revisions May Impact WIC's Share of Infant Formula

In December 2007, program regulations governing the WIC food packages were revised to better reflect advances in nutrition science and dietary recommendations and to address current supplemental nutritional needs of WIC participants (*72 Federal Register* 68965-69032). WIC State agencies were required to implement the new provisions by October 1, 2009.

WIC's food package revisions have the potential to impact WIC's share of the infant formula market in two ways. First, some revisions were specifically designed to strengthen WIC's breastfeeding promotion efforts and provide additional incentives for mothers to initiate and continue to breastfeed. For example, WIC mothers who fully breastfeed their infants are offered greater quantities of a larger selection of foods in an effort to encourage both breast-feeding initiation and duration. Simultaneously, related revisions aim to minimize early supplementation with infant formula, to facilitate the successful establishment of the mothers' milk supply and increase breastfeeding duration, and to encourage mothers who feed their infants both breastmilk and formula to increase the intensity and duration of their breastfeeding.

Second, in an effort to promote and increase duration of breastfeeding, the new WIC food packages provide different amounts of infant formula depending on the infant's age and "feeding method." Among fully formula-fed infants, those younger than 4 months of age receive the same amount of formula under the new food package as under the old food package. However, infants 4-5 months of age receive greater amounts of formula than before, while infants 6-11 months of age receive smaller amounts of infant formula under the new food package than under the old food package.[17]

We used data provided in the interim rule revising the WIC food packages (*72 Federal Register* 68965-69032) on the projected number of fully formula-feeding, partially breastfeeding, and fully breastfeeding infants, by age, and amounts of infant formula in each food package, to estimate changes in infant formula use. We estimate that the new food package would result in a 20-percent reduction in the amount of infant formula purchased through the WIC program, assuming the same number of fully formula-feeding, partially breastfeeding, and fully breastfeeding infants (see appendix D). A reduction in infant formula use by WIC would decrease the WIC share of the infant formula market and, as hypothesized above, may lead manufacturers to offer larger rebates to WIC State agencies.

It is not clear what impact these revisions will have on breastfeeding initiation, intensity, and duration among WIC mothers and, therefore, infant formula use. For example, the reduced amount of infant formula that partially breastfed infants may now receive—only about half the amount that is prescribed to fully formula-fed infants—could lead some WIC mothers to choose to breastfeed even less—or not at all—in order to qualify for the full amount of infant formula.

If the food package revisions are effective in increasing breastfeeding rates among WIC mothers, WIC's share of the infant formula market is likely to decrease. Manufacturers might respond by offering higher rebates, resulting in lower net wholesale prices for WIC. Additionally, retailers may respond by lowering the retail price of the WIC contract brand, which also could lower WIC's formula costs.

CONCLUSIONS

Results from this study indicate that nearly all WIC State agencies were paying more for milk-based powdered formula (the primary type of infant formula) in their current rebate contracts (those in effect in December 2008) than under their previous contracts, even after adjusting for inflation. On average, real net wholesale prices increased by 73 percent or 21 cents for 26 fluid ounces of reconstituted formula (WIC's maximum daily allowance during the study period). Higher wholesale prices accounted for 72 percent of this increase; smaller rebates accounted for the remaining 28 percent. As a result of the increase in real net wholesale prices, WIC paid about $127 million more for infant formula over the course of a year.[18] This was equivalent to the cost of supporting 134,200 persons in WIC for a year, or about 2 percent of all women, infants, and children participating in WIC in fiscal 2008.

This trend of increasing real net wholesale prices, if it continues, will cost the program even more in the future as current contracts expire and WIC State agencies negotiate new contracts. The share of the infant formula market going to WIC may be an important factor in determining if this trend of increasing net wholesale prices will continue. As the WIC share of the infant formula market increases, manufacturers have less to gain from the additional shelf space that results from winning the WIC contract and are likely to respond by reducing their rebates and increasing the net wholesale price offered to WIC. Conversely, if WIC's share of the infant formula market decreases, manufacturers may respond by increasing their rebates and decreasing the net wholesale price offered to WIC.

Weak economic conditions have the potential to increase WIC's share of the formula market if sufficient funding allows the program to meet the increased demand for WIC services. On the other hand, the new food packages have the potential to decrease the relative size of the WIC infant formula market by reducing the total amount of infant formula that formula-fed infants receive over a year, and by possibly increasing breastfeeding rates among WIC mothers. The extent to which these factors affect WIC's share of the infant formula market may play a major role in determining future infant formula costs to the WIC program.

APPENDIX A: ESTIMATING WIC'S SHARE OF THE INFANT FORMULA MARKET

We estimated WIC's share of the infant formula market using two different methods. The first method was based on formula needs of infants, the second was based on market sales data.

Method Based on Formula Needs among Infants

This method is based on estimates of formula needs of WIC infants relative to the formula needs by both WIC and non-WIC infants. The analysis uses data from the National Immunization Survey (NIS) on breastfeeding and formula-feeding practices for WIC and non-WIC infants.

The NIS, conducted by the Centers for Disease Control and Prevention (CDC), uses random-digit dialing to survey households with children aged 19-35 months. CDC provided ERS with data for the 2006-07 survey, which includes infants born between January 2003 and July 2006. The survey categorized infants by whether (a) the infant received WIC; (b) the infant was eligible for WIC but did not receive it; or (c) the infant was not eligible for WIC. We combined the two latter categories into a "non-WIC" category using a simple weighted average.

The household telephone survey asks three questions about breastfeeding:

1. Was [child] ever breastfed or fed breast milk?
2. How old was [child's name] when [child's name] completely stopped breastfeeding or being fed breast milk?
3. How old was [child's name] when (he/she) was first fed formula?

We converted data on monthly breastfeeding rates (the proportion of children that were breastfed at each month) into formula-feeding rates by subtracting the breastfeeding rate from 100, under the assumption that infants who were not breastfeeding received infant formula (and only infant formula, with no breastmilk). For example, if the data showed that 66 percent of the WIC infants were ever breastfed, we assumed that the remaining 34 percent of WIC infants received formula from birth.

We assumed that once infants started receiving infant formula they continued receiving it for the remainder of their first year of life. Therefore, infants who started receiving formula at birth received formula for a total of 12 months, infants who started receiving formula at 1 month received formula for a total of 11 months, and so forth. Therefore, the estimated formula-feeding rates are cumulative, in that each month's rate includes all infants that received formula the previous month (table A1).

To simplify the analysis, we also assumed that all infants consumed the same amount of formula regardless of WIC status, age, weight, etc. We further assumed that the amount of formula provided by WIC was sufficient to meet the infants' formula needs over the first year of life (so WIC families did not have to purchase formula with their own funds).[19]

We estimate that an average of 63 percent of WIC infants are formula-fed (without any breastmilk) over the first year, compared with an average of 46 percent among non-WIC infants. Given that WIC infants account for half of all infants in the United States, and assuming that all infants are fed equal amounts of formula regardless of WIC status, age, or weight, this results in formula-fed WIC infants accounting for an estimated 58 percent of the total formula used by both WIC and non-WIC infants (table A1).

Since some WIC participants are likely to purchase some formula out of pocket, the assumption that WIC families do not purchase any formula with their own funds may result in an overestimate of the WIC formula share. However, this is likely offset by the fact that the analysis also underestimates formula use, since it only measures formula use among infants who are not breastfed. NIS data show that a large proportion of breastfed infants also receive some formula (table A1). In fact, nearly 25 percent of all breastfed infants received some formula supplementation within 2 days of birth, and 31 percent of all breastfed infants received some formula at 1 month of age. The NIS data indicate that a higher proportion of breastfed WIC infants receive formula supplementation than do non-WIC infants each month. If we assume that supplemented breastfed infants receive equal amounts of formula regardless of WIC status or age, the higher proportion of formula supplementation among WIC infants suggests that the underestimate may be larger for WIC infants than for non-WIC infants. In addition, one might expect that breastfed infants on WIC receive greater amounts of formula than those not on WIC, since infants on WIC receive formula for free. This would further increase the underestimate of formula use among WIC infants relative to non-WIC infants. Therefore, our estimate that WIC infants account for 58 percent of total infant formula use should be considered a lower-bound estimate.

Method based on Nielsen Market Sales Data

The Food and Nutrition Service reports that WIC paid $2,333.5 million for infant formula before rebates in fiscal 2005 (USDA, 2007). Unpublished proprietary data that the Nielsen Company prepared for ERS indicate that total infant formula sales in 2005 totaled $3,404.6 million (Nielsen, 2008). Dividing WIC's infant formula costs by total infant formula sales results in an estimate of WIC's share of the infant formula market of 68.5 percent.

The Nielsen data collection occurs at both the store and household level. The primary source is from Nielsen Scantrack, which collects scanner-based retail sales information (i.e., point-of-sale information) from a sample of grocery stores with annual sales over $2 million, drug stores, and mass merchandiser stores (excluding Walmart). This data is supplemented with Nielsen Homescan data that provides food-purchase information from additional outlets from a panel of U.S. households (food-at-home purchases from all individuals in the household are captured using a scanning device in the home). However, since the Homescan data may underrepresent infant formula sales from some sources—such as toy stores and Internet sales—that are not included in the Scantrack data, the Nielsen data may underestimate total infant formula sales in the United States. As a result, the 68.5 percent should be considered an upper bound estimate of WIC's share of infant formula sales.

Table A1. Rates of breastfeeding, formula feeding, and formula supplementation

Initiation/duration of breastfeeding (time length)	Breastfeeding rates		Formula feeding rates		Rates of formula supplementation among breastfed infants	
	Percent					
	WIC	Non-WIC	WIC	Non-WIC	WIC	Ineligibles[1]
Ever	66.1	81.5	33.9	18.5		
Within 2 days of birth					28.5	18.8
1 month	59.2	76.0	40.8	24.0	34.7	27.9
2 months	52.7	70.4	47.3	29.6	37.9	30.9
3 months	46.9	66.3	53.1	33.7	42.1	34.6
4 months	39.9	60.5	60.1	39.5	45.8	38.7
5 months	35.4	55.5	64.6	44.5	48.2	41.5
6 months	33.1	52.0	66.9	48.0	49.6	43.0
7 months	26.8	43.8	73.2	56.2	52.5	47.9
8 months	24.5	40.5	75.5	59.5	52.8	48.3
9 months	21.8	36.3	78.2	63.7	53.2	48.8
10 months	19.0	32.0	81.0	68.0	53.4	48.7
11 months	17.7	28.5	82.3	71.5	54.5	49.2
Average rate			63.1	46.4	46.1	39.9
Share of total			0.58	0.42	0.54	0.46

[1]Due to lack of information on sample sizes, it was not possible to combine the data for "eligible but not on WIC" and "not eligible for WIC" in order to estimate a weighted average for a "non-WIC" category. The data presented in this column on infants ineligible for the program account for about 90 percent of infants not receiving any WIC benefits. Rates of formula supplementation for infants eligible but not receiving WIC were fairly similar to rates of formula supplementation among infants ineligible for the program.

Source: USDA, Economic Research Service calculations based on 2006-07 National Immunization Survey (NIS) data from U.S. Department of Health and Human Services, Centers for Disease Control and Prevention.

APPENDIX B: START DATES OF CURRENT AND PREVIOUS REBATE CONTRACTS BY STATE

State or multistate alliance	Start date of most recently completed contract	Length of original contract	Length of extension	Total length of contract	Start date of current contract
		Years			
AL	10/1/2004	3	0	3	10/1/2007
CA	8/1/2003	3	1	4	8/1/2007
CO	1/1/2003	3	1	4	1/1/2008
FL	2/1/2002	3	2	5	2/1/2008
GA	10/1/2002	3	1	4	10/1/2006
IL	2/1/2001	5	2	7	2/1/2008
IN	10/1/2003	2	2	4	10/1/2007
KY	7/1/2001	2	3	5	7/1/2006
LA	10/1/2004	3	0	3	10/1/2007
MI	11/1/2001	3	2	5	11/1/2006
NJ	10/1/2004	3	0	3	10/1/2007
NY	7/1/2003	3	0	3	7/1/2006
ND	7/1/2001	2	2	4	7/1/2005
OH	10/1/2002	3	1	4	10/1/2006
PA	10/1/2003	5	0	5	10/1/2008
Puerto Rico	2/1/2004	3.67	0.33	4	10/1/2008
SC	4/7/2000	2	3	5	4/7/2005
TN	7/1/1999	1	4	5	7/1/2004
VA	6/29/2001	2	3	5	7/1/2006
WI	1/1/2001	3	2	5	1/1/2006
NEATO[1]	10/1/2001	3	0	3	10/1/2006
OK	10/1/2005	1	2	3	10/1/2008
AR, NM, NC	10/1/2003	3	0	3	10/1/2006
IA, MN, TX,	10/1/2002	3	2	5	10/1/2007
WSCA[1]	10/1/2001	3	3	6	10/1/2007
MO	10/1/1998	3	2	5	10/1/2003
NE, SD	10/1/1999	3	1	4	10/1/2003
Average		2.8	1.5	4.3	

Note: Current contracts are those in effect in December 2008. Most recently completed contracts (i.e., previous contracts) are those that were in effect immediately prior to the current contract.

[1]NEATO and WSCA are multistate alliances. For a list of members of each alliance, see box, Multistate Alliances," p. 14 " .

Source: USDA, Economic Research Service calculations based on USDA, Food and Nutrition Service data.

APPENDIX C: ANALYSIS OF THE CHANGE IN REAL NET WHOLESALE PRICE OF MILK-BASED INFANT FORMULA IN LIQUID CONCENTRATE FORM

Although powdered formula is now the predominant form of formula provided through WIC, in previous years most WIC formula was provided in concentrated liquid form. For example, a study by the U.S. Government Accountability Office (2006) of 29 States, found that concentrated liquid accounted for 55 percent of all WIC formula in 2000, but only a third of all WIC formula by 2004. This section examines the change in real net wholesale price of milk-based infant formula in liquid concentrate form. In general, the change in real net wholesale prices of milk-based infant formula in liquid concentrate form mirrored the changes in real net wholesale prices of milk-based powder.

Comparison of the previous and current infant formula rebate contracts for milk-based formula in liquid concentrate form indicate that the real net wholesale price increased in 23 of the 27 contracts (figure C1). Some of these contracts reflect multistate alliances. Excluding Mississippi and Vermont, which do not distribute WIC foods through retail stores, 42 of 48 States, the District of Columbia, and the 5 territories saw an increase in their net wholesale price. Among those States in which both the current and previous contracts were based on DHA/ARA-supplemented formula, 7 of the 10 contracts experienced an increase in real net wholesale price.

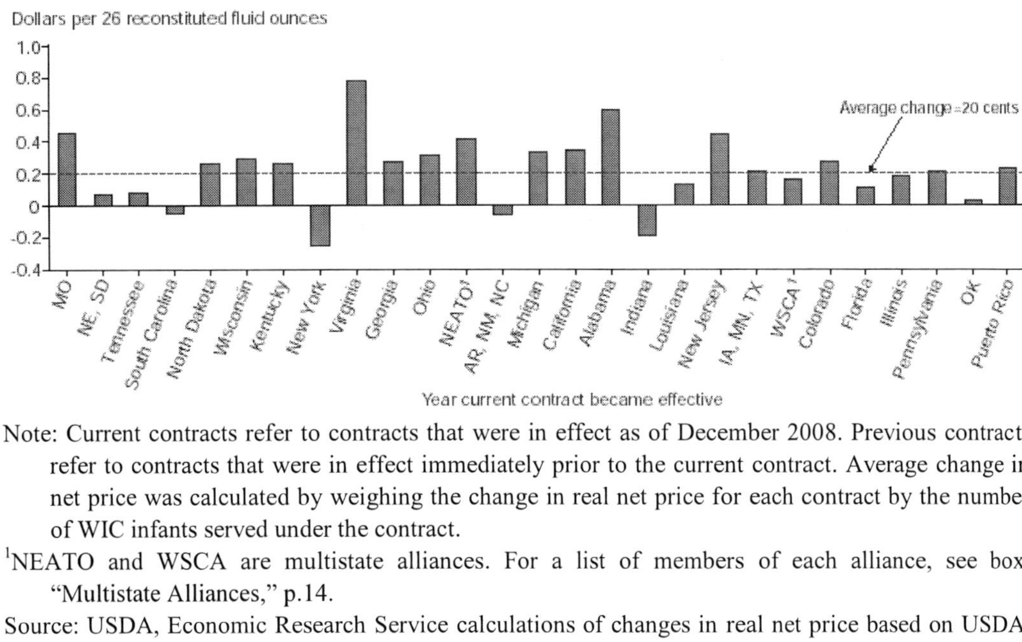

Note: Current contracts refer to contracts that were in effect as of December 2008. Previous contracts refer to contracts that were in effect immediately prior to the current contract. Average change in net price was calculated by weighing the change in real net price for each contract by the number of WIC infants served under the contract.

[1]NEATO and WSCA are multistate alliances. For a list of members of each alliance, see box, "Multistate Alliances," p.14.

Source: USDA, Economic Research Service calculations of changes in real net price based on USDA, Food and Nutrition Service estimates of net prices adjusted by U.S. Department of Labor, Bureau of Labor Statistics' Consumer Price Index for All Urban Consumers for All Items.

Figure C1. Change in real net wholesale price between current and previous contracts, by State (Liquid concentrate, December 2008 dollars)

The average percentage discount (weighted using the State agencies 2008 infant caseload) for the liquid concentrate formulas decreased from 93 percent for the previous contracts to 88 percent for the current contracts. In 20 contracts, the discount rate for the current contract was less than the discount rate for the previous contract. The discount rate increased in three contracts (representing five States) and in four contracts (representing five States), the discount rate did not change.

On average, real net wholesale prices increased by an average 20 cents for 26 fluid ounces of reconstituted formula between States' previous and current rebate contracts.[20] If all WIC infants received milk-based formula in liquid concentrate form, this increase of 20 cents for 26 fluid ounces of reconstituted formula would result in increased annual costs to WIC of $123.3 million.

This estimated increase in real net wholesale prices of 20 cents for 26 fluid ounces of reconstituted formula was based on the current and previous contracts for all the States (except Vermont and Mississippi). Some of these States switched from unsupplemented formula in their previous contract to DHA/ARA-supplemented formula in their current contract. Estimating the change in net wholesale price in only those 10 States (or multistate alliances) whose previous and current contract were based on DHA/ARA-supplemented formula (that is, controlling for the higher wholesale prices of the DHA/ARA-supplemented formulas) resulted in an average increase of 18 cents for 26 reconstituted ounces.

Appendix D: Estimated Change in Infant Formula Use by WIC under the New Food Packages

The WIC food package revisions change the maximum monthly allowances for infant formula for some infants, depending on the infants' age and feeding method. We estimated total infant formula use by WIC infants under the old food package (which was totally phased out as of October 1, 2009) and under the new food packages using data provided in the Interim Rule (USDA, 2007). For both the old and the new food packages, we multiplied the number of infants projected to be participating in WIC in 2008, by age and feeding method (fully formula-feeding, partially breastfeeding, or fully breastfeed-ing) by the estimated average amount of formula prescribed by WIC for a given age and feeding method, and summed across age and feeding methods to obtain the estimated quantity of infant formula used under each of the two packages (table D1).[21] The results show that the total quantity prescribed under the new food package is about 20 percent smaller than the quantity prescribed under the old food package. Reductions in infant formula use are observed across most age and feeding methods. Fully formula-fed infants 4-5 months of age are the only group where infant formula use is higher under the new food package than under the old food package.

Table D1. Estimated monthly infant formula use under the old and new food packages[1]

Infant's age	Estimated number of infants (FY 2008)	Old food package		New food package		
		Estimated average prescribed amount per infant	Total quantity	Estimated average prescribed amount per infant	Total quantity	Difference
			Reconstituted fluid ounces			
Fully formula-fed						
0-3 months	426,994	906.33	386,997,472	842.65	359,806,494	-27,190,978
4-5 months	283,539	906.33	256,979,902	931.37	264,079,718	7,099,817
6-11 months	840,456	906.33	761,730,486	656.66	551,893,837	-209,836,650
Subtotal	1,550,989		1,405,707,860		1,175,780,049	-229,927,811
Percent reduction						-0.16
Partially breastfed[2]						
newborn (0 months)	28,205	546.55	15,415,443	0.00	0	-15,415,443
1-3 months	84,616	546.55	46,246,875	390.14	33,012,086	-13,234,789
4-5 months	31,566	613.76	19,373,948	470.66	14,856,854	-4,517,095
6-11 months	56,380	637.89	35,964,238	355.32	20,032,942	-15,931,297
Subtotal	200,767	2,344.75	117,000,504		67,901,881	-49,098,623
Percent reduction						-0.42
Fully breastfed						
0-3 months	199,996	79.58	15,915,682	0.00	0	-15,915,682
4-5 months	56,262	77.38	4,353,554	0.00	0	-4,353,554
6-11 months	98,114	77.12	7,566,552	0.00	0	-7,566,552
Subtotal	354,372		27,835,787		0	-27,835,787
Percent reduction						-1.00
TOTAL	2,106,128		1,550,544,151		1,243,681,931	-306,862,220
Percent reduction in total formula use						-20

[1]These estimates assume that the number of infants in each category does not change.

[2]FNS interim rules provide data on 0-3 month old infants (n=112,821). We assume that one-fourth of these are newborns (n= 28,205) and three-fourths are 1-3 months olds (n= 84,616).

Source: USDA, Food and Nutrition Service. Special Supplemental Nutrition Program for Women, Infants, and Children (WIC): Revisions in the WIC Food Packages; Interim Rule (7 CFR Part 246); *Federal Register*, December 6, 2007 (table 4, p. 69018, and table 5, p. 69020, for estimated average prescribed amounts; table D, p. 69031, and table E, p. 69032, for projected participation in the WIC Program by food package type.

(For more detailed information, see http://www.fns.usda.gov/wic/regspublished/wicfoodpkginterimrulepdf.pdf)

REFERENCES

American Academy of Pediatrics. (1999). "Iron Fortification of Infant Formula (RE9865), Policy Statement of the American Academy of Pediatrics," *Pediatrics*, Vol. *104* (1), July.

Besharov, D. & Call, D. (2009). The Expansion of WIC Eligibility and Enrollment, Good Intentions, Uncontrolled Local Discretion, and Compliant Federal Officials, AEI working paper, March 5,.

California WIC Association. (2009). "*Concerns about Infant Formula Marketing and Additives*," Unpublished paper, March.

Centers for Disease Control and Prevention (CDC). (2009). "*Breastfeeding Among U.S. Children Born 1999-2005, CDC National Immunization Survey*." http:// www.cdc.gov/breastfeeding/data/NIS_data/, accessed, March 23,.

Davis, David. (2008). Unpublished Dataset on WIC Infant Formula Rebates (Preliminary), South Dakota State University.

Fomon, S. (2001). "Infant Feeding in the 20th Century: Formula and Beikost," *The Journal of Nutrition* (Supplement), Vol. *131*.

Hamilton, B., Martin, J. & Ventura, S. (2009). *Births: Preliminary Data for 2007*. National Vital Statistics Reports, Vol. *57*, No. 12, National Center for Health Statistics, March 18.

Institute of Medicine, Food & Nutrition Board. (2002). *Dietary Risk Assessment in the WIC Program*, National Academy Press.

Institute of Medicine, Food & Nutrition Board. (2005). *WIC Food Packages: Time for a Change*, The National Academies Press.

Martin, J., Hamilton, B., Sutton, P. & Ventura, S. (2009). *Births: Final Data for 2006*. National Vital Statistics Reports, Vol. *57*, No. 7. National Center for Health Statistics, January.

National WIC Association. (2009). *2009 WIC Reauthorization Legislative Agenda*, February.

Neuberger, Z. & Greenstein, R. (2004). *WIC-Only Stores and Competitive Pricing in the WIC Program*, Center on Budget and Policy Priorities, May.

Nielsen Company. (2008). Unpublished data provided to USDA's Economic Research Service..

Oliveira, V. & Davis, D. (2006). *Recent Trends and Economic Issues in the WIC Infant Formula Rebate Program*, Economic Research Report No. 22, U.S. Department of Agriculture, Economic Research Service, August.

Oliveira, V. & Frazao, E. (2009). *The WIC Program: Background, Trends, and Economic Issues*, Economic Research Report No. 73, U.S. Department of Agriculture, Economic Research Service, April.

Oliveira, V., Prell, M., Smallwood, D. & Frazão, E. (2004). *WIC and the Retail Price of Infant Formula*, Food Assistance and Nutrition Research Report No. 39, U.S. Department of Agriculture, Economic Research Service, June.

Tejada-Vera, B. & Sutton, P. (2009). *Births, Marriages, Divorces, and Deaths: Provisional Data for 2008*, National Vital Statistics Reports; Vol. *57*, No 19, National Center for Health Statistics.

U.S. Department of Agriculture, Food & Nutrition Service, Budget Division. (2009 a). *Program Information Report (Keydata), U.S. Summary, March 2009,* May.

U.S. Department of Agriculture, Food and Nutrition Service, Office of Research & Analysis. (2009 b). *Personal communication*, February.

U.S. Department of Agriculture, Food and Nutrition Service, & Budget Division. Program Information Report (Keydata), U.S. Summary. Various years.

USDA, Food and Nutrition Service, & Office of Analysis, Nutrition, and Evaluation. (2006). *Analysis of WIC Food Package Prescriptions, 1998-2002*, Special Nutrition Program Report Series, No. WIC-06-PCFP, April.

U.S. Department of Agriculture, Food and Nutrition Service, & Supplemental Food Programs Division. *The Integrity Profile (TIP) Report, Fiscal Year 2005.* Available at http://www.fns.usda.gov/wic/tip/tipreport2005.htm.

U.S. Department of Agriculture, Food & Nutrition Service. (2007). *WIC Food Package Costs and Rebates Summary: Fiscal Year 2005,* September.

U.S. Department of Health and Human Services, U.S. Food and Drug Administration, Center for Food Safety & Applied Nutrition. updated April 3, (2006). Website on "Infant Formula: Frequently Asked Questions," accessed on April 7, 2009 at http://www.cfsan.fda.gov/~dms/inf-faq.html.

U.S. General Accounting Office. (1998). *Food Assistance: Information on WIC Sole-Source Rebates and Infant Formula Prices*, GAO/RCED-98-146, May.

U.S. Government Accountability Office. (2006). *Food Assistance: FNS Could Take Additional Steps to Contain WIC Formula Costs*, GAO-06-380, March.

U.S. Senate, Committee on Agriculture, Nutrition, and Forestry. (2004). 2nd Session 108-279, Report to Accompany S. 2507, June 7.

End Notes

[1] In contrast, USDA's Supplemental Nutrition Assistance Program (SNAP)—formerly the Food Stamp Program—is an entitlement program, whereby everyone who meets the eligibility criteria may receive benefits if he or she so chooses.

[2] The term "net wholesale price" used in this report is equivalent to the term "net price" referred to in WIC regulations (*7 Code of Federal Regulations* (CFR) 246.2). We chose to use this term to highlight the fact that net wholesale price is only one component of the cost of infant formula to WIC and does not include the cost associated with the retail markup.

[3] The WIC food packages were revised in December 2007. WIC State agencies were required to implement the new provisions by October 1, 2009. All States implemented the new food packages after December 2008, which was the end of the time period examined in this report.

[4] Vermont uses a home delivery system, while Mississippi, parts of Chicago, IL, and two Indian Tribal Organizations' State agencies use direct distribution.

[5] The price comparison was based on the relative prices of Mead Johnson's Enfamil LIPIL, Abbott's Similac Advance, and Nestlé's Good Start Supreme DHA/ARA in powder and liquid concentrate as of September 2007.

[6] Protein hydrolysate formulas make milk proteins more digestible and less allergenic and thereby provide alternative sources of protein to children who are allergic to milk and soy proteins.

[7] The U.S. Food and Drug Administration (FDA) claims that the scientific evidence on whether the addition of DHA and ARA to infant formulas is beneficial is mixed (U.S. Department of Health and Human Services, 2006). FDA states that "Some studies in infants suggest that including these fatty acids in infant formulas may have positive effects on visual function and neural development over the short term. Other studies in infants do not confirm these benefits. There are no currently available published reports from clinical studies that address whether any long-term beneficial effects exist."

[8] Note that a change in the national wholesale price does not affect the net wholesale price to WIC because the WIC infant formula contracts include inflationary provisions that keep the net wholesale price of formula to a WIC State agency fixed over the entire span of the contract.

[9] Although the WIC program usually issues formula in powdered or liquid concentrate forms, formula may be issued in ready-to-feed form in special situations, such as when the participant's household has an unsanitary or restricted water supply or poor refrigeration, or if the person caring for the infant may have difficulty in correctly diluting concentrated forms or reconstituting powdered forms (7 CFR 246.10).

[10] The California WIC Association (2009) has expressed concerns that Federal law requiring WIC to accept bids for higher priced infant formulas containing additives "with no demonstrable health benefits" may be the beginning of a trend whereby WIC pays more for new formula product lines.

[11] The previous rebate for New York that took effect in July 2003 specified a rebate that was 65 percent of its wholesale price. In January 2004, a contract amendment changed the rebate to 75 percent of its wholesale price. The data for New York used in this study reflect the net wholesale price in effect after the 2004 amendment.

[12] Throughout this report, all averages refer to weighted averages where the weights reflect the State agencies' 2008 infant caseload. That is, if one State served twice as many WIC infants as another State, that State received a weight that was twice that of the smaller State.

[13] Nine of the 10 contracts in which both the current and previous contracts were based on DHA/ARA-supplemented formulas experienced an increase in real net wholesale price. The one State that experienced a decrease in net wholesale price—New York—may be a special case. Its previous contract took effect in 2003. Prior to that time, most contracts offered rebates that were over 90 percent of the wholesale price. Mead Johnson was the only manufacturer to bid on the New York contract, and therefore won despite a rebate bid that was only 65 percent of the wholesale price for milk-based powder. In January 2004, the contract was amended to increase the rebate to 75 percent of the wholesale price.

[14] This is the latest data available and there is no information suggesting that it may have increased or decreased.

[15] To estimate the number of WIC participants supported by $126.7 million, we divided the $126.7 million by the sum of total WIC costs in fiscal 2008 ($6.209 billion) and the amount of the rebate in fiscal 2008 ($2.008 billion) and multiplied the result by the average monthly number of participants in fiscal 2008 (costs and participation figures based on USDA, 2009a).

[16] The U.S. Government Accountability Office (2006) interviewed the formula manufacturers participating in WIC's rebate program and reported that all three "manufacturers noted the importance of shelf space and product placement to their marketing strategies."

[17] In all cases, the revised food packages aim to balance the reduced amounts of formula with greater amounts and varieties of foods to the infants' mothers, as well as to older infants.

[18] As discussed in appendix B, if all the formula provided to WIC infants were milk-based liquid concentrate instead of powder, the estimate of the increase in real net wholesale price would have been about $123 million.

[19] On average, the amount of formula provided by WIC is sufficient to meet all of the infant's energy needs, particularly since the number of cans of powdered formula necessary to provide the full authorized nutritional benefit actually provides more than that amount (see discussion of the rounding-up option in the chapter on "Characteristics of the Infant Formula Market"). For those older infants who consume more than the monthly allotment of WIC formula, parents may be able to stock excess WIC formula provided during the first few months—when the infant's energy requirements are likely less than the amount of formula provided by WIC—for use in later months.

[20] Unlike the results based on milk-based powder, the average change in real net wholesale price of milk-based liquid concentrate in those States in which their last two contracts were based on the DHA/ARA supplemented formulas (15 cents) was less than that in States that switched to the DHA/ ARA supplemented formulas in their current contract (23 cents).

[21] Although WIC has a maximum allowance of 806 fluid ounces of reconstituted infant formula, some infants can actually receive more, since the number of cans of powdered formula necessary to provide 806 fluid reconstituted ounces provide more than that. On the other hand, mothers of breastfed infants may choose to receive less formula. Rather than using the maximum allowances we use the average estimated prescribed amounts as our measure of the amount provided by WIC (USDA, 2007).

In: Child Nutrition and the WIC Program
Editor: Dominic J. Lombardi
ISBN: 978-1-61209-142-6

Chapter 5

WIC AND THE BATTLE AGAINST CHILDHOOD OVERWEIGHT

Michele Ver Ploeg

One of the most worrisome aspects of the growing tide of obesity in the United States is the high rate of overweight among children. Over one in five young children, ages 2 to 5, are at risk of being overweight—meaning their Body-Mass-Index-for-age is at or above the 85th percentile. These children face both current and long-term health problems, and their numbers have grown in the past two decades (Must and Strauss, 1999). Th e number of young children whose families participate in the Special Supplemental Nutrition Program for Women, Infants, and Children (WIC) also grew in that time period, more than doubling from 1.7 million in 1988 to 4.0 million in 2007 (USDAERS, 2008).

Are these increases connected? Does WIC participation contribute to the problem of overweight among U.S. children? Although causes of the increase in childhood overweight and obesity are complex, the answer to both questions appears to be "No." Results from data covering almost 20 years show no association between WIC participation and Body Mass Index (BMI) or the probability of being at risk of overweight (see box, "Calculating Body Mass Index," p. 4). However, low-income status, especially for Mexican-American children, does raise the probability of a child's being at risk for overweight.

This brief examines trends in the relationship between WIC participation and weight status by updating the results of *Food and Nutrition Assistance Programs and Obesity: 1976-2002* (ERR-48, Ver Ploeg et al., 2007). Th at analysis has been updated to include more recently released data from the 2003-2006 National Health and Nutrition Examination Survey (NHANES, 1988-1994 and 1999-2006).

BACKGROUND AND METHODOLOGY

The percentage of boys ages 2-5 at or above the 85th percentile of BMI-for-age rose from 15.2 percent to 22.5 percent between 1988-1994 and 1999-2006 (see figure 1). Te increase for girls was smaller, but still sizable, increasing from 16.1 percent to 20.6 percent over the same time period, according to NHANES.

Economic Research Service (ERS) analysts examined the relationship between WIC participation and BMI over the past two decades. Data from the National Health and Nutrition Examination Survey (NHANES) covering the years from 1988-1994 and 1999-2006 were used to explore whether or not there is a relationship between WIC participation and body weight and whether that relationship has been consistent over time as the number of children who participate in the WIC program increased. (The 1988- 94 NHANES oversampled Mexican Americans, but not other Hispanic Americans. The sample size does not support separate estimates representative of all Hispanic Americans, only Mexican Americans.)

The analysis compared boys and girls separately. Further, the analysis compared children who reported receiving WIC benefits with children who were income-eligible but did not receive benefits (income less than or equal to 185 percent of Federal poverty guidelines), with children who had moderate income levels (income between 185 and 300 percent of Federal poverty guidelines) and higher income levels (income above 300 percent of poverty).[1] Race, ethnicity, and age were also controlled in the analysis.

BODY WEIGHT IS NOT RELATED TO WIC PARTICIPATION

The only instance in which WIC participation was associated with the probability of overweight was in 1988-1994 for girls—showing that WIC participants were less likely to be at risk of overweight than moderate-income children.

Boys—Estimates for both sets of years of data showed that young boys who received WIC benefits had similar BMI and were as likely to be at risk of overweight as income-eligible nonparticipants. Further, there were no significant diff erences between WIC participants and higher income nonparticipants.

Mexican-American boys had significantly higher BMI than non- Hispanic White boys in both 1988-1994 and 1999-2006, even after controlling for income, food stamp participation and age (figure 2). Mexican-American boys were also more likely to be at risk of overweight than non-Hispanic White boys in 1988-1994, but this diff erence was no longer statistically significant in 1999- 2006. There were no diff erences between BMI and the probability of being at risk of overweight between non-Hispanic White and non-Hispanic Black boys.

Girls—Girls who received WIC have similar BMI as income- eligible nonparticipants and as higher income nonparticipants. No diff erences in BMI between these groups were found in either 1988-1994 or 1999-2006. Similarly, there were no diff erences in the probability of being at risk of overweight across WIC participation and income level. There was one exception, however—1988 to 1994 data show that moderate-income girls were more likely to be at risk of overweight than WIC participants. T is diff erence was no longer present in 1999-2006.

Race and ethnicity were important predictors of BMI and the probability of being at risk of overweight among girls as well. Compared with non-Hispanic White girls, Mexican-American girls had greater BMI. T is result is consistent for both time periods. In 1988-1994,

Mexican-American girls were also more likely to be at risk of overweight than non-Hispanic White girls. T is diff erence, however, was not significant in the more recent period, 1999-2006. Non-Hispanic Black girls had similar BMI as non-Hispanic White girls for both survey periods. However, in 1999-2006, non- Hispanic Black girls were more likely to be at risk of overweight than non-Hispanic White girls.

One area for concern among young children regardless of income is that young Mexican-American girls and boys had greater BMI than non-Hispanic White children and non-Hispanic Black children. Figure 2 shows diff erences in BMI across race and ethnicity for boys in 1999-2006. In 1988-1994, this translated into greater likelihood that young Mexican-American boys would be at risk of overweight than their non- Hispanic White counterparts, but the latest data showed no statistically significant diff erences for the probability of being at risk of overweight. Another potential area of concern was that in 1999-2006, non- Hispanic Black girls were more likely to be at risk of overweight than non-Hispanic White girls.

Although these results do not show evidence of a relationship between WIC participation and body weight, ERS analysis methods cannot ascribe (or deny) causal links between WIC participation and overweight status. Selection bias may exist because families and individuals who choose to participate in food assistance programs may be systematically diff erent in unobservable ways from those who do not participate.

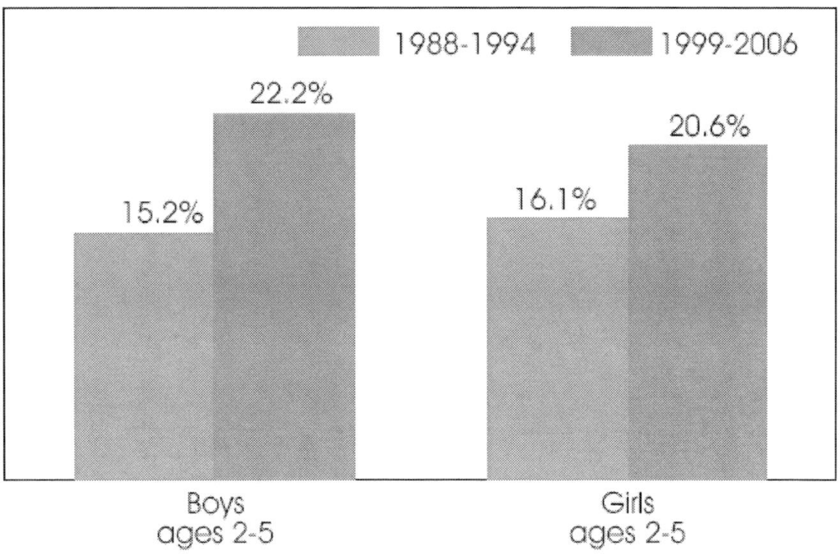

Source: ERS estimations using National Health and Nutrition Examination Survey data.

Figure 1.Children with Body-Mass-Index-for-age at or above the 85th percentile

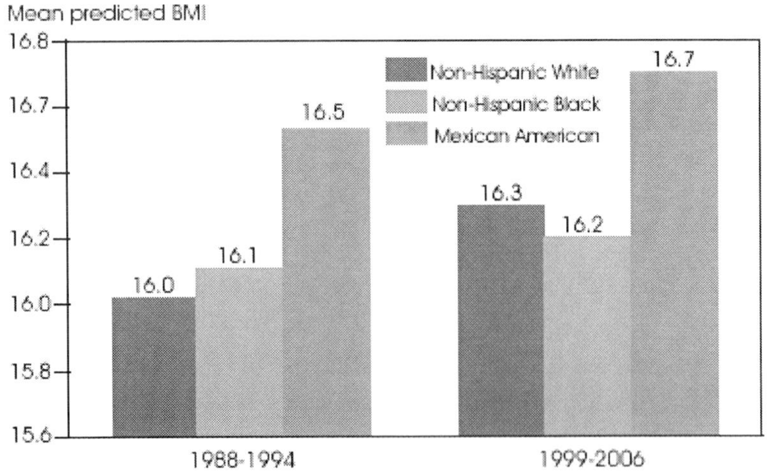

Note: Differences among groups and between years are not statistically significant.
Source: ERS estimations based on regressions of BMI on age, race/ethnicity, WIC, and income status.

Figure 2. Mean BMI by race/ethnicity for boys ages 2-4 who were enrolled in WIC, 1988-1994 and 1999-2006

Conclusions

The WIC program appears not to be a major cause of the childhood obesity problem, but the program could be part of the solution. WIC could be used as a tool to combat the problem of overweight among children, at least for those low-income children whom the program primarily serves. By October 1, 2009, the WIC program must implement recently approved changes to the types and amounts of foods the program off ers, including a voucher for the purchase of fruits and vegetables.

State WIC agencies now are implementing the changes in the types and quantities of foods that can be purchased through WIC. The new WIC food package for children 2 years and older eliminates whole milk and makes available only lower fat milk, reduces the maximum monthly amount of juice and eggs, adds whole-wheat bread, and includes a voucher for $6 per month to buy fruits and vegetables. Such changes could be important for reducing the risk of obesity if they encourage consumption of more fruits and vegetables and lower fat milk while reducing consumption of less healthy foods.

The revisions to the food package also attempt to encourage breastfeeding. The changes include:

- making the food package for postpartum women who exclusively breastfeed relatively more generous than the food package for partially breastfeeding and nonbreastfeeding postpartum women (off ering more juice, milk, eggs, whole-wheat bread, canned fish, and off ering a $10 voucher for fruits and vegetables compared with an $8 voucher for partially breastfeeding and nonbreastfeeding women).
- eliminating the provision of infant formula for fully breastfed infants
- reducing the amount of formula provided for partially breastfed infants

If these revisions are successful in promoting breastfeeding, a longer term impact of reducing childhood obesity could occur, since breastfeeding may protect babies against becoming obese later in life (Arenz et al., 2004). Future research and evaluation should assess the eff ectiveness of these policy innovations in changing dietary patterns, as well as others that may be proposed as a way to reduce the prevalence of child obesity.

Recommended Citation format for this Publication

Ver Ploeg, Michele. *WIC and the Battle Against Childhood Overweight*. EB-13, U.S. Department of Agriculture, Economic Research Service. April 2009.

CALCULATING BODY MASS INDEX

Body Mass Index (BMI) is a function of weight and height. In English units, it is measured as pounds divided by inches squared, multiplied by 703.

Adults

As an example, a 5-foot, 5-inch (65 inches) adult weighing 150 lbs would calculate his BMI by: dividing 150 by $(65)^2$ and multiplying the result by 703, for a BMI of 24.96. That is just within the high end of the healthy-weight range, as shown below.

BMI $<$ 18.5 = underweight
18.5 $\leq$ BMI $<$ 25 = "normal" or healthy weight
25.0 $\leq$ BMI $<$ 30 = overweight
BMI $\geq$ 30.0 = obese

Children

For children, the calculation is more complex, involving date of birth (month/day/ year), date of measurement (month/day/year), gender, height (to nearest one-eighth of an inch), and weight (to nearest one-quarter of a pound). That number is placed on a Centers for Disease Control and Prevention BMI-for-age percentile chart that places the child within a BMI range for the child's peers.

As an example, the BMI calculated for a 7-year-old girl who weighs 55 pounds and is 48 inches tall would be done the same way as an adult's BMI. The result, a BMI of 16.8, would be placed on the CDC chart, showing she is just above the 75th percentile, meaning her BMI is higher than 75 percent of girls her age in the United States.

Children and Adolescents Ages 2-19

BMI $<$ 5th percentile of BMI-for-age = underweight
5th percentile of BMI-for-age $<$ BMI $<$ 85th percentile BMI-for-age = healthy weight
85th percentile BMI-for-age $<$ BMI $<$ 95th percentile BMI-for-age = at risk of overweight
BMI $>$ 95th percentile of BMI-for-age = overweight

To calculate specific BMIs for adults, children, and teens, see: http://www.cdc.gov/nccdphp/dnpa/healthyweight/assessing/bmi/index.htm

REFERENCES

[1] Arenz, S, Rückerl, R., Koletzko, B. & von Kries, R. (2004). "Breast-feeding and Childhood Obesity—A Systematic Review," *International Journal of Obesity,* Vol. *28, 1247-1256.*

[2] Must, A., Strauss, R.S. (1999). "Risks and Consequences of Childhood and Adolescent Obesity," *International Journal of Obesity,* Vol. *23*, Suppl. 2, S2-S11.

[3] National Health & Nutrition Examination Survey (NHANES). 1988-1994 and 1999-2006. U.S. Department of Health and Human Services, Centers for Disease Control and Prevention, National Center for Health Statistics. Available at: http://www.cdc.gov/ nchs/ nhanes.htm/.

[4] U.S. Department of Agriculture, Economic Research Service. (2008). Average Monthly Participation in WIC: Fiscal 1980-2006. Available at: http://www.ers.usda.gov/ briefing/ FoodNutritionAssistance/ gallery/ wic.htm/. Accessed June 3, 2008.

[5] Ver Ploeg, M., Mancino, L. & Lin, B.H. (2007). *Food and Nutrition Assistance Programs and Obesity: 1976-2002,* U.S. Department of Agriculture, Economic Research Service, ERR-48, September 2007.

End Notes

[1] The Federal poverty threshold for a family of 4 in 2008 was $21,200 and the 185-percent eligibility limit for WIC was $39,220.

In: Child Nutrition and the WIC Program
Editor: Dominic J. Lombardi

ISBN: 978-1-61209-142-6

Chapter 6

ECONOMIC LINKAGES BETWEEN THE WIC PROGRAM AND THE FARM SECTOR

Kenneth Hanson and Victor Oliveira

The Special Supplemental Nutrition Program for Women, Infants, and Children (WIC) is one of the central components of the Nation's food and nutrition assistance programs. With Federal expenditures of $5.5 billion in fiscal 2007—or almost 10 percent of total Federal Government expenditures for food and nutrition assistance—WIC is the third largest food assistance program, trailing only the Supplemental Nutrition Assistance Program (SNAP, formerly the Food Stamp Program) and the National School Lunch Program (USDA, 2008). WIC serves over 8 million participants per month, including almost half of all infants and a quarter of all children ages 1-4 in the United States.

WIC provides program participants with supplemental food, as well as nutrition education and referrals to health care and other social services. WIC is based on the premise that early intervention programs during critical times of growth and development in a child's life can help prevent future medical and developmental problems. WIC also has economic ramifications that extend beyond program recipients. To the extent that WIC increases total food expenditures, WIC also affects the country's farm sector. This report estimates the revenues that farmers derive from sales of WIC foods and the number of farm jobs needed to produce these foods. It updates the analysis reported in Hanson (2003) by taking into account the 2007 revisions in the types and amounts of food provided in the WIC food packages.

WIC FOOD PACKAGES ARE REVISED

Participants in WIC receive one of seven food packages, depending on their recipient category (infants 0 through 3 months; infants 4 through 12 months, children 1 to 5 years; pregnant and breastfeeding women, nonbreastfeeding postpartum women, breastfeeding women-enhanced, and children/women with special dietary needs). The foods included in the packages are high in nutrients that have been determined by nutritional research to be lacking in the diets of the population served by the program (7 CFR 246.2). A lack of these nutrients may result in adverse health consequences.

Before 2008, WIC food packages included combinations of the following foods: iron-fortified infant formula; iron-fortified cereal (infant and adult); vitamin C-rich fruit juice and/or vegetable juice; eggs; milk; cheese; peanut butter, dried beans, or peas; tuna fish; and carrots. In December 2007, program regulations were revised to better reflect advances in nutrition science and dietary recommendations and to better address current supplemental nutritional needs of WIC participants (72 *Federal Register* 68965-69032) (see box, "Summary of Major Revisions to WIC Food Packages"). Reductions in the maximum monthly allowances for some foods (e.g., milk, cheese, juice, and eggs) and the addition of new groups (e.g., fruits and vegetables and some whole grain products) are anticipated to improve the nutrition and health of the program's target population. Allowing more flexibility in food selection (e.g., soy-based beverages and tofu as alternatives to milk in the women's packages) should also provide greater incentives for families to participate in WIC and consume the prescribed foods. The new food packages were designed to be cost-neutral—that is, to cost no more than the packages they replaced. WIC State agencies are required to implement the new provisions between February 4, 2008, and October 1, 2009.

Summary of Major Revisions to WIC Food Packages

- Addition of fruits and vegetables (as commercial baby foods for older infants and as cash-value vouchers for children and women).
- More whole grain foods—at least half of the cereals in a State's list of approved WIC foods must be whole grain, and new whole grain products are allowed, including breads, brown rice, tortillas, and bulgur.
- Addition of baby food meats for fully breastfed older infants.
- Greater variety of choices, such as soy beverages and tofu, as substitutes for milk for women.
- Less milk, cheese, eggs, and juice. New constraints on choices include reduced amount of cheese that may be substituted for fluid milk; no whole milk, except for 1-year-old children or children with medical documentation for other participant categories; no juice for infants.
- Delayed provision of complementary infant foods for children ages 4-6 months (only infant formula will be provided until the infant is 6 months old).
- Less infant formula for partially breastfed infants and for older infants (6-11 months), more infant formula for fully formula-fed infants ages 4-5 months (to compensate for the elimination of complementary infant foods for this age group).

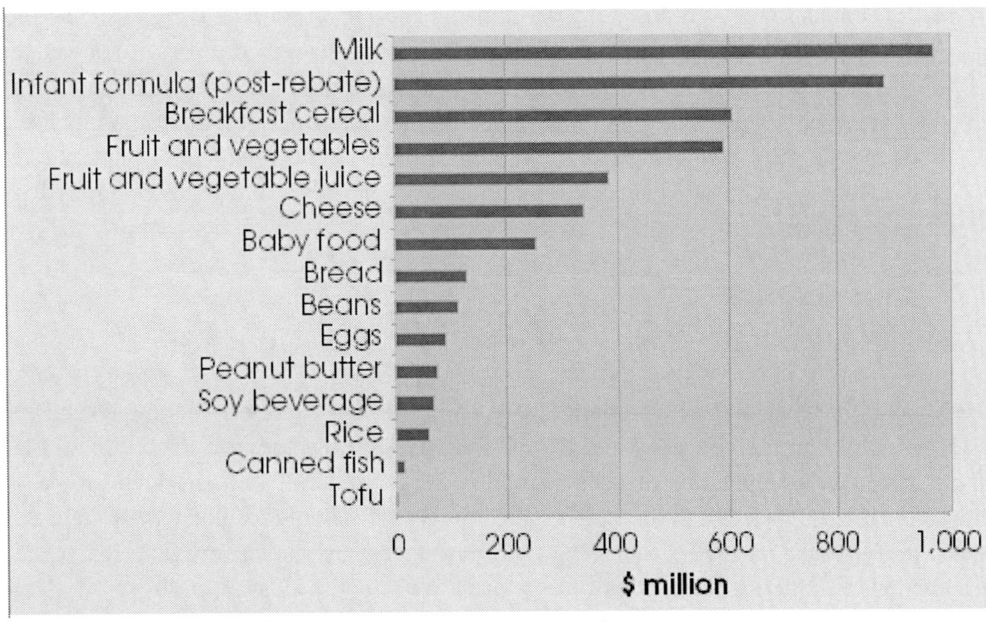

Note: Estimated post-rebate WIC sales in 2008 sum to $4.6 billion.
Source: ERS calculations.

Figure 1. Estimated WIC sales by food item based on revised food packages, 2008

Table 1. Farm revenue from WIC food sales by type of farm, 2008

Type of farm	Farm revenue	
	From producing WIC foods	Net increase due to additionality[1]
	$ million	
All farms	1,274.2	331.3
Type of farm:		
Livestock	707.3	183.9
Dairy	568.9	147.9
Poultry and eggs	92.8	21.5
Meat animals	55.6	14.5
Crops	566.9	147.4
Grains	171.2	44.5
Fruit and vegetables	292.2	76.0
Other crops	103.4	26.9

Note: Based on the revised WIC food packages.
[1]Based on an additionality value of 0.26. Additionality is the amount by which a dollar of program spending results in additional food spending.
Source: ERS calculations.

Most States distribute WIC foods to participants via a retail food delivery system. Under this system, WIC provides participants with food instruments—in the form of a voucher, check, or Electronic Benefit Transfer (EBT) card—which specify the types and quantities of foods the participants may obtain. WIC participants then exchange the food instruments for WIC foods at over 44,000 approved retail vendors (usually grocery stores or supermarkets) across the country. WIC State agencies reimburse the vendors for the foods purchased with the food instruments.

$1.3 Billion in Farm Revenues Are Linked to WIC Foods

Although States have until October 1, 2009, to implement the revised food packages, this analysis assumes that the revisions in the WIC food packages were implemented in all States in fiscal 2008. We estimated retail sales of food in the revised WIC food packages to be $4.6 billion after rebates in fiscal 2008 (see box, "How Was the Study Conducted?"). WIC sales by food item—based on the revised WIC food packages—are shown in figure 1. Even with the reductions in milk associated with the revised WIC food packages, milk has the largest sales—$978 million. About two-thirds (67 percent) of all WIC food sales are accounted for by milk (21 percent), infant formula (19 percent, measured on a post-rebate basis), breakfast cereal (13 percent), and fruits and vegetables (13 percent).

Our analysis indicates that farmers receive almost $1.3 billion from the sale of commodities that are used in producing the $4.6 billion in WIC retail food sales. A food's path from its raw form at the farm to a finished product in a WIC household may take various routes with few or many stops along the way. WIC foods that undergo minimal processing, such as eggs and fresh fruits and vegetables, which essentially go from the farm through the wholesale trade and transportation system to retail vendors, account for $289 million (23 percent) of farm revenues realized from the sale of WIC foods (figure 2). The largest share of farm revenue ($585 million, or 46 percent) is from farm commodities that undergo one stage of processing into WIC foods—for example, raw milk from the farm processed into the milk we drink. WIC foods that involve two stages of processing—for example, wheat and other grains processed by the miller and ultimately made into whole grain bread or breakfast cereal—contribute $149 million of farm revenue (12 percent).

In addition to farm commodities used by food processors to produce WIC foods, the production of these farm commodities may also involve the use of other farm commodities. Examples include feed for dairy cows and poultry (whether in the form of raw grains and hay or processed grains) and seed for grain production. These farm commodities account for $177 million (14 percent) of farm revenue. The remaining $75 million (6 percent) in farm revenue are from other uses of farm commodities in the production of WIC foods that are not accounted for above.

Of the estimated $1.3 billion in total farm revenue from WIC food sales, livestock and crop farms receive $707 million and $567 million, respectively (table 1). Dairy farms receive the most revenues at $569 million (45 percent), fruits and vegetables are second with $292 million (23 percent), and grains are third with $171 million (13 percent).

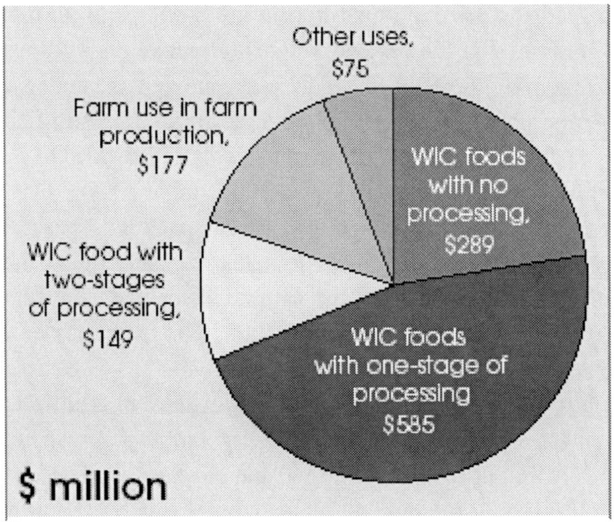

Note: In 2008 dollars.
Source: ERS calculations.

Figure 2. Estimated revenue from the sale of farm commodities used in the production of WIC foods

WIC Generates a Net Gain of $331 Million in Farm Revenues from Increased Food Spending

The estimate of $1.3 billion in farm revenue generated from the sale of WIC foods does not represent the net impact of WIC on the farm sector because many of the foods purchased through WIC would have been purchased by WIC participants even in the absence of the program. That is, without the program, the people now participating in WIC would have purchased some of these foods with their own money. Stated another way, although participants who receive a dollar of benefits from a program are likely to spend the entire dollar on food, at the same time, they are reducing the amount they spend on food from their own cash income. As a result, the increase in food expenditures resulting from a food assistance program will be some fraction of the total dollar amount of benefits provided.

How Was the Study Conducted?

The first stage of the analysis involved estimating the total dollar sales of WIC foods in fiscal 2008. At the time of this analysis, data on the sale of WIC foods was available for only the first 8 months of 2008. Therefore, a linear trend from October 2006 through May 2008 was used to estimate the remaining 4 months of WIC sales in fiscal 2008. The result is an estimate of $4.6 billion in WIC sales after rebates (WIC receives about $1.7 billion in rebates from infant formula manufacturers for the infant formula purchased through the program). Given the assumption of cost neutrality of the revised WIC food packages, the fiscal 2008 estimate of WIC food sales based on the revised WIC food packages is assumed to be the same as the estimated sales based on the old WIC food packages.

Stage two of this analysis involved distributing the $4.6 billion of total WIC sales across the individual foods contained in the revised WIC food packages (although States have until October 1, 2009, to implement the revised food packages, we assume for this analysis that the revisions in the WIC food packages were implemented in all States in fiscal 2008). The basis for our estimate of WIC food sales is the estimates developed by USDA's Food and Nutrition Service (*Federal Register* 72:234, December 6, 2007, table 18, p. 69029). FNS estimated sales of the foods contained in the revised WIC food packages based on 2005 cost data. Because the FNS estimates reflected pre-rebate sales, we subtracted out rebates for infant formula and then proportionately adjusted the estimates for each food item to derive a total estimate of post-rebate WIC food sales for fiscal 2008. The estimates of WIC sales shown in figure 1 reflect these adjustments.

In the third and last stage of this analysis, an Input-Output Multiplier Model developed by ERS was used to estimate revenues received by the various sectors and derive farm revenue (and farm jobs) linked to the WIC food package sales. The model is based on the 2002 Benchmark Input-Output Account published by the U.S. Department of Commerce, Bureau of Economic Analysis (2007). The account provides information on the dollar value of commodities used by industry as inputs into production, as well as their use in final demand by consumers. The account consists of over 400 industries and commodities, including 14 in farming and about 30 in food processing. For the analysis of the farm revenue linked to the WIC food package, we treated farm revenue as the value of production (output) in the farm sectors. Farm revenue directly linked to processed foods in the WIC food package were derived from the input-output coefficients, after taking into account trade and transportation margins. The Input-Output Multiplier Model estimates the indirect farm revenue associated with the WIC food package. For analysis of 2008 WIC food package sales with a model based on 2002 data, we deflated the WIC food sales from 2008 to 2002 dollars using the Consumer Price Index (CPI) for food at home, and then we inflated model results from 2002 to 2008 dollars.

Thus, the net impact of WIC on the farm sector depends largely on the program's additionality (that is, the amount by which a dollar of program spending results in additional food spending). If WIC's additionality is zero—that is, if all foods purchased with WIC vouchers would have otherwise been purchased with the participants' own funds—then WIC would have little overall impact on the farm sector. Any effect from WIC on agriculture would be due to a different mix of foods being purchased (for example, more milk and juice and fewer other beverages) rather than from a difference in the total amount of food purchased. On the other hand, additionality occurs if participation in WIC results in participants purchasing more food (that is, spending more money on food) than they would otherwise in the absence of the program. The degree to which WIC results in additionality is not known. A comprehensive literature review of USDA's food and nutrition assistance programs' impact on participants' health concluded that, because of data and methodological issues associated with previous empirical research, it is difficult to draw conclusions about WIC's impact on household expenditures for food (Fox et al., 2004).

In light of the lack of a widely accepted estimate of WIC's additionality, we assume that the economic behaviors by WIC participants resemble those of SNAP recipients. A number of studies have found that SNAP increases participants' food purchases (Fox et al., 2004). After reviewing the literature on the additionality associated with SNAP, we chose to use an additionality value of 26 percent based on a study by Levedahl (1995). This estimate is a conservative value among the values cited by Fox et al. (2004), which ranged from 17 percent to 69 percent. Thus, we assumed that the WIC program increases WIC participants' food expenditures by 26 percent of the value of the WIC food package. Under this scenario, we estimated that the net addition to retail food sales due to the WIC program (i.e., sales beyond that which would have been purchased if there were no WIC program) in fiscal 2008 was $1.196 million (26 percent of the $4.6 billion of WIC retail food sales). The net addition to farmers' revenues was $331 million (table 1). Of this $331 million, $184 million went to livestock farms—predominantly dairy farms—and $147 million went to crop farms—mostly fruit and vegetable farms.

WIC Affects the Number of Farm Jobs

This analysis also examined the amount of labor—as measured by number of jobs on U.S. farms— needed to produce WIC foods, regardless of whether the work is performed by hired farmworkers, self-employed farm operators, or unpaid family members. Because of differences in the seasonality of farm jobs by type of farm (e.g., jobs on dairy farms are often year-round, while jobs on fruit and vegetable farms are often seasonal) and because many farm jobs are only part-time, our estimates of farm jobs are reported in terms of full-time equivalents.

Table 2. Farm jobs required to produce WIC foods, 2008

Type of farm	Farm revenue	
	To produce WIC foods	Net increase due to additionality[1]
	Number	
Total farm jobs[2]	10,155	2,640
Type of farm:		
Livestock	5,149	1,339
Dairy	4,101	1,066
Poultry and eggs	214	56
Meat animals	834	217
Crops	5,006	1,302
Grains	1,573	409
Fruit and vegetables	2,563	666
Other crops	871	226

[1]Based on an additionality value of 0.26. Additionality is the amount by which a dollar of program spending results in additional food spending.

[2] Full-time-equivalent jobs.

Source: ERS calculations.

To produce the $4.6 billion in WIC retail food sales, an estimated 10,155 full-time-equivalent farm jobs were required (table 2). These jobs are almost evenly split between livestock and crop production. Once again assuming an additionality of 26 percent for WIC, the program resulted in a net addition of 2,640 full-time equivalent farm jobs during the year. Dairy accounted for 40 percent of the total increase in jobs, whereas fruits and vegetables accounted for another 25 percent.

The number of farm jobs associated with the production of WIC foods, either with or without the additionality adjustment, is relatively small, due partly to the efficiency of U.S. agriculture. Increased mechanization and other technological advances have greatly reduced the labor input per unit of output on U.S. farms over time. Because of the seasonal nature of agriculture, many farmworkers do not work year round in agriculture. Consequently, the number of full-time-equivalent farm jobs reported here may underestimate the actual total number of full-time plus part-time farmworkers involved in producing WIC foods.

WIC May Affect Nonfarm Sector also

This study estimates that the $4.6 billion of food purchased with WIC vouchers in fiscal 2008 generated $1.3 billion in farm revenue, based on the assumption that the recent revisions in the WIC food packages were implemented in all States in fiscal 2008. Given that WIC participants would have purchased some of these foods with their own money in the absence of the program, we estimated that the net addition to farm revenue from WIC was $331 million and the net increase in full-time- equivalent farm jobs was 2,640. Note that WIC may also impact the nonfarm sector if funds that WIC participants normally would have spent out of pocket for food are spent on nonfood items instead.

References

Fox, M., Hamilton, W. & Lin, B. (2004). *Effects of Food Assistance and Nutrition Programs on Nutrition and Health: Volume 3, Literature Review*, Food Assistance and Nutrition Research Report No. 19-3, USDA, ERS, October.

Hanson, K. (2003). *Food Assistance Research Brief—Importance of Child Nutrition Programs to Agriculture*, Food Assistance and Nutrition Research Report No. 34-12, USDA, ERS, July.

Levedahl, J. (1995). "A Theoretical and Empirical Evaluation of the Functional Forms Used to Estimate the Food Expenditure Equation of Food Stamp Recipients," *American Journal of Agricultural Economics, 77*(4), 960-68, November.

U.S. Department of Agriculture, Food & Nutrition Service. (2008). *Program Information Report (Keydata), U.S. Summary, FY 2007-FY 2008* (through May 2008), July.

U.S. Department of Commerce, Bureau of Economic Analysis. (2007). "U.S. Benchmark Input-Output Accounts, 2002," *Survey of Current Business, 87*(10),1 9-48, October.

CHAPTER SOURCES

The following chapters have been previously published:

Chapter 1- This is an edited reformatted and augmented version of a Congressional Research Service publication, report R40397, dated March 12, 2009

Chapter 2 – This is an edited reformatted and augmented version of a united States Department of Agriculture publication, report 73, dated April 2009.

Chapter 3 – This is an edited reformatted and augmented version of a Congressional Research service publication, report R41354, dated August 6, 2010.

Chapter 4- This is an edited reformatted and augmented version of a United States Department of Agriculture publication, report 93, dated February 2010.

Chapter 5 – This is an edited reformatted and augmented version of a United States Department of Agriculture publication, report 13, dated April 2009.

Chapter 6 – This is an edited reformatted and augmented version of a United States Department of Agriculture publication, report 12, dated March 2009.

INDEX

A

B

C

D

E

F

G

H

I

P

R

S

T

U

V

W

Y

Z